'This journey captures an important moment in time as a new National Trail around the coast of England reaches completion. The King Charles III England Coast Path will help millions of people to connect with nature. Martyn champions the transformative power of walking, and his insights reveal a culturally rich and dynamic coast under threat from development, climate change and nature crisis.'

Julian Gray, Co-Chair World Trails Network

'A remarkable journey of the boundary between the sea and land, and the inner and outer self.'

Marcus Vergette, Sculptor and Musician, Time and Tide Bells.

'A beautifully composed account into a special coastal journey, from start to finish, an example of the importance of the outdoors and how this freedom and expansion of knowledge only adds to our happiness and the experience of our existence on this earth.,

Adam Bridgland, Artist

# THE COAST is our COMPASS

A pilgrimage along the
world's longest coastal path

To my wife, Alison, who continues
to encourage me to live my dreams

# THE COAST is our COMPASS

A pilgrimage along the
world's longest coastal path

MARTYN HOWE

First published in the UK in March 2026 by Journey Books, an imprint of Bradt Travel Guides Ltd
31a High Street, Chesham, Buckinghamshire, HP5 1BW, England
www.bradtguides.com

Text copyright © 2026 Martyn Howe
Edited and project managed by Gail Simmons
Cover artwork by Debbie Lyddon
Cover layout, text layout and typesetting by Ian Spick, Bradt Guides
Production managed by Sue Cooper, Bradt & Page Bros

The right of Martyn Howe to be identified as the author of this work has been asserted by him in accordance with the Copyright, Designs & Patents Act 1988.

'Sea to the West' from Collected Poems by Norman Nicholson (Faber & Faber); reproduced by permission of David Higham Associates.

Every effort has been made to obtain the necessary permissions with reference to copyright material, both illustrative and quoted. The author apologises for any omissions in this respect and will be pleased to make the appropriate acknowledgements in any future edition.

All rights reserved. All views expressed in this book are the views of the author and not those of the publisher. No part of this book may be reproduced, scanned or distributed by any means without the written permission of Bradt Travel Guides, nor used or reproduced in any way to train artificial intelligence technologies/models. Bradt Travel Guides and the author unequivocally reserve this work from the text and data mining exception, as per Article 4(3) of the Digital Single Market Directive 2019/790.

ISBN: 9781804693858

British Library Cataloguing in Publication Data
A catalogue record for this book is available from the British Library
Importer to the EU: Freytag-Berndt u. Artaria KG, Ölzeltgasse 3/10, 1030 Wien, Österreich
Digital conversion by www.dataworks.co.in
Printed in the UK by Page Bros

To find out more about our Journey Books imprint, visit www.bradtguides.com/journeybooks

| | |
|---|---|
| Introduction | viii |
| Digital Map | xii |
| Chapter 1 – Cromer to Felixstowe | 1 |
| Chapter 2 – Harwich to Rochester | 14 |
| Chapter 3 – Rochester to Dover | 24 |
| Chapter 4 – Dover to Chichester | 32 |
| Chapter 5 – Chichester to Swanage | 44 |
| Chapter 6 – Swanage to Teignmouth | 57 |
| Chapter 7 – Teignmouth to Par | 68 |
| Chapter 8 – Par to St Ives | 80 |
| Chapter 9 – St Ives to Bude | 95 |
| Chapter 10 – Bude to Minehead | 106 |
| Chapter 11 – Minehead to Chepstow | 116 |
| Chapter 12 – Chester to Fleetwood | 129 |
| Chapter 13 – Fleetwood to Barrow-in-Furness | 139 |
| Chapter 14 – Barrow-in-Furness to Gretna | 151 |
| Chapter 15 – Berwick-upon-Tweed to Horden | 164 |
| Chapter 16 – Horden to Bridlington | 175 |
| Chapter 17 – Bridlington to Boston | 187 |
| Chapter 18 – Boston to Cromer | 203 |
| Further Reading | 213 |
| Acknowledgements | 214 |
| List of Artists | 215 |
| About the Author | 220 |

# INTRODUCTION

My passion for long-distance walking started in the mid-1970s when I completed the Pembrokeshire Coast Path with a school friend. We were complete amateurs, but the experience left a lasting impression until, in 2006, I found the time to walk that coastal path again. My youth rekindled, I spent the next 10 years walking 19 UK National Trails, finding time by leaving corporate life and going freelance. I wrote about that journey in *Tales from the Big Trails*, published in 2021.

The UK has an unrivalled network of paths, of which 20 are designated National Trails. I had walked them all except one, which would follow the coast of England. The new King Charles III England Coast Path is an ambitious 2,700-mile project that will become the longest managed coastal path in the world in 2026. I couldn't wait for its completion, and set off in September 2021, just after the pandemic, finding 17 weeks to walk contiguous sections from Cromer in Norfolk, clockwise, until I arrived back at the pier in June 2024.

The first National Trail, the Pennine Way, was opened in 1965, as the popularity of outdoor recreation increased. Its post-war genesis developed alongside the National Health Service – promoting access and understanding of nature through new National Parks (now 15 in total and growing) and National Trails (a total of 21 in 2026, with the further addition of the 'Alfred Wainwright' Coast to Coast route), in England, Scotland and Wales. National and local organisations were created to manage this natural wealth, promoting, maintaining and protecting it for future generations – for what is life, if we lose our foundations in the natural world we live in?

It is of huge value, for studies confirm the benefits of walking for mental and physical health, but what is less known is that coastal walking amplifies those benefits. Being near blue space touches our psyche, restoring and revitalising our body, mind and soul in powerful ways we have yet to understand fully. This has been my experience, and it is why I have become addicted to coastal journeys by foot and by bicycle. This book explores what it feels like to walk along the littoral boundary, a wild belt between sea and land, a journey rich in art, culture, heritage, community and natural beauty.

## INTRODUCTION

As I learn more about our nation's boundaries, curiosity encourages me to explore further, examining externally what I see and internally who I am – enriching my life in many ways. I choose to invest in physical, mental and cultural wealth in preference to financial wealth and status. By taking time to walk, you will receive a healthy return from an increased understanding of the world, greater fitness and contentment. Unfortunately, I discovered a planet under an unprecedented threat from climate change and biodiversity loss, with consequences understood by many, but not everyone. What does this mean to us personally? Are we in denial, relying on the media for explanation and comfort? How important is it for us to understand the interconnectedness of the world and our place in it?

I believe we are disconnected, living in cities and blinded by online addictions – both factors that undermine understanding and our resolve to do something. From what I see, market forces and a twisted economic model reward the unsustainable consumption of our resources. This insatiable human appetite is like a fire, gorging oxygen and fuel until all that remains are ashes – almost unstoppable. We are the dominant species and there is nothing (yet) to counterbalance our progress. As this natural capital slips through our fingers, we face an existential crisis. It will creep up to our door and knock more loudly in the coming decades. What will we answer, and what excuse will we construct to explain our part in this tragedy?

Yet, I am hopeful and optimistic and believe there is a way forward. The solutions lie within us. We are adaptable, intelligent, and capable of incredible things in times of crisis. The accelerating pace of industrial and technological change is extraordinary, but it must be directed to solve these challenges. This will not be easy against a backdrop of self-interest and greater inequality, leaving those without means to suffer the most.

The rate of change exceeds our ability to evolve. We should take things more slowly. Our natural pace is to walk, which is the speed at which our minds process, memorise and experience the world. If we travel too fast, we lose time and miss things. We should slow down and absorb the immense wonder that surrounds us. Our lives are not chopped up into minutes, hours and days (measurements of our own invention) and should synchronise with the sunrise, sunset, tides, seasons and weather cycles. Walking outdoors, you reconnect with this circadian rhythm, and your senses align with nature. Sounds that soothe, smells that excite, touch that connects, and sights that enthral. You encounter new people and cultures, hearing what they have to say; many voices willing to share their thoughts with a solitary stranger on the path. You are a transient traveller in their world, and the words flow freely in absence of judgement from others. The frank and open conversations surprised me, as if we both needed to vent pent-up pandemic frustrations.

The coastline is a commons – a public space (at least in this country), and the physical boundary of our world, where we stop, settle and gather to trade, relax and wonder. Why is it that so many are drawn to our shores? Why do we stare in awe at the vast unknown expanse from the edge of a cliff or a sandy beach? Are we staring at our shadow mind, seeking answers to our existence? Do we have an ancestral fear of land predators, or are we facing our destiny, contemplating the final chapter in the cycle of life?

People ask me why I walk alone. Like many, I was born an introvert, one who seeks energy from within, but as I get older, I have learned the value of external contact. Walking alone, I am more approachable, open and less threatening. This lowers barriers, making it easier to engage in conversation. We can take as much time as we need, speaking without interruptions, being free to walk on if we must, remaining strangers, but often becoming new friends, if only for a moment. Walking alone, your ego is unclothed, you are vulnerable and exposed, enduring the hardships of walking, sleeping and eating outdoors without comforts. After a few days, this experience becomes your new life, an older and slower way that takes a certain amount of courage to endure. Yet, I feel more alive and active, in possession of my soul, not passive and disengaged, as I walk with an open heart and mind.

On this journey, I began to think about the connection between walking and my growing interest in art and philosophy. Being outdoors encourages a virtuous loop of learning, curiosity and adventure. The more you see, the more observant you become, and you start to understand the relationship between industrialisation, militarisation, energy production and agriculture, and its impact on wildlife and the natural world. Art helps you see the bigger picture through a new lens, to see this mindless destruction and the negative impacts on social inequality, physical health and mental wellbeing. Likewise, philosophical concepts resonate with the experience, many written by those who walk. Their wisdom opens new

## INTRODUCTION

channels of thought, and many stoical quotations stick like brainworms in my mind, somehow brought to life through the direct, unfiltered and meaningful experience of repeatedly placing one foot in front of the other. Walking helps us understand what the artist and philosophers are trying to say. Walking helps us to think, process and create.

I believe this creativity and inspiration comes to us most powerfully when we explore an edge, and walking the coastal edge produces wonderful thoughts and ideas – exercising the mind and body in a stunning landscape. Public art acts as a catalyst, opening a bridge between our conscious and unconscious minds, awakening emotions, processing our hidden selves, allowing us to connect with our inner worlds and process our thoughts. The artists helps us answer questions, often drawing attention to our planet's plight and the impact of our collective actions on nature and our health and, ultimately, our survival. Being outdoors, we can take a step back and experience the overview effect, where astronauts see borderless continents and connected lands and oceans in the vast blackness of a lifeless universe. We only have one Earth, but are we too preoccupied to notice how that thin arc of atmosphere that surrounds our planet sustains us? Like the bark of a tree, it helps us grow and will be fatal to all species if it is cut or removed.

This ambivalence towards our foundation in nature must change. Will we remain in denial, constructing false narratives to explain a complex, interconnected world and assuage our guilt? Are we becoming disconnected, seeking solace in a virtual world increasingly influencing our lives with beliefs that polarise our communities? We are both victims and perpetrators and must explain that paradox to ourselves. This isn't a climate crisis – it is a human one, which only we can solve by connecting to nature, people and community to find new ways to live in this world. We need to be more vocal about our hopes and fears and encourage others to understand this threat through greater access to the outdoors.

Walking and writing about the experience is one small way I can add to this conversation. I hope to inspire you to walk a National Trail – and, like me, take a pilgrimage, a spiritual journey connecting to nature and society. Let the coast be our compass to help us navigate these future challenges.

# DIGITAL MAP

A digital map accompanies this written work which aims to show the interplay between public art, culture, news, science, nature, geology and the organisations that protect the landscape along the route I walked. It shows the paths I walk alongside the official routes, and the coastal margin established when the path was opened.

This map (and future maps) can be found on my website, which details other journeys I have made by foot, bicycle and campervan. *trailplanner.co.uk*

# 1
# CROMER TO FELIXSTOWE
## You are the dawn after my dark

*'Solitude is for me a fount of healing which makes life worth living.'*
Carl Jung

### Distance walked: Nil

I am staring at the acorn waymark in Cromer, a reminder of the end of my journey in 2016. The easterly extent of the Norfolk Coast Path once terminated here; now, it will take you to Suffolk and even further around England along the England Coast Path. My original journey over 10 years covered 3,000 miles of glorious British countryside along all the National Trails, in England, Wales and Scotland. A similar distance lies before me. As one journey ends, another is about to begin.

The pandemic delayed my start and the proposed path completion, but now I am fit and eager, and many sections are approved and open. It should fully open in 2026, with only a few irritating sections remaining unwalkable due to planning difficulties, coastal defence civil works and funds for bridges and complex paths. I can't wait that long, and the Ordnance Survey maps suggest that the majority is walkable. My rules allow for public ferries, so I will miss a few estuaries and attempt to keep the sea to my left, saving perhaps 400 miles of official walking. There will be diversions due to flooding, path closures and safety considerations that will take precedence, as this is a dynamic environment, constantly changing and fought over by nature and man.

Walking alone, along a knife edge between the sea and the land, you teeter between worlds: the familiar and the unfamiliar, security and danger, the conscious and the unconscious. Living on this edge is thrilling, exploring the envelope of existence and connecting with the natural world along a coastal margin where sea-dwelling vertebrates adapted to living on land, and ultimately evolved into who we are today. As with all boundaries, this is where creativity, thought and inspiration happen. The tension between the realms, both physical and philosophical, are bridged, allowing us to explore the opposites.

Enough procrastination. It is September 2021, and I take my first step from Cromer. The coast will be my compass, curiosity a lure, and progress will mark a transition from a modern world until the path becomes my home, life and companion, where I can connect with nature, speak to people outside of my community, and spend time alone to connect with who I am.

I have walked the South West Coast Path, Wales Coast Path, and Cleveland Way, so I know what to expect. However, walking again in a different direction at different times of the year will be a new journey. I am no longer a slave to official routes, confident that the trail will unfold, so I try to relax and use my experience to deal with adversity. I want the landscape to dictate the rhythm, where time is replaced by a harmonious symphony of heartbeat, breath and walking cadence, in tune with the natural vibrations of wind, trees and waves. A flow state where I stop being in nature and become nature.

If I can achieve this flow state, my mind empties and fills with new thoughts, stimulated by new senses, unprocessed memories, worries, and how I feel. I am not in a rush as, counter-intuitively, I have learned that I walk further and more easily if I let go of expectations, plans and schedules. Have you ever noticed how you get tired at the end of a journey, no matter how long it might be?

I plan to camp (official and wild) and use hostels wherever possible, with occasional hotels and B&Bs in urban areas. Later, I will saunter around the coastline in my campervan and clean up a snagging list of beaches, islands and estuaries unwalked. That will be a deferred pleasure, an opportunity to reflect, to take it slowly and observe more deeply – another approach entirely. For now, my backpack will carry my shelter, kitchen and wardrobe – a bare minimum, travelling light, as I walk self-contained and unencumbered along cliffs, dunes, beaches, riverbanks, seawalls and promenades over the next few years when opportunity allows me to live the life of a nomad for a few weeks at a time.

## CROMER TO FELIXSTOWE

I take the first most difficult step, without encouragement from Winston Churchill. An artwork written into the promenade in steel contains the words 'I am not enjoying myself very much' – his emotion when he visited Cromer aged 13. Maybe he was thinking more about pleasing his father and getting a place at Harrow School. I am thinking of relaxing and enjoying the Norfolk coastline: an area so flat that it appears to be nailed to the continental shelf by numerous churches in the landscape, like wooden pegs holding down the pelt of the land, preventing it from floating into the North Sea. The coast here erodes frighteningly, requiring significant investment to defend, notably the shoreline at the Bacton Gas Terminal – a strategic energy facility. This is understandable yet ironic, as it pumps the hydrocarbons that burn and impact our climate and sea levels. But the sea is not concerned; it will be what it will be, doing what it has always done, seeking rest through any passage and over any terrain, breathing in and out twice a day, washing away the sins of the land dwellers.

The campsite is a little further than Walcott. I have stretched my legs for half a day along pebble shorelines, hopping over groynes, avoiding pillboxes, taking new paths around the fields, cleaving into the sea. My pitch is cosy and my neighbours welcoming, although it is far too early to announce that I am walking around the coast of England. I assemble my tent and lie in it to rest but jump out of my skin as the pole snaps with a loud crack. It is a fatigue fracture succumbing finally to overuse – the pole recording the memory of every pitch, wind buffet and storm I survived. Luckily, the repair sleeve I have carried for thousands of miles earns its keep, perfectly sheathing the broken ferrules. This accident is an unwelcome start, but it wakes me from my urban slumber.

At least my home is portable, unlike the homes of Happisburgh (pronounced 'Hayz bruh'), a village being undermined by the sea. Its lighthouse, church and manor house are perilously close to the edge. The 'road ahead closed' sign merely states the obvious, for the tarmac has sheared cleanly at the cliff face. Static caravans can be towed and rescued, but other residents of permanent dwellings will certainly lose their homes to the sea. It looks calm and gentle now, but storms accelerate the destruction, and a combination of surge, wind direction and high tide can devastate this coastline. The one-in-a-hundred-year events are now more frequent as the probability increases and the consequential impact of a changing climate becomes more real. In 1953, a devastating event claimed 531 lives, lost on land and at sea in the UK, and many more in the Netherlands and Belgium. Over the next few weeks, this flood risk will be evident as I walk south: eroded coastline, exposed utility cables and piping, cornfields hanging perilously at the edge, with crops unharvested. Soil and buildings are orphaned, murdered by entropy, and are now unrecognisable as pebbles and sand.

Sea Palling has impressive coastal defences, where the 'hold-the-line' strategy is critically important to protect vast inland marshland areas. Offshore reefs absorb wave energy before they reach the beaches, the waves carving tombola sand formations. These and more substantial options are used along this coastline: expensive concrete seawalls, gabions, revetments and groynes – all in stages of decay as the sea nibbles away at their foundations. If these dunes are breached, the infinite sea will flood deep into the Norfolk Broads, consuming villages, towns, farmland and nature. Residents along coastal areas without defence funding are angry and unable to accept the policy decisions that will destroy their homes. Major works along the coast often shift the issue to another shoreline: unforeseen and unintended consequences from hard-nosed economic decisions favouring commerce over minority livelihoods.

It is no use arguing with nature. It will not listen and will only act. We are victims and perpetrators, unable to accept how our collective behaviours are leading to catastrophe. We are the only ones to come to the rescue in this trauma triangle – to solve the 'tragedy of the commons'. When a disaster is an act of God, we tend to forgive; if it is an act of man, we fight in wars. We should recognise that climate impact is an existential human crisis, where only we can make the changes needed to survive. If we continue in denial, nature will remind us and our illusions will be shattered. But, by then, it might be too late.

Out of season, the villages along the coast are desolate. I walk inland to the Post Office mini-market and get buzzed by a lunatic on a powerful motorised scooter, clearly illegal. He is wearing so much aftershave that I should call Porton Down for an emergency decontamination team. He struts into the store like a peacock, seeking attention, but he hasn't noticed me yet. After he leaves, I try to eat a tepid cheese pastie, but the musk atmosphere makes me retch. I walk away, keen to breathe the sea air, but get buzzed again along the path.

'Do you like my scooter?' he demands to know.

'Err, yes. Quite fast, is it legal?' I ask.

'Nah, don't worry about things like law around here, mate,' he replies, twisting the throttle in case I pull out a badge. I was not about to start a conversation about the laws of nature with someone so in love with their new toy. The contrast between my journey and his unnerves me, as I do not know where to start to see his perspective.

My sense of smell, hearing and taste is restored within a few minutes as I coax three kestrels along the dunes as they hunt into an onshore breeze. I snuggle into a sandy hollow near Horsey and hide behind the grasses. Uncountable grey seals, some pregnant and waiting to pup during winter, arrive, settling on the beach to rest. This tranquil nursery would, at another time and in an alternative history, have witnessed an invasion in the 1940s. It is peaceful now, but the pillboxes and tank traps remind me of what could have been a living hell during a seaborne assault from continental Europe – the power of automatic weapons and artillery destroying nature and man in a moment.

The inland dune path is easy-going, filling my boots with sand, which I stop to empty at California, so named when a hoard of coins was discovered here during the US gold rush, prompting a similar frenzy in a time before metal detectorists. I am starting to ease into a walking routine, my body adapting to life outdoors: a hint of tan lines on my calves and hands from socks and pole straps. It is not far to Great Yarmouth, but I stop to read about the Caister-on-Sea lifeboat, Britain's first independent rescue service, formed after the RNLI decided to close the station after 124 years. 'Caister men never turn back' is their motto. They have saved 395 lives since 1969. Lifeboat stations will be a constant theme of my walk, each with stories of bravery and heroism in the face of an unforgiving sea. I meet many coastal fundraising walkers who visit them all, but I wonder if they overlook the independents, lacking a powerful brand and central resources of the Royal National Lifeboat Institution (RNLI) and perhaps forgotten.

Arriving at a campsite in the middle of a racecourse, I wait for horses to gallop by with the monotone commentary. 'Papa Stour' and

'Molly Shaw' battle for the lead and finish. The gates open, and I can cross to the reception hut. I cook an evening meal, watching the 16:30 and 17:00 races conclude. The racing community then packs up for the day: horses, jockeys, owners and punters exhausted after their excitement and exertions. Joy and elation, financial loss or gain – familiar emotions repeated at this and other venues during the season.

I awake with the horses, stretching their legs before their day's events, and head for Great Yarmouth. Britannia Pier dominates the beach, somehow impervious to the ravages of the sea. It is closed, and the promenade is deserted, save for a few dog walkers. An over-enthusiastic short-legged dachshund with a labrador brain pesters me as I take a photograph. Its owner is lost in a conversation with a neighbour about its genetic makeup. 'I'd like one with longer legs next time,' she says, as if you select them from a catalogue. No wonder the mongrel trying to mount my leg seems so manic – he may be replaced at any moment for the sake of fashion. People care a great deal for their pets for the unconditional love and joy they bring. At Sea Palling I'd noticed a BRITA-sponsored filtered water point for dogs, with a sign saying that any other users (I assumed that meant me) would be prosecuted. Water points are a welcome sight on my journey, and it is encouraging to see refill points popping up so you can avoid the £1.50 a litre plastic bottle option. Now it seems dog owners are getting in on the act, and the simple bowl outside a house got an upgrade.

The walk along the industrial quayside of the River Yare is rewarded at Gorleston-on-Sea, the winner of many a 'best beach in England' competitions and tabloid Top 10 advertorials and listicles for hotels and bougie B&Bs. It has a perfect cafe for breakfast. As I pay, the waitress asks me where I am going, and I now feel able to say I am walking around the coast of England.

'Ooh, I saw a group at Lowestoft setting off along the coast path to London a few weeks ago; they all carried flags. Something to do with the Festival of Light, I think.' She adds, 'They were beautiful'.

I make a mental note and head south to what I assume to be a county border, for the Norfolk Coast Path ends after Hopton-on-Sea. Now, I follow a series of unmarked desire paths and cycleways until I pick up the Suffolk Coast Path at Lowestoft, which I navigate until dropping down to a seawall to the most easterly point of the British Isles. I fall into conversation with a couple cycling to the UK's four cardinal points, something I did in 2001. Their bikes are draped around a toposcope, where we can read the distances to notable European cities as we walk around its perimeter. Berlin is due east, 490 miles away.

'The route over the Pennines is tough, but you'll enjoy the ferries across Mull to Ardnamurchan,' I offer.

'No ferries for us; we'll cycle to Fort William and then up the west coast.'

'Impressive. What a journey. It is more interesting than the direct Land's End to John o' Groats route as it cuts across the grain of the landscape and takes you through stunning scenery. It is nice to touch the coast at the four points of a compass.'

We chat for a while until I weave through the industrial estate and into town, over pedestrian crossings and the bridge beside the marina, on to another long stretch of beach. I recall that cycling journey 20 years earlier, and a good luck card the child of a campsite host handmade and presented to me when they learned of my destination. This treasured possession, a cartoon stickman and bicycle, with panniers and tents lovingly coloured with wax crayons, now lies buried in a biscuit tin with the maps and tickets I acquired as I cycled from the Lizard to Lowestoft to Ardnamurchan and finally to Dunnet Head.

South from the harbour is where the Festival of Light is held on the solstice in June each year, the idea being to party all night and watch the dawn, a rising sun – a pagan-inspired event marking the transition of a year. A plywood art installation, with letters carved by a jigsaw, remains erect on the beach, and I am struck by its message:

YOU ARE THE DAWN AFTER MY DARK

It is a work by Adam Bridgland. The idea, I assume, is to watch the sunrise through the cutout letters. This gets me thinking. Why do people prefer sunsets to a sunrise? Isn't it more optimistic to know you have a day ahead rather than enter the dark of night? Is it *my* dawn or *my* dark? Have I come from *the* dark into the light? Such permutations preoccupy my mind for weeks. The east coast is remarkably beautiful in the mornings, and waking before dawn is a real pleasure; seeing the sun rise over the horizon fills me with joy, knowing I have a day ahead – I am still alive, I have survived the dark of night. I have also survived a pandemic, which is perhaps the darkness implied in the work. Yet have you ever heard someone say *carpe noctem* (seize the night) instead of the familiar *carpe diem*?

I experience this first-hand with a stunning dawn from the campsite at Kessingland, where I'd stopped earlier to avoid the inland Suffolk Coast Path route to catch a low tide along the beach to Southwold. Those feelings expressed in the artwork have come to life: you *are* my dawn; you were the dark. This is a glorious day, walking along the beach – a raw, wild, stunning coastline with a hint of danger. There are only a few escape routes if the wind blows hard from the east and an incoming tide threatens; this would be impassable in such conditions. But today, I am in another country; the sun is warm, the sea is calm, and the beach and cliffs glow a subtropical orange. The foam-laden waves unfold from an aquamarine sea, wiping my footprints from the shoreline. Above the cliffs, undermined trees and their foundations are washed away by a fatal salt sea that earlier crossed the line I now walk. Unable to scale the cliffs or swim in a cold sea, I am also on the edge between life and death, navigating a narrow path that would be a very different experience in a winter storm.

Inland, Benacre and Covehithe Broads are home to wild birds, resting and feeding in a haven, half of their defensive border provided by the sea, the other by woodland. A marsh harrier floats in the air, patrolling the reed line. I wish I had binoculars, as many interesting dabbling fowl float in the waters, but I must make progress, for tide and time tarry for no man, and for once, a schedule is important. Adrenaline kicks in and powers me south to clamber up slippery rocks to Southwold. This shortcut has saved me hours of inland walking, and I am exhilarated, on a high, and ready for a late breakfast. I try the local putting green cafe, but that only serves light snacks. The owner helps me with a few suggestions:

'Can you recommend somewhere for a full breakfast?' I ask.

'Try this cafe; it is the one the locals use,' he replies. We confirm with my smartphone map for directions. 'It has few tables, but you might be lucky.'

It is a farmhouse bakery serving superb full English breakfasts and a range of filled rolls for lunch. It is a one-stop brunch wonder. I snuggle into a corner seat, fuel up for a long day ahead and then walk to the ferry crossing the River Blyth. A one-mile diversion to a bridge would be needed if it were not running. But, £2 later, I am walking through marshlands along boarded paths, a few feet above the muddy gullies, watching a great white egret step gently to stalk prey, striking swiftly, the hapless fish upended and swallowed whole, head first. Looking inland, the marsh is lined with gorgeous white-leaved poplar trees that shimmer in the sea-reflected sunlight; their susurrant sound soothes my thoughts – nature is meditating, the land in conversation with the softly lapping waves. She invites me to join in, enveloping me with mesmeric rustlings and sea whispers as I walk on.

I reach Dunwich, a town submerged after a great storm in the 13th century – a lost Atlantis, a world that crossed a line to the otherworld, claimed by the sea. I make haste, having visited before, for the National Trust car park, which I hope has a cafe. It does, and has a welcome water point (neither filtered nor sponsored) at the coastguard cottages. I fill up before the beach walk beside RSPB Minsmere, one of the finest bird reserves on the east coast, to Sizewell B, one of the largest nuclear power stations in the UK. Without a fashionable dome, its predecessor, Sizewell A, no longer generates electricity and will soon be decommissioned, demolished and inert. They sit together, buildings of function, lacking architectural considerations, attempting to look bland to hide their secrets.

I try to reconcile the presence of a town destroyed by coastal erosion, a significant nature reserve, and atomic reactors – is something wrong with this picture? Protesters agree, and their 'Oh, we don't want to be beside the C side' sign confirms their concerns, seeking to stop the construction of Sizewell C's two new 1.6GW reactors. This juxtaposition of nature and science: the beauty of evolution and the consequence of manmade technology sitting alongside each other. Our insatiable demand for energy, with decommissioning debt deferred for future generations, is unpaid by those who benefit. I wonder how our children will look upon our decisions in 10, 100, 1,000 and even 10,000 years (if the human species lives that long), as a legacy of nuclear waste accumulates, not necessarily on-site, but via a processing facility and ultimately hidden and buried from view, but no less dangerous.

Huffing in thought, I enter Thorpeness, a delightful faux village with the Meare boating lake and tempting pub in no way ameliorating the hidden poisons of the power station. I press on to Aldeburgh, feeling the 25 miles under my belt. Maggi Hambling's *Scallop* is perfectly placed on the beach. 'I hear those voices that will not be drowned,' it declares, a passage from the opera *Peter Grimes* by Benjamin Britten, a narrative poem about a small town bearing a resemblance to Aldeburgh. The beach is quiet, and I am undisturbed as I shelter in its wings. The waves echo against the blades of the shell, somehow enveloping and protecting a coastal traveller for a moment from the sea, from the world. The scallop form, a symbol of pilgrimage, my own spiritual coastal journey in nature.

I make a rookie error of not booking ahead for accommodation. Contemplating wild camping options, I relent and blow my budget on a comfortable room in a sea-facing hotel. It is money well spent: the food is excellent, and the people-watching even better. A narrow demographic of retired, permatanned, regularly exercised and healthy looking guests float in the sea – their evening dip before dinner. It is like a scene from the 1985 film *Cocoon* where some alien energy revives octogenarians. Perhaps they know something more about a nuclear elixir nearby, for they have a vitality that betrays their years.

Suitably refreshed and sorely tempted by a lie-in, I depart and head inland towards Snape Maltings along the Sailors' Path. Maybe one day there will be a shorter route via a ferry across Westrow Reach, but that would avoid the delight of the calming woodland paths through Black Heath. It seems the area north of here is also threatened by industrialisation, with a land-based substation and interconnect for offshore wind farms. These green energy projects plan to destroy a natural landscape, regardless of what their corporate statements might declare. It is worth scrutiny to decipher the corporate double-speak and PR spin. A large SASES (Substation Action Save East Suffolk – *sases.org.uk*) banner announces the desecration of pilgrim footpaths, medieval villages and the heritage and natural landscape we should fight to protect. Who would have thought that this part of sleepy Suffolk would be a hotbed of activism – aiming to expose a planning scandal that significantly impacts local communities?

The mudflats and marshes hide a wealth of wildlife, striving to live and completely unaware of their potential fate. I hear unfamiliar bird calls, perhaps water rail, hiding in the reeds. The Sandlings Walk path weaves to the Maltings, a focal point for art and music in an Area of Outstanding

Natural Beauty (AONB). I sit alongside Henry Moore and Barbara Hepworth sculptures, enjoying a coffee before returning to the coast. All this is amid future construction vandalism in a protected landscape that will never recover.

The path follows the River Alde before heading into farmland and an industrial piggery. A piglet has escaped beneath an electrified fence and cowers in the hedgerow, trembling and frightened. I feel obliged to return it to the fold, as it will surely die without its mother. I pick it up, and it squeals loudly; it is like holding a small naked baby, and I must resist an urge to drop it as I walk towards the fence, its mother alert to the rescue. She pokes her head out of the pigsty, grunts loudly, and looks in my direction. She is huge, so I do not delay placing it in the field while avoiding an electric shock between my legs. It scampers away to be reunited. I celebrate a good turn for the day as I walk on, reflecting upon their fate as pork chops, bacon or sausages.

After that excitement it is a relief to enter Tunstall Forest, a sandy-floored peaceful woodland that leads to open farmland, housing enormous grain silos with attendant articulated lorries. Signs warn of adders as I ascend an unusual hill to Butley Ferry (one of the 'four foot ferries'), a service I would have taken from Orford if it were running. Butterflies take flight in their hundreds as I walk along the field boundaries. They lie unseen, wings folded, until the last moment when they fill the air around me. A vintage bicycle guards a small bench at the ferry. It is a perfect spot for lunch, its Brooks saddle weathered from use, a bygone agricultural-community patina reflecting the values of durability, tradition and hard work. It is a pity the ferryman is not around for a chat, for I am sure the conversation would have revealed many secrets of the landscape.

A seawall protects the land, which is my first introduction to the experience of walking on a raised path. It is exposed, and I am chilled by the wind blowing up the river, which changes from the River Alde to the River Ore as it flows towards the sea. A classic yacht is tacking inland, making slow, steady progress against an outflow towards nowhere in particular, for they are sailing for pleasure and the challenge of the estuary. Rare and important coastal plants thrive in the saltings – bird's-foot trefoil and sea campion. Oystercatchers and ringed plovers peck away at the mud. The landscape recalls J. A. Baker's book, *The Peregrine*, which

I have been reading. I am not convinced he witnessed the behaviours of this wonderful falcon in the landscape I am walking through. The hardest thing seems to be to see what is hidden, and I would need years in this landscape to tune in as he did. The bird in question was shot during the war so that carrier pigeons could do their work. I feel his work is an imagined landscape – a personal and perhaps private coping mechanism for a modern world. I aspire to his descriptive writing and powers of observation, perhaps the ultimate achievement for someone who spends so much time in nature. Yet, there is no evidence of the falcon.

Orford Ness, isolated from the mainland by the river, shimmers in the haze, merging with ripples in the shingle and the gentle swell of the North Sea. It is a surreal landscape, the location for airborne weapons testing and radar experiments from 1913 until the military and research agencies departed in 1987. The River Alde/Ore secures Europe's largest shingle spit from prying eyes, ironically creating a haven for wildlife. It would have witnessed nuclear weapons testing to ensure bombs went off when they were supposed to and did not explode accidentally (not actual nuclear detonations, thankfully). The brutalist concrete test buildings succumb to nature: organic decomposition and mineral erosion act patiently, slowly erasing the evidence of technology from the memory of man as they become a part of the shingle drift.

I reach the first of many Martello Towers, crunching through the pebbles with effort along the appropriately named Shingle Street. A couple in a holiday home asks where I am walking and offers water and a Soreen malt loaf bar (a hiker's favourite). At Bawdsey my path heads inland, and I march along the road to the ferry terminal, avoiding huge sprinklers watering the turf fields. My timing is perfect for once, to avoid a soaking and to catch the ferry. My only task now is to reach Felixstowe and watch for wayward golf balls as I walk beside the fairways.

I could have done with a bang on the head, as, like a fool, again I have not booked accommodation as the weekend starts. I am far too relaxed and complacent: everywhere is expensive. The ferry to Harwich is not running, and I am considering a cheeky wild camp at Landguard Point and an improvement in the weather. But the forecast suggests otherwise, delaying the service for days. After a quick check on *trainline.com*, I realise staying home for the weekend is cheaper. Plan C becomes Plan A.

## CROMER TO FELIXSTOWE

I can attend to a few blisters and collect a new tent pole. I still have a few wild foraged plums and apples in my outer pockets for the journey and savour their taste as the carriage rocks towards Liverpool Street.

# 2
# HARWICH TO ROCHESTER
## Beach hut 103

*'One foot in front of the other. Repeat as often as necessary to finish.'*
Haruki Murakami

### Distance walked: 110 miles

The weekend at home is just what I need at my age. Even though I am walking as well as I ever have, creeping fatigue builds after multiple 20-mile days. Recovery needs more than one night's rest. The body keeps the score, and I must listen to avoid an injury I know will follow. Over the years, I have suffered shin splints, twisted ankles and aching hips, but the consistent injuries are blisters. I have been lucky with knees, and I am sure walking poles have helped a great deal. Long-distance walking is not a sport, where you can recover from a day of abuse, for you must pay attention and pre-empt injury with action. Unfortunately, I often fail to do this, marching on as if the pain will go away and suffering the consequences.

Such thoughts cross my mind as I take the train to Harwich, skipping the estuary. The England Coast Path will guide you one day from Felixstowe along the River Orwell to Ipswich, returning to Shotley Gate and up the River Stour to Manningtree and back to Harwich, but my rules permit the use of the public ferries or, if they are not running, to use public transport. It is a strong north-easterly, and the Harwich Harbour Ferry is moored up for the day, so returning to the opposite shore by train is acceptable. In the future, I will return to complete a circular walk around three estuaries, if I add the River Deben to that list. My younger departed brother lived nearby, and I will walk it in his memory. His cancer diagnosis was a shock to me, and with a memory of other close friends who died too early, I feel a loneliness that needs more walking to process my grief. The river edge in winter would be an ideal journey to take slowly, listening to the sounds of the wading birds, treasuring what it means to be alive in their company – reflecting on our friendships.

The train passes RRS (Royal Research Ship) *Sir David Attenborough*, undergoing final checks before her first voyage to Antarctica on 16th November 2021. She is carrying *Boaty McBoatface,* an autonomous underwater vehicle (AUV), to remind everyone of the comedy error of running a public poll to name the new vessel. I would love to sneak on board as a stowaway, for their journey will be epic and fundamentally important. Telling a story of climate change to the world, measuring and recording evidence and investigating the powerful negative loop tipping points that accelerate change: ice sheets sliding into the oceans lubricated by invisible underground rivers, thawing permafrost releasing methane, and the shifting, incomprehensibly named Atlantic Meridional Overturning Circulation (AMOC) that makes our weather milder than it should be through its influence on the Gulf Stream. As the world gets warmer, we should not say it has been the warmest month this decade; we should think of it as the coldest month of the next decade. Each year establishes a new baseline, and the 'new normal' narrative implies this is somehow acceptable. It is the Lucretius Problem, a cognitive bias that assumes the worst that can happen is within the boundaries of our experience. Yet records are broken each year, some that flabbergast scientists as they try to understand what they thought was not possible.

The port of Felixstowe unloads thousands of containers from MSC and EVERGREEN shipping lines. They enable the transportation of material goods in one direction and recycled waste in the other, feeding a voracious consumer economy and sweeping up the mess afterwards – a capitalist circulation not unlike those ocean currents. The scale is beyond comprehension compared to the coastal trade before the invention of the shipping container in 1956. The ruthless logistical efficiency of the 20-foot equivalent unit (TEU) steel box compares to the invention of the jet engine as a transformational technology, enabling a global economic model. As I turn the corner and head south, a possible Banksy artwork reflects that interconnectedness, depicting a boy catching a facemask with a fishing rod – a contrast between local leisure, mass industrialisation, globalisation and imported pandemics.

The restored Dovercourt lighthouses signal entry to the harbour and the marshlands. I take a picture of a number 103 beach hut. Why? Well, my friends have a beach hut at Milford-on-Sea with that number. I have decided to photograph as many as I see and construct a montage. It is an eccentric English thing. You may have seen *Roundabouts of Great Britain* or *A272, an Ode to a Road*. Silly yet passionate narratives. I love the fragility of a beach hut on the coast – a little home from which you can contemplate the eternity of tides, weather and sea. A marker too, of the coastal erosion that will one day sweep them away.

It is a messy inland road walk around an explosives factory on Bramble Island to Beaumont Quay, and back on to the seawall into Walton-on-the-Naze. The quality of the light is exceptional as I pass Horsey Island, an unbridged tidal retreat for geese and seals, one of many Essex islands that will be included in the official route. The interplay of reflected colours from the sea, cloud and sky paint subtle hues and tones, as if the sea and sky are inverted. The mudflats hold decaying wrecks. Wooden boats and barges are succumbing to nature, their carcasses, fibres and sinew absorbed by time. The tides flow in, and a cocktail of decay flows out of their skeletal structures.

My accommodation at Frinton-on-Sea retains its 1970s decor and furniture, hidden in an unfashionable cul-de-sac, forgotten. It protects me from an autumnal overnight storm, and the host offers a simple room with a Goblin Teasmade that I dare not touch. Headwinds persist into the morning, making progress to Clacton-on-Sea challenging. An angry vertical storm tower hangs in the sky to the east, the backdrop to silhouette the wind farms that survived the night. Number 103 beach huts are frequent, and hut names amuse me. *Vitamin Sea, Bathing Bellies,* and *Shore Thing* – the humour is uplifting and playful. A full English is demolished for £4.50, accompanied by a bucket of coffee. The promenade bin collectors join me, having made a much earlier start. This is their routine break and a chance to catch up with the news they read in the streets they clear.

I'm collecting spooky *what3words.com* navigation square addresses, words that reflect their environment by chance: *///sand.reader.regretted* points to the promenade, *///giant.mass.crush* is nearby, appropriate for the crowds that gather in summer. This useful smartphone app is popular for emergencies where rescue services can pinpoint a location with three simple words instead of complex grid references or latitude/longitude measurements. I use waymarks, common sense and my OS map app to confirm location when I am lost. My sense of direction is informed by observation, wind, sun and smell – a developing unconscious ability to recognise when I have taken the wrong path. Even though the sea over my left shoulder would be the biggest clue, I am surprised how often I miss an important bridge or diversion from the coast.

The path into Jaywick is obvious, a cycle track above the breakwaters. This coastal community is often quoted as being the poorest in England, with its shanty town vibe of collarless cats and dogs, and semi-permanent structures repaired with the flotsam found on the shoreline. It has a friendly atmosphere, hippy and alternative, and is an outpost from accepted norms. Maybe my feelings are deceived by the sunshine, for it could be quite different in winter, yet the community seems more approachable than some of the wealthy areas I have passed through. Someone has painted a poignant mural on the breakwater, a sentiment of the impermanence of their home:

> *Throw at me nature's fury & I'll stand firm. Keep the sea at bay & your paradise safe. Our seaside shield defender. Help me help me cold 6ft giant I divide sea from settlements. How much longer can I do the job? A friend in tides of need the restless sea has won.*
> #tidesoftendring

This sums up a battle between the sea and the village of Jaywick, a community that evolved from a holiday resort to one housing East End families who had lost their homes to the bombers of World War II. Some bloke on a deckchair asks why I have taken an interest in the mural as he cracks open a tin of lager.

'Nice to see you reading about Jaywick,' he says. 'Where are you walking to?'

'The plan is to reach Mersea this afternoon, but I am not sure about the ferry,' I explain. 'I'm walking the coast of England.'

He takes a sip after the spilt warm foam settles around his hand. 'We had a bunch of people walk through here a few weeks ago; they all had flags,' he says. 'Something to do with storytelling.' It's a funny coincidence, I think. That is what the waitress in Gorleston said. I'm curious.

I pass another three Martello Towers (there are 29 along the Essex and Suffolk coastline), built as a defence against invasion by Napoleon in the early 19th century, and then a final tower at St Osyth Stone Point, in the vain hope of catching the ferry to Mersea. At this late time of year the ferry is not running, so I catch a bus to Colchester and then take a taxi to the campsite in East Mersea after shivering at the bus stop, waiting for a cancelled service until my patience expired.

There is a path around the island, but the route to Salcott is missing. The map comes out, and I explore options using roads and footpaths around a maze of estuaries and military ranges. A deep red sunrise accompanies me to West Mersea with its unpretentious seafood huts and shucked oyster promises. It is too early to savour, and I have a tide to miss at the island causeway – a tide stick measures six feet, and watermarks indicate the extent of a spring tide. Written signs warn trespassers not to enter the samphire beds from the seawall, which will one day be a faster route around Feldy Marshes. I march along busy back lanes via Peldon and Great Wigborough, sporting a bright yellow microfibre towel tied to my backpack for visibility (everything carried should have multiple uses). A few muddy fields remain until I enter Salcott and a new England Coast Path fingerpost. I resume my coastal trek in the haunting landscape of Old Hall Marshes National Nature Reserve – a paradise for wildfowl, waders and walkers in search of tranquillity, and a relief after dodging the traffic.

As I reach the River Blackwater, a surreal illusion appears in the form of two large sugar cubes, for Bradwell Nuclear Power Station dominates the views to the east. As the light changes, their abstract forms vanish; their colour merges with the grey sky until they disappear altogether. The sunlight emerges again, and they pop out of the magician's hat: intense, brilliant white foreign forms. Nature is painting these blank canvases with a light reflected by the sea and mirrored back to you – an optical trick that confuses your visual perception.

It is a long haul into Tollesbury, around the Wick Marshes. Endless monotonous grass-banked seawalls keep you dry alongside the Blackwater Estuary, home to the lonely historic Osea and Northey Islands: natural defensive geography occupied by invaders from another millennium. It has been a tiring day, and it is a relief to reach Maldon Travelodge only to be greeted by a robotic vacuum cleaner, achieving sentience and making a bid for freedom through the automatic doors. I can barely walk to McDonald's opposite as there is no footpath, priority given for the drive-in and car-bound. I should have followed my robotic friend, savouring its newfound freedom as it tried to break into Greggs for a sausage roll, its algorithms overwhelmed by the aromas. I sleep deeply after a restorative bath that would be divine if the tub were two feet longer.

My journey around the Dengie Peninsula will take two days, with a certain wild camp. I need to stock up before departure. It is raining hard as I stand in the supermarket aisles, chilled by the air conditioning. Taking the first step into the deluge is difficult, but my fate is to be soaked, so why delay? Thames barges are moored along the quayside; the dreich, dreary scene subtracts 100 years from my mental calendar and their wooden decks bleed a sepia tint into a grey watercolour-wash seascape. This painting is dramatised by the sight of a huge red sail making its way to the port, tacking gracefully as the river bends and the tide floods – a colour focal point in the landscape that draws my eye to it. I am a lone walker in this weather, against this backdrop of marshland, islands and estuary – a resident of another world, another time, another reality.

The weather improves as I double back into the creeks of Marylandsea, which thwart easterly progress. The reality of a modern world re-emerges as the power station appears again. It is eerily quiet, yet hums a synaesthetic sound, assaulting the senses with unnatural energies – more perceived than actual. I walk on by, sitting on the seawall and contemplating the shores of Mersea opposite. A short-eared owl sits on a fence post and stares at me; a wing beat from resuming a patrol of the arable fields. Foxes skip along the hedgerows. No doubt small rodents will scurry from this twin threat as the evening descends, their position betrayed by the movement in the grasses and stubble.

Around the headland, the Othona Christian community has found sanctuary adjacent to the stunning Chapel of St Peter-on-the-Wall, constructed by St Cedd in AD654. I turn a huge latch into the chapel to sit out of the wind and drizzle. I close the door. Silence envelops me. This simple shelter is a spiritual trigger, a pilgrim's shelter. My psyche connects, reflecting, and unconsciously praying – not to a conventional god, but to the voices of nature I collected that day. A few miles further, I pitch for the night. The roosting wildfowl startle me as they glide inland, perhaps missing my head by only a few feet in the dark. They are resting too and will depart with me before dawn. I catch up on emails. My wife has sent me a passage from a poem by Lord Byron, perfect reading before I fall into a deep sleep, cradled by the grasses and reeds:

> *There is a pleasure in the pathless woods,*
> *There is a rapture on the lonely shore,*
> *There is society where none intrudes,*
> *By the deep Sea, and music in its roar:*
> *I love not Man the less, but Nature more,*
> *For these our interviews, in which I steal*
> *From all I may be, or have been before,*
> *To mingle with the Universe, and feel*
> *What I can ne'er express, yet cannot all conceal.*
> Lord Byron, extract from *Childe Harold's Pilgrimage* (1812)

I wake and pack an hour before dawn – instinctive wild camp behaviour. The dew soaks my feet in the half-light as I take in the wide vista from the elevated position on the seawall. A farmer is raking a field in the distance and the lights from the triangular-track tractor confuse me – they look like the probing beams of a UFO, looking for an abductee. Only when the sun rises can I see the pilot and its true form emerge, completing a night shift. I walk along the grass mound wall around the sluice gates that protect the high-yield reclaimed fields. The fractal tide-cut gullies of the marsh contrast with the geometric lines of the huge fields – one tended by nature, the other by man, each the architect of their designs. David Hockney once said that landscape has no perspective, yet the farmer has drawn one with his GPS-guided tractor. The light of this alien technology cannot compete with the rising sun as a deep orange glow intensifies to announce the new day, and the UFO departs to the yard for breakfast, its identity exposed.

Dropping down to a track that services the seawall I see a kestrel hovering ahead, its motions pivoting around a transfixed gaze, searching for prey. I approach slowly and observe, but it twists and flies ahead to a branch. I do not expect it to linger, yet it lifts again and settles in the grass bank. Again, it lifts just 10 metres from me as I walk, finding a post to perch on. It is watching me but also watching the path. Unbelievably, this continues for almost 20 minutes. What behaviour am I observing? Am I disturbing rodents on which it will pounce? It feels like more – a symbiotic connection and a thrilling experience. My prayers to nature at the chapel are being answered, and I begin to understand what J. A. Baker experienced during his time on the Essex coastline, details observed and captured in *The Peregrine*.

It is just past lunchtime as I reach Burnham-on-Crouch. The ferry is not running so I take a train home. I decline to walk to South Woodham Ferrers to return to the marina opposite a few days later, remembering that it is cheaper to pop home than stay locally – like a daily commute to work. Foulness and Wallasea Islands will have to wait for a summer's day and more detailed plans to include walking the Broomway on Foulness – a long-held ambition. You can't just rock up and walk it; a guide and restricted access permissions are needed. Instead, I ease my way along the seawalls to Rochford for lunch, admiring the fields of wintering geese in huge numbers. I use the spires of the Little and Great Wakering churches to guide me around the intricate creek-side paths into Southend-on-Sea. The land to the east is a military range, and I can the hear gunfire and explosions which will be familiar for a week or so, even across the Thames Estuary in Kent.

I stay in an anonymous hotel, where the host seems surprised by my booking, passing me a key worn and bent with overuse. The room overlooks the promenade, where all seems quiet at first but later erupts into a glitter-fest, furry-dice, car Armageddon of strutting vehicles, their sound systems shaking the ground, percussion provided by snare drums and ignited unburnt fuel in their exhausts. There is no need for a TV tonight as the entertainment is provided in real time – a live people-watching show below my window, backlit by the neon lights and a colourful cackling banter from a town that sleeps by day and parties by night.

I emerge to the promenade at 7am, contemplating the 1.34 miles of the world's longest pleasure pier. It needs a train to reach its terminus, and to walk it this early in the morning will lengthen my day if I am to reach Tilbury. Breakfast is found at a no-nonsense, surprisingly good vegetarian cafe in Leigh-on-Sea, a former cockle-fishing community. The *Endeavour LO41*, a cockle bawley built in 1926, lies in the mud, seemingly fully operational. With breakfast inside me, I walk past Two Tree Island, named after two huge elm trees that were felled by storms in the 1960s. Ramshackle houseboats lying in mud-drained marinas guide me through Benfleet to Bowers and Fobbing Marshes before an abrupt interruption of immense commerce at London Gateway Port, seeking to de-throne Felixstowe and Southampton as the UK's busiest port.

Leaving Canvey Island for another day to reach Tilbury, a Thurrock Thameside Nature Park ranger guides me around the colourfully named Mucking Marshes to Coalhouse Fort, broadly following the Thames Estuary Path. The birdlife is unfazed by the industrial landscape, which is overwhelming in places. The walking is surprisingly pleasant, and the views across the contracting estuary calm me as coastal vessels glide to London. A city is coming – you can smell it, feel it, sense it.

The shoreline here contains the spoils and rubble of the Blitz in the 1940s; shards of glass and ceramics glisten on the beach. I learned later that this inspired the *Beach of Dreams* project I had inadvertently encountered – those flags that locals carried, each telling a story about their coastline. 'What dreams were shattered when the bombs went off? This is the beach of broken dreams,' a journalist muttered when he visited this spot, with the artist Ali Pretty, who conceived the project, replying, 'If this is the beach of broken dreams, where is the beach of dreams?' My interest was piqued, and I later met the Kinetika team that organised a 500-mile walk from Lowestoft to Tilbury, where a silk flag had been made for each mile, each telling a story about the coast. What a wonderful idea: a community art project that follows a path around our coastline. It has an emotional power to transcend and communicate: a subliminal call to action, a statement with undeniable integrity – the concerns of our coastal communities made tangible in a visual form.

My walk takes me to the ferry and Gravesend, the landing point for the Windrush Generation, whose expectant and fearful faces adorn the glass as you walk down the pier. I passed the Worlds End pub, mentioned in *The Diary of Samuel Pepys* in 1669, a location that will have witnessed a rich and colourful history: wars, commerce, and the taming of the Thames. As I approach the metropolis every wall, timber and building reflects history and heritage, a spectrum of patina that colours the path side. One day, I will walk on to Tower Bridge to link with the Thames Path National Trail, but today, a public ferry can take me to Gravesend.

The hotel is very comfortable but a financially unsustainable luxury. I need a plan for the Kent section, as campsites are rare and accommodation expensive or hard to find. The Luftwaffe made a mess of this town during the war, as pilots dropped bombs early in fear of the flak hell ahead – a creep-back phenomenon that destroyed many homes before they reached their intended targets. Pre-war photographs in the breakfast cafe are difficult to match with the streets outside the window. The walk east, through a sickly industrial aroma, is unpleasant: tyre dumps, scrap heaps and recycling yards block the paths until I reach the seawall. The Thames mist veils the ghostly coastal ships as they rumble past, heard long before they are seen – surreal spaceships on their final approach to docking points or steaming into the North Sea with increasing urgency, throttles nudged open to 'ahead full'.

I'm walking along the Saxon Shore Way, my occasional companion until Reculver, instead of a completed England Coast Path National Trail. It is an endless seawall to the Isle of Grain, a no-man's-land of mud and sand that Magwitch would recognise (*Great Expectations* by Charles Dickens, 1861). It is a messy route, the path incomplete, leading to a dead end on the Isle of Grain, necessitating an awkward navigation to Hoo Flats and a path again. Darnet and Hoo Forts guard Gillingham Reach. I progress along the shingle banks to Rochester, the brent geese gurgling away on the mudflats for company. A high tide means a higher path to the pretty village of Upnor. Its cobbled high street descends to the riverbank, beyond the King's Arms pub. Even without a few pints inside, I am perplexed by the strange sight of Foxtrot B-39 U-475 *Black Widow*, a Cold War Soviet Navy submarine that served in the Baltic until 1993. It lies moored and forlorn in the Medway, a discreet distance from the historic naval shipyard at Chatham.

I cross the bridge and catch a train home through London. My journey around Essex, the second longest county shoreline, is complete, as estuaries, islands and restricted ways remain for a later day – an unconscious decision to draw me back to the beguiling estuary landscape of mudflats, sands and channels full of wildlife.

# 3
# ROCHESTER TO DOVER
## Groundhog Day

*'Home is not where you were born; home is
where all your attempts to escape cease.'*
                                              Naguib Mahfouz

### Distance walked: 270 miles

I am searching online for accommodation from Rochester to Dover and beyond, looking for affordable campsites and hostels in the winter months, but these facilities are scarce: urban environments have no demand for such accommodation, and the seaside holiday towns are closed for the season. Another strategy is to use public transport and base myself in a single location. Fortunately, good bus and rail services connect this coastline to Canterbury, which has a nice all-year campsite where I can park my ageing campervan for a week.

The advantages are numerous: I can carry a day pack, take only what I need, shop for and cook home meals, and sleep inexpensively. A local No. 43 bus leaves the campsite each morning at 07:04 to the train station for services east and west. In the twilight, I board the bus and join city commuters on the train to Rochester. As I alight, the exit barrier eats my paper ticket, and I can walk east to any convenient station to return to the campsite. Sittingbourne is achievable, even Faversham if I feel good and the paths are easy.

Weaving past the historic docks and Royal Engineers Museum, the Saxon Shore Way follows a seawall on the south bank of the expanding Thames Estuary. Flocks of brent geese chatter away, like endearing tribbles from the famous *Star Trek* episode in 1967. There are curlews, redshanks and little egrets, undisturbed by the outline of a walker on the grass bank. The birds probe the mud and shallows, looking for a morsel. Each has a specialised bill, adapted to find worms, fish, shells and crustaceans, with tweezer, dagger, scissor and spoon designs. Buzzards and kestrels are daily sightings, looking for something less salty. Other waders are happy sifting through seagrass and weed, inelegantly wiggling their upturned rears as they sift the shallows or stamping in the mud to wake their prey. The cormorants seek more nutritious protein as they plunge headlong to the depths, their wings and feet now powerful flippers. In one moment, they skim the surface like a ground-effect aeroplane; the next, they are sea predators, efficient, agile and deadly. The speed at which they swim defies belief as they plunge to the depths. They master two worlds, a marvel of evolutionary existence.

There are signs that I am leaving the capital city: the industrial aroma is replaced by clean air, the commuter hum turns to birdsong, and the unnatural architectures fade to nature. The solitude returns, and my mind empties of the mundane, allowing new ideas to pop into my head spontaneously. My freed synapses now explore new connections and patterns. I habitually write down the unusual conclusions that have finally processed memory into creative insight – small snippets that would never emerge were I to allow distractions to preoccupy my headspace. It doesn't happen often, as if some computer is silently looking for an answer in the background but has no idea how long that process will take – popping up an answer at any moment.

The sun breaks through the low fog in the estuary to light up the orchards in Upchurch, the trees groaning with ripe apples and pears. Tractors pull gangs of pickers in one direction and full loads in another. No one will miss one fallen apple – its label-free form saved from a four-pack plastic wrapper, variety label and barcode sticker. This is a garden of England, a fruit basket for supermarket chains seeking genetically husbanded varieties, standardised, polished and flawless.

Loud, deep explosions can be heard at odd intervals, almost certainly from Shoeburyness across the estuary. Their booms are quieter than I experience in Essex but still make you uneasy. It is a reminder that a catastrophic explosion could occur at any time, for frightening energy is contained within the rotting hull of SS *Richard Montgomery*, lying on the sea bed a mile from Sheerness. It contains 1,500 tonnes of unexploded ordnance and would break every window in the town if it were to detonate

– an unresolved legacy of World War II. I will leave the Isle of Sheppey for another day when the England Coast Path is opened, for the path has yet to find a route along the eastern and southern shores, requiring bridges and signposts across their marshes to return to the Kingsferry Bridge.

I continue walking, re-entering an industrial landscape. An incinerator power station and recycling plants discreetly deal with our discarded and forgotten waste. It is unappealing, unattractive and unpleasant until I exit Sittingbourne through an unexpected country park via the 'Head' and the 'Mouth' of Milton Creek. Even in this environment, egrets, redshanks and curlews will find something along the polluted mudbanks. Boats long-forgotten rot in the mud: modern fibreglass hulls resist natural decomposition, becoming ugly, shattered remains, bleached of colour and strength as the tide does its best to erode their glass-and-resin structures. Wooden-framed ancestors succumb to their graves with dignity and grace, the Earth reclaiming nutrients for another day, unlike the manmade plastics and chemicals of modern vessels, which will permanently pollute our planet and take centuries to digest – forgotten forever chemicals.

The next day, I return to the town, reflecting on my journey in a dream state alongside the school kids and commuters, universally preoccupied with the content streaming from their smartphones: supplicants to the gods of commerce, manipulated and held captive by an addictive cocktail of social validation and echo chambers, platforms designed by psychologists and behavioural scientists to secure attention and maximise profit. During my life, the time spent online for this school-age demographic has soared to 40% of their waking day. It takes discipline to disconnect and re-engage with family, friends, co-workers and the community in a more direct and meaningful way, as we evolved to do over millennia.

The seawall and marshes give way to an expanding estuary as I walk the banks of the Swale, the channel that cleaves the Isle of Sheppey from the mainland. Walking at a pace that matches the ebbing tide, I flow like a passenger on an airport travelator. Conyer Creek diverts inland, and I correctly guess the name of the Ship Inn pub on the opposite bank. It is open, and I am tempted, but I rarely drink alcohol on a long hike – it troubles my sleep, requires nighttime pees, and has a potential to waylay my loose schedule. It is an opportunity to take a break from stimulants and experience the outdoors sober, letting its wonders provide the high.

The old ferry to the Isle of Harty would once have perfectly connected to Sheppey and the Oare Creek path to Faversham – a port with another temptation: Shepherd Neame Brewery. I snack on a bench on the wharf and drink tea. It has been a long diversion around the Ham and Nagden Marshes to reach the coastline of the North Sea again. I am leaving the Thames Estuary, an intermission in the coastal narrative. This is a river that impregnates the land with commerce, begetting London, England and, at one time, the British Empire.

Offshore wind farms in the distance confirm the more expansive seascape as the estuarial mud turns to coastal pebbles, shingle and sand. The marshes recede and the groynes return, as do beach huts and deckchairs at Whitstable. Beachgoers are wrapped in blankets, snoring, sheltering from the wind and having a pleasant afternoon nap. I have arrived in oyster town, its heritage betrayed by middens of calcium shells. Huts and restaurants tempt you to saviour their slimy delights with a chilly or acidic piquant sauce. The experience of swallowing is one moment repulsive, and then a revelation as you taste the secrets of the sea. I rest on a bench near the RNLI station, satiated yet wanting a main course. The backrest is carved with lyrics from Van Morrison's *Into the Mystic*: 'Hear the sailors cry, smell the sea, feel the sky, let your spirit fly' sums up a good day on the north coast of Kent as the bus takes me home.

Returning to Whitstable, I can see Canterbury Cathedral bathed in a temperature inversion, a beautiful scene ignored by the regular passengers through familiarity; yet, a pilgrim approaching their destination would cry at this vision of heaven. I head north to the bus stop I left yesterday, to rejoin my own coastal pilgrimage. There is a pleasant westerly wind to push me along the path, effortless walking with such a light pack. The seawall is now concrete, hosting a cycle path to Herne Bay. As the second hour passes, I open an energy bar, a routine to keep energy levels high, and throw the wrapper into a one-eyed penguin rubbish bin, its mouth open to encourage feeding. I ponder the helter-skelter that screws the end of the pier into the rising tide, securing it for winter. To twirl with gravity is a wonderful, simple seaside experience for anyone who has tried it.

## THE COAST IS OUR COMPASS

The boardwalks and promenade are deserted until I meet the bronze statue of Amy Johnson. This sculpture commemorates a famous aviatrix. Her Airspeed Oxford aircraft ran out of fuel here on 5th January 1941. She parachuted safely but was lost at sea, her body never found. Eleven years earlier, she took to the air from Croydon airfield with a pack of sandwiches and a thermos flask of coffee. Her Gypsy Moth *Jason*, registration G-AAAH, took her to Australia – quite an achievement for a typist from Hull who became bewitched by flying after a chance visit to an aerodrome. She was blessed with a curiosity that led to incredible adventures that captivated the world during the Depression – someone who refused to accept that such challenges are impossible at such times.

There are red-throated divers in the bay, confirmed by a group who are keen to know about the arrival of the brent geese from Siberia – an epic 2,500-mile journey. The volunteers have set up a stall just before the Reculver Towers to talk about the diversity of nature and the Roman fort, built to defend against Saxon raids. It once guarded the Wantsum sea channel that separated the Isle of Thanet from the mainland. This will be my destination tomorrow after I walk the northern shores of the former island to explore the delights of Margate, Broadstairs and Ramsgate.

There is quite a bit of history here, as you might expect given its proximity to Europe. The channel slowly silted up and became farmland in the 16th century; perhaps it will flood again when the sea levels rise. The path follows the base of the cliffs into Westgate-on-Sea and eventually Margate, a tired, run-down town whose regeneration started with the new Turner Contemporary gallery and the homecoming of Tracey Emin. Art once again acting as a catalyst for positive change. The tidal bathing pool sits beneath an ornate Nayland Rock Shelter, where T. S. Eliot wrote a favourite poem, *The Waste Land*, in 1921. Even though I find it hard to comprehend fully, many of the paragraphs resonate as I walk through coastal communities. The poem searches for meaning in a post-war world, and perhaps it helps me search for meaning in later life as someone disaffected by the pursuit of material wealth and status. Is it my guilt of consumption? A participant contributing to the changes in our climate – instigated, like war, by the human species?

My thoughts take a break as I dodge crashing waves driven by a strong north-easterly wind on to the concrete under-path beneath the chalk cliffs, threatening a salt soaking. Out to sea, huge turbines twist the pitch of their blades to embrace the cold air, activating to meet an unseen demand. I can sense turning the corner as I enter the Strait of Dover, letting out my main sheet to sail on a broad reach south to Broadstairs. The former lifeboat station is a moment of shelter before crossing the beach to climb back on to the cliffs. It is not a day to promenade; it is too windy along East Cliff. On a quieter day in 1866, it would have been a privilege you paid for, as the old notice declares on a tiny toll building that survives.

Ramsgate retains a Victorian charm, complemented by modern artworks and many interesting architectural gems. The stairs from the pavilion are colourfully decorated with ornate tiles, easy to miss unless you look back. Peter's Fish Factory and the Queen's Head invite you to recuperate, retaining their period decor. Then, the idle wasteland of an industrial port shatters quaint illusions until you reach Pegwell Bay, the eastern end of the Wantsum Channel, with more stories to tell.

The Romans established a bridgehead at Richborough in AD43 until they left in AD409. Then the Anglo-Saxon chieftains, Hengist and Horsa, arrived in AD449 to fill the void until the Apostle to the English, St Augustine, landed in AD597 – seeking to conquer the territory, hearts and minds of a nation wandering into the Dark Ages. The Romans secured their port, building a fort and amphitheatre to supply their land armies and guard the Wantsum Channel. Kent welcomed a replica of a Viking ship, named *Hugin,* in 1949, which sailed from Denmark to commemorate the 1,500th anniversary of the Viking invasion. St Augustine became the first Archbishop of Canterbury. The legacy of all these settlers remains with us – in our collective memory, in our beliefs, customs, values and behaviours.

A sign reroutes around a scrap metal site that has blocked a path. The dispute is unresolved with the council, a boundary battle that stirs emotions, with the property owner refusing to back down. The alternative is a long, dull walk along a busy dual carriageway, then past the Pfizer factory, where Viagra was first formulated – a little blue pill that has changed the sex lives of many couples. I wonder if those earlier settlers, with much shorter lifespans, could have imagined such a perplexing remedy.

I arrive at Sandwich, where a preoccupied gambler invented *the* sandwich. The 4th Earl needed a quick meal and suggested his beef be served between two slices of bread. To his delight it tasted wonderful, as anyone who enjoys a steak sandwich will affirm. The town is a medieval gem, one of the Cinque Ports, and at one time a hive of trade and commerce. The delightfully named 'No Name Shop' on 'No Name Street' serves an excellent French baguette, perfect for my meal on the bus back to Canterbury and worthy of the tradition it maintains, albeit with a continental twist.

Walking late into the season means more time during the golden hours with perfect light at the start and end of the day. The short contrails of transatlantic flights are visible in the clear, crisp, cold sky, enhanced by the light. Radiant sunburst rays converge to their vanishing point, back through the woodland to the morning sun. The sky fades to deep blue, blending with the orange sunrise as I approach the shoreline near the River Stour that now reaches the sea, the last meandering remnants of an inland waterway that isolated the Isle of Thanet. I am alone walking south past the famous golf course of Royal St George, where the morning dew is cleared from the greens, ready for competition. The private estates along this coastline are deserted, devoid of traffic and people, exclusive yet unused, even by hardy dog walkers unable to park their cars nearby.

The day comes to life at Deal, which didn't receive the tacky seaside town memo. It retains an old-fashioned character: fishing boats hauled on to the shore, a castle and a modest pier – nothing too flashy, and very 1920s. There is a 5k Park Run, where I keep pace with the slower runners; it is a sunny Saturday, not a time to spend indoors. The runners turn around at the outskirts, and I ascend on to the downs and a glorious view of the French coastline. It is a crystal-clear day, and the visibility is perfect, for every vessel transiting the Strait of Dover is visible.

Channel Rescue human rights observers sit on deckchairs, binoculars in hand, watching for migrant boats. They log any sightings and observe the activities of the Border Force vessels. They will call out the RNLI if the more sophisticated 'official' cameras and radar equipment miss anything. They are holding the government's response to account; its semi-permanent military-like camera installations nearby connect to a monitoring room manned by people sipping tea and munching bacon rolls. It will be a busy day. The sea is calm and the winds are slight – ideal conditions to cross the Channel in a small boat. Perfect conditions to be seen and rescued.

I descend to St Margaret's Bay to touch the shoreline where many oversized rubber boats and scenes of migrant desperation have been witnessed. I climb again to the White Cliffs of Dover for a final run into the port, its position betrayed by a fleet of cross-channel ferries with their cargo of drivers and passengers in buses, lorries and cars, passports and entry visas ready to hand. Dozens of tourists have climbed from the town to take pictures; their selfie sticks point to the sky as they pout. This is a viral social media location, overpopulated by those seeking to prove attendance at one of England's iconic geographical locations – a white band of chalk announcing England, a border defended at great cost over generations. They may have missed Dame Vera Lynn Way and the First and Last, the voice of these cliffs and the self-proclaimed last pub in the civilised world, but these sidenotes don't compete with the Instagram hashtags.

On the bus back to Canterbury, I reflect on the non-linear nature of the walking week, constantly returning to my campervan base. It doesn't feel the same, like the *Groundhog Day* movie, waking, moving, repeating, as if I am going to work. I will make amends when I return later as the familiarity of the repeated nightly accommodation dilutes the sense of progress that doesn't fit well with a long-distance traveller.

# 4

# DOVER TO CHICHESTER
## To see the world in a grain of sand

*'The greatest of all follies is to sacrifice health
for any other kind of happiness.'*

Arthur Schopenhauer

**Distance walked: 360 miles**

The HS1 train from St Pancras to Dover takes but a moment to transport me back to a choice of trail, for the England Coast Path overlays the last miles of the North Downs and Saxon Shore Way. The fingerposts barely have space for the walking permutations from this Cinque Port. It is a truism that you could reach anywhere in the British Isles from this point (a ferry or two may be needed), as a few long journeys start from Dover. For example, the Sustrans National Cycle Network Route 1 will take you to Shetland, and the North Downs Way will connect you a huge network of pilgrim paths from Canterbury. I climb through the Western Heights, past substantial forts and defensive structures, under the busy A20 to reach the coastline and the free air on Shakespeare Cliff. It is early November, and the weather is glorious. I have chosen to follow the England Coast Path west and will see how far I get before winter takes hold.

The Battle of Britain Memorial cafe, in the shape of a Spitfire wing, reminds us of the summer of 1940 when aircrew fought bravely to defend these shores. Concrete parabolic sound mirrors still stand, a primitive form of audio radar used to detect incoming bomber formations. The path is unnervingly close to the cliff edge and foot placement between treasured private gardens and the sheer drop to the sea takes concentration. I feel safer after descending to the Martello Tower in Folkestone, the risk of a landslip behind me.

The town is full of subtle artworks, and one makes me think. The *Folkestone Mermaid* is a bronze statue like the famous *Little Mermaid* sculpture in Copenhagen, but with her watchful gaze on the sea. Created by Cornelia Parker, in the likeness of Georgina Baker, a local mother of two children, it alludes to the threat of rising sea levels. The mythical sea creature defends our oceans and seas: a siren to lure those who plunder her home to early graves. This water world has mysteries yet to be discovered, and we should be cautious, for it is of profound importance to all life on Earth. We are connected to it, dependent on it, even if we cannot see into its depths.

Then, I can't help laughing at a memorial plaque to Don Thompson, the only male gold medallist for Great Britain at the 1960 Olympics. He competed in the 50-kilometre walk (31 miles), finishing in an astonishing 4 hours, 25 minutes and 30 seconds – that is seven mph! If I walked at that pace, I'd return to Cromer in a month. No amount of hip wiggling, gait lengthening or cadence increase gets me even near that speed. I can reach four and a half miles per hour with effort, but I generally sustain three and a bit miles per hour for an eight-hour day. This aligns with my rule of thumb: mere mortals are half the speed of in-form professional athletes, be they swimmers, cyclists, walkers or runners. I'll suspend my 'walking is not a sport' mantra for a moment, for the plaque is a starting mark for the annual one-mile race organised by Thompson's former club. It takes me 14 minutes (a satisfying 4.3 mph) to reach the finish mark. I am exhausted, but my prize is a deep red sunset, which guides me to Hythe for the night.

The next morning, the path takes an inland route, following the Royal Military Canal before returning to the coast at Dymchurch Redoubt, a Napoleonic fortification built to defend the sluice gates. There is a wealth of historic structures to protect marshlands from an easy victory from an angry sea or determined enemy. Only the concrete sluice and earthen berm protect a vast inland area of Romney, Walland and Denge Marshes, all once salt flats flushed by the sea until a great storm of 1287 reshaped the coastline dramatically. Ports became landlocked, towns gained new harbours, and poor (Old) Winchelsea village drowned completely.

The walk is flat, and the skies open, my pace marked each mile by another Martello Tower to New Romney, once a Cinque Port at the entrance to the River Rother. The quayside is now inland, dry and demoted, a road now inelegantly named the B2071. A stunning water tower and more substantial concrete sound mirrors are worth a diversion from otherwise bland architecture that subtly evolves into bohemian-style cottages and fishing huts as you venture deeper into the shingle. Boardwalks invite you to the shifting, drifting shoreline. Inland, Derek Jarman's well-known Prospect Cottage intrigues, a black structure with yellow window frames sitting in an unusual desert garden that blends with the landscape. The southern wall hosts a decaying poem, made of wood block letters on a tar-painted wall. I can discern *The Sunne Rising* by John Donne, which tells a story of lovers still in bed, their romantic post-coital bliss interrupted by the warming sun:

> *Busy old fool, unruly sun,*
> *Why dost thou thus,*
> *Through windows, and through curtains call on us?*
> *Must to thy motions lovers' seasons run?*
> *Saucy pedantic wretch, go chide*
> *Late school boys and sour prentices,*
> *Go tell court huntsmen that the king will ride,*
> *Call country ants to harvest offices,*
> *Love, all alike, no season knows nor clime,*
> *Nor hours, days, months, which are the rags of time.*
>
> John Donne, extract from *The Sunne Rising* (1633)

I break for lunch at a shipping container pop-up seafood shack – the type you immediately sense has the highest-quality fresh produce, cooked without pretence. A scallop bun with chilli jam is exquisite and lifts my spirits for the walk to the old and new lighthouse structures and the terminus for the Romney, Hythe and Dymchurch Railway – an excellent return route for a day's linear walk. Like Sizewell and Bradwell further north, Dungeness hosts two huge nuclear power stations, visible for miles and sitting in a National Nature Reserve: the Magnox (Dungeness A) is defuelled, while the Advanced Gas-Cooled reactor (Dungeness B), beset by technical problems, is being prematurely decommissioned. They no longer generate power, even though the huge transmission lines pointing arrow-straight inland are connected by subsea cable to the French nuclear electrical network. Again, the contrast between rising sea levels, a nuclear facility that will take generations to decommission, and the natural world is perplexing. I am sure there is an approved risk assessment document that explains this, but I, for one, need reassurance. Something is wrong with this picture. Reading about storms and floods and examining OS map contours only heightens my anxiety.

My beach walk abruptly ends as a soldier shouts obscenities at me from the guard tower, assuming I cannot see the red flag, or read the signs indicating that Lydd Ranges are in use. He must be bored, peppering his day with angry outbursts, chalking up wins on his noticeboard for a laugh. I sit down in protest and have a cup of tea from my flask before heading inland to Lydd, past an open marshland full of wild birds, an RSPB reserve (more contrast between beauty and destructive power) that will see rarities during the year. Bitterns will boom, hobbies will catch dragonflies, and cuckoos will call. Many migrating birds will be thankful for the lakes and this shingle desert following a channel crossing, refuelling before venturing into the British Isles and beyond.

After a pleasant night at the hotel, I am eager to leave early to return to the coastline at Jury's Gap, along a cycle track past lakes full of geese and dabbling ducks. The upgraded seawall is an easy walk to Camber Sands, then across a grass-carpeted golf course to the River Rother. The views of the town are jigsaw-box perfect, a medieval scene with depth, mystery and a timeless quality. A seal swims against the flow, happily fishing and ignoring my presence. I follow it to Rye Bridge and wave goodbye before walking to town to look for a cafe. Nothing is open, so I have the supercalorific pecan cake (from that lovely fish pop-up) for breakfast and then opt to follow the 1066 Country Walk to Winchelsea, perched above the landscape. This new village has an unusual modern grid-pattern street layout, and an elevation to survive future floods (although it may one day become an island). I stop to chat with a man who has walked along the canal with a chair to sit and read a newspaper.

'The best decision I ever made, retiring at 56,' he says.

'You've found a lovely spot to read, and to watch the birds,' I say as I point out a kestrel hovering and a heron floating with long beats along the canal. He has found his relaxation, and I have found mine – one static and the other in motion.

## THE COAST IS OUR COMPASS

The ascent to the community of Fairlight and into Hastings is novel, I say to myself, having not seen a climb for a while. A bench is perfectly placed to rest to reflect on this new geology:

*Come sit a-while, come take some rest*
*And think of those in their quest*
*To be together, were always discreet,*
*And met nearby at Lover's Seat.*

Tall, thin, black wooden buildings greet me on the shoreline at Hastings. They are used to store fishing gear and designed to comply with old planning restrictions, maximise the limited space on the shore, and yet meet the requirements to dry nets, vertically. I have time to visit the local museum to learn more. Built in 1835, they are called 'netshops', and stand in neatly lettered rows like enormous beach huts. It is a unique sight in England which brings a distinctive character to a town that gave its name to the famous battle in 1066.

I watch the sunset, picking at a fish supper, rather than stare at the insides of a Travelodge and answer *Pointless* questions on TV. I study the map and realise I will be in a seaside urban landscape for a week, with only the Seven Sisters chalk cliffs to entertain me. This will be a change from dilapidated piers, retirement complexes, promenades and the endless visitors looking at the sea from the comfort of their cars, reading a paper, munching on chips.

The Sustrans National Cycle Network Route 2 (another that starts from Dover), will be my friend for a few days. I fantasise about the sheer pleasure of riding a bicycle – but it is not the same. A walking pace is relaxed; your mind absorbs the experience and sensual inputs, ticking along at your natural pace without interruption from foreign technological aids (a bicycle wheel). I am more observant and alert to the unusual in this state, seeing so much more in the landscape. The more I see, the more I notice. The familiar is ignored, opening my mind to new movement and shapes. Cycling is just too fast, yet it is thrilling to sacrifice observation for speed. To quote William Henry Davies: 'Now shall I walk Or shall I ride? "Ride," Pleasure said "Walk," Joy replied.' Today, a balance of those two modes would be perfect.

St Leonards-on-Sea and Bexhill-on-Sea are cycle path-on-sea hosts that end abruptly at Pevensey with a snotty notice declaring a private beach. I am not sure how the route will be determined in the future, as the beachfront owners are proud of their shingle gardens. It is a pointless boundary dispute with the sea, which cares little for what is private or public. Yet, after miles of shingle skating, I am happy to take a firmer inland road, where I can observe the backsides of the beachfront second home Shangri-la.

It is time for a treat, so I wait for a restaurant to open at Eastbourne Marina. My taste buds are insulted by what should have been a pleasant meal, so I leave early. I progress into the town, marvelling at the coastal defence work in progress. Massive trucks and diggers, superscale versions of a holiday child with a Tonka truck and bucket and spade, are rearranging the shoreline shingle. Period beach shelters, piers and artworks entertain visitors and locals alike in this beautiful coastal community. There is a nice vibe on Sunday, amplified by the warm sun – a location with the most sunshine days in a year in Britain. I reach the start of the South Downs Way and call it a day. The nearby B&B is traditional in every sense, tucked in the backstreets of the western part of town: its shade is welcome, my host is lovely, and it's clean and comfortable.

But I skip what looks like a delicious breakfast, for I am not feeling well. My energy levels are low. Something is wrong. Nevertheless, I head up on to the downs, taking the cliffside route to the Bomber Command memorial, a tribute to the 55,573 aircrew who lost their lives during World War II. This headland, for some, was their last view of England. The walk is exhilarating and adrenaline compensates for my condition and propels me past the landmarks of Beachy Head and Belle Tout lighthouses and into the roller-coaster ride that is the Seven Sisters. The folded rolling chalk hills are cut like an undulating cake, revealing their sugary white interiors. The views inland of ancient downland are as beautiful as the sea views. My eyes are torn between the two contrasting worlds as I walk the path between the fold of a sea/land diptych. My mind wants to close the scene together – a memory to keep and treasure later.

The inland route at Cuckmere Haven interrupts the coastal joy until I can marvel at the downland scene one last time. With the foreground of the famous coastguard cottages it's a clichéd holiday brochure picture.

I walk in a coma-like state, my stomach making strange noises, into Newhaven and pop into a supermarket for a bottle of Lucozade, my go-to cure for sickness and an energy boost. The chemical reaction is immediate and violent. I find a drain just in time to catch the eruption. I have food poisoning. A caring woman at the estate agent rushes outside to ensure I'm ok, not judging my behaviour.

'I'm sorry, I've eaten something dodgy,' I say. 'I'm ok; it is out now. Thank you so much for checking.' I complete my sentence just before another eruption, my frail body hanging from my walking poles to keep me upright. 'Don't worry, it is definitely all out now,' I declare, trying to man up.

After flushing out my mouth with water, I carry on to Newhaven Fort in a dream-like state and take a deep breath of the sea air near the breakwater. I should stop, but walk blindly on until my body continues to purge the poisons into a nearby drain. I rue this self-inflicted harm as I cross the Meridian Line and sit every hour for a sip of energy drink until I reach the outskirts of Brighton. I must stop soon, so book the Premier Inn for an unusually low price, as if some god has compensated for my condition. Knowing I have a haven, I adopt a flâneur walking style to disguise my exhaustion, wandering along the promenade, observing the arrival of vintage vehicles on the London to Brighton annual run. The uplifting smell of oil, coal and other combustibles is sweet, countering my sickly odour, when it should really have the opposite effect. I feel better when I reach my bed, having walked 28 miles in a sorry state. I recall that for some perverse reason I have a history of walking long days while feeling unwell. Is it grim determination or anger that I have made a mistake? I am not sure, but it has introduced me to my limits.

I get up early and walk, trying to reclaim my system. Brighton's seafront is alive with interest, sculpture, art and colour. The Georgian buildings, upside down cottages, ornate shelters and fancy hotels are lit with a clean, clear light, the sun rising above the burnt-down pier structure sitting orphaned in the sea. I can count my miles westward, watching the height of the i360 observation tower diminish, its gondola rising like a Polo mint on a straw.

Portslade-by-Sea and Shoreham-by-Sea (what is the difference between -on- and -by-, I wonder) shield an unexpected working port. I should have brought my trail shoes, as my boots are heavy on the cycle path. The day is awakening, and my empty fuel tank demands a refill as a fancy cafe appears. Cautious that treats can have consequences, I have a lovely bowl of porridge and eggs on toast and return to the path – but barely make it another mile before I disgorge 20 quid's worth of delicious food on to the pavement. I am unhappy. This can't continue, so I vow to take 24 hours drinking only water and nibbling plain bread. This is becoming Type 3 fun.

Worthing looks very fancy, with new architectural wonders and a clean beach. Yet a sign recalls quite a different scene on 17th December 1944, when an Avro Lancaster PB355 EA-B narrowly missed the rooftops and crash-landed on the beach, its ordnance exploding, making rescue difficult. The pilot, F/O Edward Gordon Essenhigh, 151969, only 24, was to be married 11 days later; his body and that of five others were never found. Many streets of newly built homes nearby are named after the crew.

Humbled, I progress westwards, reflecting on the lives of others and my good fortune to be born after a war and to grow up in a period of prosperity that is easily taken for granted. I calculate that being a boomer of the early 1950s is almost ideal: the hippy hedonism of the late 1960s (who wouldn't want to be 19 in 1969?), defined benefit pensions and the economic growth of the 1980s at the peak of your career – all without the complication of smartphones, digital technology or social media. They are the sweet-spot decades, if we forget the turmoil of the 1970s. The trauma of the events in Japan in 1945, when as many as a quarter of a million people lost their lives, brought a peace that is almost outside living memory. The hibakusha, survivors of those events, are dying of old age – the last witnesses who can attest to the horrors of nuclear war. Those weapons had a twentieth of the power of a single warhead in today's strategic arsenal. We need to be reminded that we live in a nuclear age that has the power to destroy life on Earth. Such thoughts occupy my mind until I see another number 103 beach hut to add to my photographic collection, which is coming along nicely since Folkestone. Modern and post-war seaside architecture is rampant elsewhere, and housing claims the shingle beach, diverting the paths inland. I am happy to reach Littlehampton and cautiously read the fishermen's recipes on the railings leading into town.

My stomach has stopped complaining, and the B&B is perfect. The hosts are attentive, attending to small details with a care that cheers me up. They serve up a light, healthy breakfast that should not interfere with my digestion. Or so I hope.

Rejoining the coastline, I wish for hills as the path is flat and without elevation. Butlin's has sucked the character out of Bognor Regis, homogenous and explicit in its version of a seaside experience. At least a Felpham Beach information board mentions William Blake, who lived nearby, a poet in tune with his surroundings:

*To see a World in a Grain of Sand*
*And a Heaven in a Wild Flower*
*Hold Infinity in the palm of your hand*
*And Eternity in an hour*
      William Blake, extract from *Auguries of Innocence* (c. 1803)

Those words resonate as I open my gaze along the fractal coastline. The forms mimic and multiply: headlands are larger versions of coves and inlets, cliffs are textured in the same way. Then an outcrop, a rock, a pebble, then a grain of sand – the same shape, structure and pattern repeated. What appears to be so small can multiply to the limit of imagination, from the microscopic crystal of sand to the salt-and-peppered night sky. Mathematics is universal at any scale, the very mechanism of existence, nature's divinity.

Maybe my delirium hasn't cleared, as thoughts replace hallucinations induced by lack of food. I welcome the inland route around Pagham Harbour back to the shoreline, squelching through the low-tide salt-flat route to Sidlesham and the tempting Crab & Lobster pub, as my mind seeks influence over my body. The brent geese are abundant, plodding on the marsh and pecking at the vegetation. I rest above an abandoned yacht that has succumbed to a storm on the shingle bank. The waves nudge the fractured hull, dismantling any rigging left after the salvage men have stripped away precious brass and stainless steel. It is dying a slow death, cracks creep at angles along its form as the salt water and sun bleach its decks of colour. The relentless surf is the ultimate victor in this contest between nature and the leisure toys of mankind.

Selsey was once served by a tramway from Chichester. This service could not compete with the automobile and closed in 1935, yet former carriages live on, incorporated into ramshackle cottages along the shoreline. Once you spot the shape of a carriage window, you can see their form appearing along the beach road. Eric Coates stayed here and was inspired to compose *By the Sleepy Lagoon*, a tune that opens every episode of *Desert Island Discs* on BBC Radio 4, a radio programme that has run almost continuously since 1942 – over 3,400 episodes. The place has that remote desert island feeling, an ideal place to contemplate the eight tracks of music in your life, and the object you would take with you to treasure.

A fisherman hauls his boat on to the shingle, the rusty motor winch somehow still working. His modest catch, flapping in the plastic box, will feed friends and family. Bass and mackerel look bright-eyed and shiny; the freshest flesh awaits a lucky diner. I reach the southerly extent of the shoreline, and the Isle of Wight announces its presence, silhouetted against a resting sun. I stop and admire a wonderful seal sculpture, styled in a likeness of Sir Patrick Moore, the famous astronomer and host of *The Sky at Night*. It is the longest-running TV series, first broadcast on 24th April 1957. The sculpture is quirky, joyful, humorous, eccentric and fits perfectly to the character of a monocled stargazer, looking both east and west, observing the sun's daily arc. Selsey, or the old name Silsey, retains the ancient name for a seal, for this was Seal Island long ago. It is a fitting location that has inspired the enduring and comforting nature of these iconic BBC programmes.

As I rest in a cosy pub bedroom, I scour the internet for tomorrow's accommodation. The rates in Chichester are exorbitant, so I will take a train home and call it quits for a year on the England Coast Path. After breakfast, I skirt around Medmerry Nature Reserve, another inland bird haven, and march down the Wittering Beaches to East Head. Some houses look dilapidated, like ideal target practice for the Royal Navy gunners, standing exposed on the shoreline, incongruous monstrosities now decaying. The area is under threat of uncontrolled greenfield development without concern for road infrastructure, flood risk or protection of the natural world – developers seeking profit at the expense of others, having identified the next lucrative second-home hot spot. No doubt these structures will be replaced with something less hideous.

Having once lived in the area I know this coastline well, but its familiar paths emerge now in the context of a coastal journey and surprise me with their beauty. I sit on a timber log to reflect on where my home is now, sensing the longing for place so beautifully captured by the Welsh word *Hiraeth*. I wonder if the path is my home, as I let the emotions of reconnecting to a former life wash over me, embracing the inevitable changes as I get older.

I nibble a plain white roll and sip from my water bottle, simple nourishment that feels like culinary freedom. It makes me rethink my walking diet. I must use more freeze-dried food (even in hotels, not just when camping) to avoid expensive restaurants and risky food. This guarantees taste and quality, adding variety to a diet that can be repetitive. This approach appeals to me after I try a local cafe at East Wittering for a coffee. The floor is so filthy with grease that I almost slip, which is ironic given the mud paths I have walked without incident. It is wise to be cautious about what you eat when you cannot control the source.

The Hinge at East Head, around which a sand spit pivots, constantly changes. Its tip is now 1,500 metres from where it was in 1786, when it was less than 500 metres from Hayling Island. A lifeboat was once stationed there, serving the harbour. Occasionally, when I visit the beach for a day or two, I record a GPS outline of the mean high-water line, as marked by the seaweed pushed up the beach by the tide. I have recorded surprising changes, even in the past five to ten years. These small increments of dune shift can only be measured and not experienced, like the proverbial frog boiling in the saucepan on a gently increasing heat. More recently, anyone would notice the decaying groynes, dramatic erosion and reshaping of the sea channels. If the neck is breached, the mouth of Chichester Harbour will change dramatically. This seems certain as sea levels rise, impacting the ecosystems in this precious harbour. The area is very sensitive to change, and it will be heartbreaking to see what happens during the few years I have left to live. Changes taking place in a former home I care so much about.

The walk towards Chichester along the channel is peaceful and relaxing, until it is interrupted by the sailing boatyards and marinas of Itchenor, Birdham and Dell Quay. Tidal locks protecting millions of pounds of idle assets in a thriving yachting community. This wealth fades as the channel weakens, all the way to Fishbourne and its Roman Palace – confirming this harbour's strategic and historical importance over centuries, if not millennia. The last few miles follow the boundary of what remains of RAF Appledram (Apuldram) airfield: a pop-up Polish and Czechoslovakian fighter base in World War II – its wartime days now hidden beneath the fields of West Sussex. Numbers 302, 308, 310, 312, 313 and 317 fighter squadrons fought with our nation's airmen, their engines now silent. The fields cover any evidence of their contribution during the war, unlike the iconic Tangmere airfield and museum nearby, tended to by its enthusiastic volunteers.

I walk into Chichester, but the ticket gate will not accept my barcode. I am too early for my timed train and cannot catch an earlier service. This is a blessing, as I spend my hours visiting Chichester Cathedral, primarily to see the colours of my father's disbanded No. 46 Squadron flag hanging in a side aisle. To my delight, the nave contains an enormous model of a full moon, some seven metres in diameter. It is a backlit artwork, *Museum of the Moon* by Luke Jerram, which leaves me breathless. To see such a vivid depiction of a celestial body in a vaulted religious building is a spiritual experience. The object is the companion for our planet, its symbiotic orbit with the Earth drives the tides – the zone where vertebrates discovered land. This littoral and liminal ecosystem is so crucial to life and the world I am living within and walking through. I shed a tear, humbled by the scale of the universe and my place in it.

# 5
# CHICHESTER TO SWANAGE
## The back of the Wight

*'The real voyage of discovery consists not in seeking new landscapes, but in having new eyes.'*

Marcel Proust

**Distance walked: 520 miles**

I am restless over the winter months, itching to get back on the path, planning accommodation options and a route around the Isle of Wight. In a modern world, the vast resources of the internet make this easy: online maps, accommodation options, weather and tides – all at your fingertips with a sophisticated smartphone. I miss the early 2000s when it was sufficient to have a map, let curiosity guide me, and ask the people I met for recommendations. The thrill of the unknown seems to be the essence of adventure, encouraging engagement with the community and making you feel alive. The social media world sets expectations at the expense of an undiscovered vista or serendipitous encounter. As an Arabic saying goes – 'one meeting by chance is worth a thousand by appointment'.

Four months later, as February closes its door for the year, I return to Fishbourne, courtesy of the 700 Coastliner bus service from a hotel base in Havant. My urban existence is washed away by the marsh rushes alongside the harbour tributary – the sounds of the whispering reeds and the chatter from my brent geese friends make me feel at home again. I could have shaved off a day's walking by taking the Itchenor Ferry last year, but that would miss the delights of Chichester Harbour on this cold, clear winter morning, as the residents and landscape recover from Storm Eunice a week earlier. Wind gusts from this extratropical cyclone reached 122mph at the Needles on the Isle of Wight, so I am under no illusion about the potential conditions ahead. Yet, if I were to worry, fuelled by dramatised tabloid news and weather forecasts from the comfort of home, I would never venture outdoors. The weather somehow is far worse when viewed from behind a bedroom window.

Many paths sheltered from the wind and rain by trees and hedges remain muddy, covering my boots with a clawing clay, until I can clean them in the puddles on the roads that pass the private estates that are unlikely to share land for a coastal path. Some prefer the ferry, which links directly to a picturesque low-tide path to Bosham, but that would miss the beauty of the deeper estuarial salt marsh channels. Rising sea levels will impact these waterways this century, testing the strength and height of the seawall defences. King Cnut (Canute), once a ruler of the North Sea Kingdoms, placed his chair in the sea at Bosham (or possibly Thorney Island, no one is sure) to demonstrate to his obsequious courtiers that he was not omnipotent. Nature cannot be reasoned with, was his message. It is in the hands of gods, not mortals. Cnut's daughter is thought to be buried in Bosham Church, a place of worship for well over 1,000 years, which is yet more evidence of the historic importance of Chichester Harbour. His message applies today, as the climate responds to the activities of man.

The path leads around Bosham Channel on to Chidham, another peninsula of land in this remarkable harbour. Thorney Channel follows, once destined to become reclaimed land, but defying attempts to seal the entrances with seawalls and dams. Ancient dykes still reach out from the headlands, breached long ago, their wooden posts melting into the mud and abandoned to the sea and salt marsh. This landscape is home to a diverse ecology: seals are resident in the harbour, and birds thrive on the remote shorelines. I reach Prinsted early but decide the 10-mile loop around Thorney Island is too much for today. I know the path well enough, having lived here for five years in the 1970s. Besides, England play Wales at Twickenham tonight, and the winter evenings are drawing in quickly. I do not want to overstretch myself with weeks of walking ahead.

England prevailed 23-19, and I read the match reviews on my phone on the bus back to the path. This will be an emotional day, as I fondly remember growing up and attending school on the island and at Southbourne. This is where my wanderlust was born: my parents would kick me out of the house on a Saturday morning and not expect to see me until Sunday for dinner at the Sergeant's Mess (it was an RAF base until

1976). During that time, my good friend Chris and I would pitch tents, light campfires, tickle mullet in the creeks, and explore the channels in dinghies and canoes. This is how I learned to use a knife, light a paraffin stove, tie knots and live an Arthur Ransome *Swallows and Amazons* existence. Like nature at many military bases, I too thrived in the presence of the machinery of war.

The paths are familiar, and I pop into the graveyard at the Norman church to pay respects to friends my father knew who died in a helicopter accident. I continue to Pilsey Island, where as a child, I once enjoyed jumping into old bomb crater pools, waded through thick mudflats and made crazy attempts to build prototype windsurfer boards with planks and old sails (ending tragically, but with bones unbroken). The memory of these experiences greatly influenced my life, and it was a sad day when we moved inland as I love the outdoors near the sea. My parents' ashes lie nearby, and I take a moment to reflect. Other memorial benches pay tribute to lives lost in the armed forces. The runway approach lights are rotting, falling into the sea now the airbase has closed. They will have witnessed many heroic missions during the war when the base was a centre for Coastal Command. I imagine squadrons of Mosquitos, Typhoons, Beauforts, Blenheims and Spitfires filling the air in the 1940s.

I walk past the Deep, the sluice-gated drainage channel that protects the military base; you must still click through a metal gate to access the Sussex Border Path. Sailors are easing their way to port on the high tide, once a channel hosting England's largest oyster fleet, shipping 100,000 shells a week to London. The decline came in 1902 when the Dean of Winchester died from bivalve typhoid poisoning from a local catch. The consequence of uncontrolled sewage is not unlike the trauma the south coast suffers today in the guise of 'permissible storm sewage overflow' from Southern Water.

This seawall leads into the harbour marina with a welcome water point at the yacht club (no dogs allowed). The Slipper Mill Pond, a tidal energy battery that powered the flour mills to feed an expanding Royal Navy at Portsmouth in the mid-1700s, is enthusiastically preserved, much to the delight of local wildfowl. Red merganser, golden eye, little grebe, kingfisher and little egret can relax in its still waters, an aquatic holiday destination for rest and recuperation.

I reach Emsworth and pop into a cafe, once a newsagent, where I used to collect my wages as a paper boy. I remember the confusion of decimalisation day in February 1971, 50 years earlier. I recall this story with a lovely Italian owner who is eager to listen.

'I wonder how much you were paid?' she asks.

'Does four shillings and six pence sound right?' A rough calculation still plays in my head as I convert shillings to modern-day currency. I think that is about 20 pence.

'I've come to collect my last wages, as I remember having to leave the island on short notice, plus interest and inflation, of course.' We chuckle together, daring to think what that figure would be (about £4, I work out later).

I describe the shop I remember; she says it was unchanged until recently. It's a cosy place, but I need a more substantial meal for the next leg. I buy a cake from her counter and then seek a local bakery. After eating my ham roll in the village square, I change my route and decide to walk to Southsea directly. I want to catch the Hayling Ferry, but it is not running and I don't fancy walking down a long cycle path and back again. The England Coast Path has work to do here on the island's eastern side. In the future, I will take an extended Solent Way circular journey to cover these gaps and the northern shores of the Isle of Wight. It will not be a keep-the-sea-on-your-left coastal walk, but part of an exploration of the estuaries of Essex, Hampshire and beyond when the England Coast Path is fully open.

Warblington Church lies isolated, bypassed by the roaring A27. I walk through the graveyard to the shoreline and into Langstone, wiggling around the sewage works and outfalls to Farlington Marshes, an unexpected paradise for birds looking out to a series of mudflat islands. South Binness, Baker and Long Island for brent geese and their wintering friends, the wigeon, teal, avocet and redshank. Warblers, flycatchers, wheatears and many more find solace in the marshland hedgerows and brambles. I envy the birders with telescopes and tripods, scanning for rarities, but make a note to return someday as I must improve my knowledge of these smaller birds.

I arrive at Portsea Island and follow the cycle path along its east coast. War memorials hint at the nature of the naval and military complex, slowly making its presence known. This architecture becomes more prominent along the Eastney Esplanade at Southsea. Victorian brick garrisons dominate. The Royal Marines have a poignant *Yomper* memorial to veterans of the Falklands Conflict of 1982 and another to the Cockleshell heroes (Operation Frankton) in 1942 – both acts of huge courage and endurance. Today, the Defence Ministry retains rights to billet, muster, march and even play cricket (although that right was removed in 1966) on the fields. Other war memorials remind us of lives lost through campaigns where this island has played a strategic role and, like many places I have walked past on the south coast, the colossal logistics of the D-Day landings.

I catch a flight on the longest-running and world's last remaining timetabled hovercraft service to Ryde on the Isle of Wight. I am expecting a noisy, rough crossing and the eyeballs to shake out of my head (like the SR.N4 *Princess Anne* service I caught to France in the late 1980s), but the Griffon Hoverwork 12000TD is a revelation – it is modern, smooth, quiet and comfortable except for the gaggle of kids that turn up at the last moment to take their daily trip to school. Ten minutes of joy is over too quickly. I must return here for my circular Solent Way walk, as the experience is a rare pleasure.

Storm Eunice has made a bit of a mess of the shoreline, with a few trees down, but it is a quiet walk east along the island's coastal path (some 70 miles) that promises to unfold into a tough three-day challenge to Yarmouth. I keep bumping into a birdwatcher with his telescope focused on the Solent as he ambles down the promenade in his small car. I can't resist questioning him.

'What are you looking for? Anything unusual?'

'Slavonian grebes,' comes a short reply, his head locked to the eyepiece.

'Oh, they're stunning. I've never seen one before. The Framlington Marshes are a revelation; lots of birds yesterday.' I try to open the conversation.

'Oh, yes, they had a sea eagle sighting recently; she has a taste for lazy ducks.'

We chat for a while, and I realise that the winter months are excellent if you are into your birds. It is not just summer seagulls stealing your ice cream and sparrows pecking at crumbs – this area has rich avian populations. White-tailed sea eagles have been introduced nearby and have a huge hunting range, popping up to Norfolk or France for lunch and holidaying in Scotland or Denmark for a change of scenery. The local birds are unhappy about that as, as the birder mentioned, they have a taste for the locals relaxing on the marshes. The sea eagles will eat most things, not just the unfortunate bass in the bay. These huge birds were once common along the south coast, and the project seeks to reinstate this apex predator over time. Opposition to these reintroduction schemes is usually brief, until the community accepts and admires them – like the red kites in the Chilterns, near to my home.

The path is muddy into Bembridge as it passes over the Duver and on to the causeway that leads to the harbour, where a yappy dog barks violently at my arrival.

'She doesn't like men!' the owner declares, projecting her own feelings, I am sure. It is a common excuse, along with other classics, such as 'we just got him from a rescue home' or the unforgettable 'he's never bitten anyone before'.

I have learned to speak to the owner in calm tones, to reassure the dog and enter the pack for a moment, whatever the owner has said. It also makes sense to face (but not look at) any dog, especially if they are off the lead, as they have a habit of attacking your tendons from behind. A few lessons in pet behaviour work wonders to diffuse a tricky situation.

The shingle path has eroded towards the RNLI station, where the views open as I head west again, towards Culver Down and its pompous monument to the 1st Earl of Yarborough, whose only achievement seems to have been to inherit wealth. It doesn't have the same gravity as the memorials I have passed on Southsea, but its location is exceptional on the eastern extent of a chalk ridge that snakes its way west to Lulworth Cove, almost 60 miles away. The inscription reads (capital letters as written):

*AS THE OWNER OF LARGE ESTATES*
*HE WAS ONE OF THOSE MOST CONSPICUOUS*
*FOR THE QUALITIES*
*WHICH PECULIARLY ADORN THAT STATION*
*AND*
*AS FIRST COMMODORE*

## THE COAST IS OUR COMPASS

*OF THE ROYAL YACHT SQUADRON*
*HE WAS EMINENT*
*IN HIS FOSTERING AND ENCOURAGING*
*BY HIS EXAMPLE AND LIBERALITY*
*ALL THAT WAS CALCULATED*
*TO IMPROVE*
*THE SCIENCE OF NAVAL ARCHITECTURE*
*AND TO ADVANCE*
*THE MARITIME INTERESTS OF HIS COUNTRY*

It carries on like that, but I can't honestly read further. No evidence of achievements was provided at all. He must have been quite a character, for an adjacent information board recalls that he insisted his crew sign documents permitting them to be flogged if they misbehaved. It was a hard life in the 1820s.

I lean into a blustery south-westerly and descend to Yaverland, whose derelict Art Deco Grand Hotel desperately needs restoration. It has started to rain hard, so I march along the promenade into Sandown and head inland to Shanklin station to catch the train back to Ryde – having overrun my booked accommodation stop. The train door closes, and I shake my head to ensure I am not on the Bakerloo Line; every sound, beep and announcement is familiar, minus the rush-hour squeeze and the meaningless advertisements above the interior windows. It's funny how sound and smells transport you to another place.

The next day, I return to the station and devise a plan to meet my uncle in Newport using the No.12 coastal bus. The weather is dreary, and it has rained hard overnight, making me nervous to walk along a coastline renowned for landslips. Sure enough, a clear 'path closed' sign at Bonchurch means a steep ascent to the A3055 through Devil's Chimney. It is a strenuous climb through geology that seems held together by vines and prayers. Exhausted, I have only a moment to enjoy the view before descending over wet, worn steps to Bonchurch, guided by the church spire into a town where I need to sit down for a cup of tea. I am resigned to a Tesco meal deal, but then I stumble upon The Better Days Cafe. Kirsty opens the door, even though I am too early. In a moment, I have toast and tea in front of me.

'Thank you for opening up,' I say. 'I could do with a cuppa after that path from Shanklin.'

'No worries,' she replies, popping behind the counter to cut a new loaf. 'It's a difficult path when it rains; it'll slide into the sea if this weather continues.'

Her warm and comfortable cafe is a local community hub, helping those with physical and mental health disabilities into the workplace – an asset for the community and far removed from the bland, branded cafes in the town.

I walk down to the shore and follow the coastal path with the Undercliff above me. Passing by Ventnor's playgrounds, I ascend sharply again through St Lawrence and on to the chalk downs. The path is like an ice rink, a thin sheen of water above hard chalk rock – very slippery and almost impossible to walk on unless you have poles. The navigation beacons and lighthouse at St Catherine's Point emerge from a sea mist 160 metres below. It is a stunning location, and I rest where Mat proposed to Gemma on 22nd March 2009 – which makes a change from the usual memorial bench.

Leaving Blackgang Chine behind me, its fibreglass pirates and dinosaurs looking sad in the rain, I can see the coastline ahead. It looks like a half-eaten, soggy pack of digestive biscuits, for the levels of erosion are alarming. I contemplate a beach walk, but the tide is high and I cannot be sure of a safe exit, so I continue along the level cliff edge in awe of massive landslips, unlike anything I have encountered since Cromer. The 'Back of the Wight Society' has jury-rigged a zip wire (to convey fishing and diving gear only) from the coastguard cottages to the beach below. The humorous notice suggests you will see eagles, condors and pterodactyls or a seal that looks like a brown football (affectionately known as Ron). The supporting cantilever pole holding the steel hawser sits too close to the edge of a field that covered 14 acres in 1976 but is now just four. A crack has appeared next to the cottage. Soon, there will be no field, zip wire or path as it falls into the sea, the last biscuit in the pack until another is opened.

Whale, Shepherd's and Cowleaze Chine are dramatic fissures on McVitie's finest coastline, with vicious gullies carved in short order by the smallest of streams. You must walk inland to get around them and resist any shortcut heroics. I chat to a couple as I read the stark warning notice.

'Some poor lady had to be rescued last week. She fell into the Chine and couldn't get out again,' he says.

'You don't ignore these diversions,' I add. 'It's been quite sketchy since Shanklin.'

'It'll be fine after Freshwater Bay,' she replies.

I call it a day and walk inland to the picturesque village of Brighstone, with its thatched shops, sub-Post Office, grocery, pubs and tea rooms – the very model of an English village. The double-decker arrives, and I sit upstairs on the front seat for the views to Newport, which I am sure are nice, but the windows are soaked with condensation and the clouds have descended over the downs.

I arrive at the care home, where my uncle recalls an unknown family history which I never knew about: my grandfather's experiences of World War I and post-war rationing, his time working as an accountant in a prison, issuing pennies to mass murderers. We chat for a while before the care home rings a bell for dinner. I leave for the Travelodge, packed with contractors who easily clear the breakfast buffet before the earliest bus back to Brighstone. I return to the soggy coastline of reddish Wealden Group sandstones, mudstones and siltstones, easing into the sea like some thick clay-quarry biscuit soup. Campsite buildings are abandoned; it is pointless to maintain them as they will topple down the cliff face this winter or next. I keep a healthy distance from the cliff edge to avoid becoming part of the beach below, for my body would lie undiscovered for at least a year, emerging from the collapsed soil as it washes into the sea.

The geology changes back to chalk at Compton Down alongside Military Road. It is at risk, too, but for now it is an easy calm descent into Freshwater Bay. This mid-19th-century bohemian retreat, home to the Freshwater Circle, revolved around Alfred Tennyson. A long list of authors, painters, photographers, artists and poets visited this bay, intoxicated by the sea air and the dramatic light cascading over the landscape. I like the beautiful mosaic in the shelter on the beach, where I stop to eat. I'll need the energy to walk up to Tennyson Down, one of my favourite coastal sections in Britain. It is akin to a three-mile-long aircraft carrier into the English Channel, the sea on either side of the chalk downs.

I have the grass fields to myself, with only cattle for company. It is an exhilarating climb to the Tennyson Monument. The sun ignites the sea with dancing pools of white – sunscalds created by nature's theatre lights, hunting for lead characters. The clouds' apertures are conducted by a weather god, casting beams of light on to the canvas of the sea. I imagine waves within waves within waves, from subatomic vibrations to the ocean swells. I feel alone in this landscape, but I am not lonely – my inner thoughts are my friends, who talk of the life-affirming experience of this journey and the overwhelming awe at such moments. This is a day to savour, so I slow the pace and open my gaze, breathing in the expanse and inhaling the rich, clean air and the sights and sounds surrounding me. It fills my mind, soul and body with joy.

I remind myself that I would have stood facing 122mph gusts of the Atlantic a few days earlier. It is frightening to comprehend that sheer power. The Needles are still standing, and the light from Goose Rock continues to guide mariners to safety, providing direction, reassurance and solace. I about-turn and head west to Yarmouth for views of Alum Bay. It is unusually dull, with the multicoloured sands reflecting only monochrome light. It reminds me of a watercolour brush pot at the end of a painter's day, diluting vibrant and pastel colours to grey.

The Solent lacks yachts, motor vessels or ferries, as the ebbing tide races over the shingle banks against the freshening south-westerly, forming wave crests in front of Hurst Castle. The views are sublime, historic and invigorating. My joyful serotonin rush subsides, replaced by tiredness as I walk through the woodlands, and I fall into bed at The Bugle. It is quiet, about to emerge from winter hibernation before the intense summer sailing months. It has been a glorious, short, 15-mile, five-hour journey, inducing a deep sleep as my muscles release the remembered effort of the day.

Catching the ferry in the morning is a challenge: there is no ticket office, functioning automated machine or call centre – only an app to download in an area with no Wi-Fi and a snotty notice saying that there's no boarding without a ticket. I feel disenfranchised, helpless and £15 lighter after waving my smartphone in the air for 30 minutes. I'd be helpless if I only had cash. The busy push-me-pull-you service is full of commuters checking emails who disembark in a hurry to catch the train or unlock damp cold cars.

It is good to be back on the mainland at Lymington. This is a pretty, well-to-do Georgian seaport market town, once famous for shipbuilding and salt, but now a marina of more idle assets with expensive maintenance schedules. The Salterns, Pennington and Keyhaven Marshes that follow are stunning homes for wintering wildfowl – each species seeking out their niche in the reeds, salt flats, marshes, channels and lakes: bar-tailed godwit, black-tailed godwit, shoveler, teal, wigeon, pintail, plovers and yes! – a Slavonian grebe. It is an enjoyable walk leading to Hurst Castle along the shingle bank and then doubling back to Milford-on-Sea and the Needles Eye Cafe. There is no rule forbidding second breakfasts, so I indulge just as the heavens open, forgoing another meal until Christchurch and staying dry for a while.

The clouds pass as I step out the doorway and walk to my friend's 103 beach hut. The photograph I take will be the centrepiece of my future collage. I have been building quite a collection since Cromer, so I carefully compose and click the shutter when the sun emerges. The winter storms have spared the row of huts for now, as they are at risk from destruction if the winds and tide combine in the right direction. The coastline suffers as the erosion is again evident, tipping golf club fairways into the bay, their white out-of-bounds marker posts upended into the sea. I skirt another internment camp-style holiday park, laying private claim to the shoreline, to stroll through Highcliffe Castle and Steamer Point Nature Reserve. The gardens are open with access for coastal walkers through the grounds to avoid an unpleasant road walk should the tide or conditions deny shoreline access.

The ferry at Mudeford is closed for the season. I have no option but to take the cycle track into Christchurch. I stop at a superb Patisserie Mark Bennett, up to French standards for pastries and cake, and then stock up at the local supermarket for a feast at the Travelodge. Any remaining nibbles are crammed into a baguette for lunch tomorrow – an unlikely backpacker/thru-hiker recipe you will not find in a magazine as it focuses on calories at the expense of taste.

With renewed energy I reach the ferry point on Hengistbury Head, crossing the river and following the Stour Valley Way markers. I could spend a day on this peninsula, but the beach to the west will not get any shorter if I dally. The scale of the walk is marked by the first hut, numbered 1379, and a promenade that curves into the distance without end, so I start marching. The huts are padlocked and empty, their locks sealed in greased plastic bags against the sea spray. There are only local dog walkers and joggers. Boscombe Pier is deserted, yet marks where the hut numbers have come to No. 1, only to start again. Number 2359 is special. It is the first municipal beach hut in the UK, constructed in 1909 by Frederick Percy Dolamore, the Chief Assistant Borough Engineer and Surveyor of Bournemouth Borough Council. The idea caught on, and I wonder how many are around our coastline. There must be tens of thousands.

Diggers are rebuilding the beach after the storm; council workers unenthusiastically sweep the promenade, in no hurry in the face of the enormity of the task ahead. Christchurch turns to Boscombe, which becomes Bournemouth, which becomes Poole, and the sun emerges. I convert my trousers to shorts and enjoy the newfound freedom of movement. I watch brave swimmers emerge in their bobble hats, swimming cozzies, neoprene gloves and booties to shiver in their Dryrobes, clutching a mug of tea (or something stronger) poured from flasks. It is time to celebrate reaching the South West Coast Path as I disembark from the Sandbanks Ferry service to South Haven Point. I pay with a £1 coin that has lived in my pocket by chance, somewhat unusual after the pandemic accelerated the move to contactless payments and a cashless society.

I've been here before, having walked the South West Coast Path in 2007. Now, it is time to do it in reverse. It is getting cold, so I do not delay the walk along Studland Bay. The naturists don't like goosebumps but some genius has built a mobile sauna, which I reach just as the sweaty occupants run screaming (and clothed) into the sea. It is a lovely stretch of sand, but it has changed dramatically in my lifetime, getting narrower. Coastal defences built in the 1980s had unintended consequences, removing sand from along the beach, but I suspect that offshore dredging for building sand may have had a role to play, too.

I climb up to Old Harry to marvel at the chalk formations and gaze across Poole Bay to their continuation on the Isle of Wight, at the Needles, where I stood two days ago. Swanage is sun-blessed, and I soak up the rays in the lee of a shelter before knocking on the hostel door to be greeted by Pam. She makes me tea, and we chat about the path ahead.

'Are you walking the South West Coast Path?' she asks.

'Yes, but I started from Chichester last week and have been timing my arrival here to reach the military ranges this weekend,' I reply. 'I'm walking around the coast of England. It's taken 33 days from Cromer.'

'Oh, wow. I'd love to do that but our health is poor, and I am unsure how long it will be before we must close.' Her husband Pete bought the former doctor's surgery a few years back, but he is not well.

I demolish a takeaway curry alongside other guests who are eating simple meals. One gent is chasing his beetroot around the plate with a knife and fork until it inevitably slides into his lap. At least he is wearing dark trousers. I can't laugh, as the turmeric-rich dal has dyed my fingers yellow as I scoop it up with naan bread, transferring its colour to my shirt sleeve as I adjust them. All a part of the developing thru-hiker look I am adopting as the miles accumulate.

# 6
# SWANAGE TO TEIGNMOUTH
## 180 billion pebbles

*'We don't see things as they are, we see them as we are.'*
Anaïs Nin

### Distance walked: 630 miles

I am excited, recalling the thrilling walk from the West Lulworth Youth Hostel in 2007 – an exhilarating day riding the roller-coaster chalk ridges to Swanage. My fitness levels after walking 630 miles of the South West Coast Path from Minehead were at a peak, and I flew along the path in a manner that surprised me. This morning, the ranges are open. Pam left me two slices of her homemade cake, and I topped up last night's curry with a bowl of porridge. Fully fuelled, I haul my pack on to my shoulders and climb out of a town yet to wake, on to the coastal path and familiar friendly acorn waymarks. This is the South West Coast Path in reverse. A quarter of my journey completed, another quarter to go on the South West Coast Path, but this time in the reverse direction.

A chilling north-easterly brings clear skies, a tailwind and a low crystal backlight that reveals the texture of the strip lynchet fields as they curve around the contours, sparkling in the morning dew. It evokes a medieval agricultural landscape of manual labour. I try to visualise the men and women tilling the fields in silence, their gaze occasionally rising to the sea views to wonder. Their connection to the land would have been deeply held and felt.

I pass Dancing Ledge, where Nicholas Crane completed a journey from Needles Eye near Berwick, following the two-degree west longitude meridian southwards as closely as possible. He wrote about that adventure in *Two Degrees West* in 1999, and celebrated the end by jumping into the sea nearby. I find the wind too cold when arriving at St Aldhelm's Head. My quads and calves complain about my choice of shorts for the day. I stop to shelter behind the chapel for a chunk of Pam's delicious fruit cake, rubbing the goosebumps away. My legs need to be warm for the brutal descent and ascent of Emmetts Hill – a taster of the terrain ahead, quite unlike the flat promenades I have marched to the east. I shepherd roe deer along the path until, in fright, they leap over the stile and vanish into the fields – they have evolved to effortlessly outrun predators and are in their element.

My legs are not used to this topography, and my illusions of pace are reset after another tough ascent of Houns-tout Cliff. This is a rugged county with stunning views where the visibility is limited by the Earth's curvature. The sea mirrors the sky, reflecting the cloud formations in the swell as it relaxes into the shore. Hydrofoil surfers are playing in a break off Egmont Point, and I wonder how they got there, for there is no road for miles. I can see Portland in the distance, its wedge-shaped shoe form terminating a geological arc of sedimentary clay, sand and gravel. Nearby, *mille feuille* cake-like layers emerge from the sea, evidence of immense forces, time and scale. It is a paradise for geologists, palaeontologists and petrologists. The latter was confirmed by the nodding donkey beam pump, slowly sucking oil from the depths since the 1960s.

Now, I pass through the open security gates for the main course – the Lulworth Ranges, the red flags tied tight to the flagpoles. This is a fascinating haven for wildlife amid the brutality of military weaponry. I clatter up Tyneham Cap to see its lost village below, keeping pace with ultra-runners on a reconnoitre for a forthcoming 120-mile race along the coast. My walking poles are an asset on such ascents, and we compete to hold a conversation between breaths.

'Walking the South West Coast Path?' asks one runner.

'... and more. I started in Cromer. I'm walking the England Coast Path, probably 600 miles done so far.'

'That's amazing; we are checking the path of an ultra-marathon in a few weeks. The Jurassic Extinction 120 – Studland to Exmouth. We need a GPS route for our watches.'

'Jeez, no, that is amazing; how long will that take?'

'Thirty to forty hours, if you can finish. It is a tough race.'

'Wow,' I gasp as we reach a summit. I now understand, an extinction event for sure.

I do a quick calculation in my head: five eight-hour days if I tried without a backpack. That's 40 hours – not too shabby for a walker if you take the proper rest stops. It seems the elite ultra events are more about overcoming sleep deprivation, not just the effort of covering the distance.

They run ahead on the ridge, and I follow into Worbarrow Bay, where a tall ship has anchored. I climb to the ancient hill fort and sit for a moment to drink in a scene from the 19th century, with its missing coastal hamlet and coastguard cottages abandoned to the army in 1943. The calls of 'mack-a-low, mack-a-low, get the boats, get the nets' will never echo again in this cove – a time when huge mackerel hauls would feed Weymouth and Swanage for a week. Nowadays, a wireless radio will be used to authorise the firing of missiles and shells at the battered, rusting tank carcasses and target boards that litter the valleys north of the ridge. The wildlife must sense these firing times and retreat to their burrows and woodlands, having made a pact with their devil (weapons of man) in exchange for the quieter, protected security of a closed range devoid of agriculture.

I descend to the limestone ledge below, a steep exposed path edging Mupe Bay. It leads to Lulworth Cove, a village protected from the gales in a hollow. I rest and decide if I should climb again or walk around the shoreline. My legs vote for the easier route and the prospect of a slice of Dorset apple cake at The Boat Shed Cafe, but the rest seizes my calves solid, and they cease to function for the climb to the campsite above Durdle Door. I muster the remaining energy to shower, pitch and change. The wind is still fresh, and I am grateful for a table at the restaurant to write my journal and eat a meal. I ask for half a pint of beer and am given a pint, as if my words did not match the demeanour of a thirsty walker – the visual message overriding the audible.

I sleep deeply and wake early for a pee. It is so cold I decide to pack and go, as the only way I will warm up again is to get moving as the northerly wind cuts holes in the windproof layers of my tent and clothing. I zip the bottoms to my convertible trousers, delighting my leg muscles. Campers are snuggled up in warm vans or have evacuated to their cars. Durdle Door beach is deserted, too early, too cold, yet at its most beautiful. The rising sun casts a long shadow on to desire paths that ascend and descend the severed grass valleys – sheep-like tracks left by walkers taking the easiest route. The sea lies still in the lee of a freshening wind. I push harder on the inclines to warm my core to reach optimal temperature. It is not a time to stop but to walk briskly for a few hours.

Weymouth grows in stature from Osmington Mills, where the Smuggler's Inn will open for lunch and a cheeky private coastal sign will take you through the bar. Walking in the opposite direction, I cannot recall the views from 15 years ago. It is like walking a new path for the first time. The perspective has changed, a new light textures the landscape, and the weather confuses your senses – a different feeling, a different journey, and a different experience.

The wind backs to a strong westerly, making me envious of the tailwind pushing 10k weekend runners to the finish line on the promenade. It's a Sunday race, and I feel exhausted, leaning into a headwind that will plague me until the evening. Entering Weymouth, with its seaside urbanity, I see a row of beach huts that I read about – the scene of a cartel of power-crazed pensioners who recently evicted long-term occupants after the local council handed them governance. Such is the quest for status of ownership. Weymouth is empty, except for brave windsurfers, gybing just feet from the shoreline before heading out to sea again. I fall into the Marlboro chippy near the footbridge over the River Wey for a lovely meal and a warming mug of tea. Fish swimming in a freshwater tank watch their seawater friends get battered and fried as I wait, clutching my mug with two hands, nudging the paper towel-wrapped cutlery with my pinkie finger. The plate arrives, phase two of the warming process, reviving my whole body as the energy drains back into my legs.

It is a short walk to The Bunker hostel in Portland, a perfect base for two days and full of love and special touches from the new hosts Tony and Sally – a welcome replacement for the nearby YHA that closed a few years ago. I must have missed it in 2007, as it has been running independently for 25 years. Their parents' adventures in hostels inspired them to take it on and realise a post-pandemic dream. It is perfectly situated for tomorrow's fast walk around the island and the East Fleet to Abbotsbury.

I sit in the bay window, people-watching as the island comes to life, nursing a bowl of too-hot porridge. I will travel around the island without my pack and return for lunch to walk on to Abbotsbury, and the Jurassic

Coaster bus back to Weymouth. Even though the Portland Coast Path and South West Coast Path have circled the island for years, it is here that the first section of the England Coast Path opened. It deviates from those former paths around the eastern cliffs and is marked by a stone spiral ammonite sculpture dated 2012. This implies Natural England has been opening sections of the England Coast Path for 10 years. I hope they will finish it in 2026 after the stay-at-home hiatus delayed progress. It is a monumental task and one of those 'painting the Forth Bridge' projects – never finished, always in need of maintenance after it has been built to protect the path along an eroding coastline.

I meet Andy, who is immediately identifiable as a thru-hiker with a weathered look and worn gear you will not see in a clothing catalogue. A style earned with effort, not bought – every torn seam and weathered sleeve a memory of a moment on his long walk.

'What is the route like ahead?' he asks.

'The ranges ahead will be closed, I think, and it's a crappy road walk around them. You might check now or catch a bus to Corfe Castle,' I recall from my pre-walk research.

'Or just hole up at the hostel and enjoy Portland,' I suggest.

'I just take each day as it comes,' he replies. 'I have time'.

'You'll have the wind behind you, at least.'

Indeed, time is a most treasured asset. Financial and social wealth are measured in money and status; freedom and physical wealth are measured in time and health – finding the right mix is one of life's challenges, but an excess in any one has consequences for the others. While he is not in a hurry, I am walking like a gazelle without a pack and progress rapidly to the headland, past numberless summer huts boarded up for winter. The lighthouse commands the channel day and night: four flashes every 20 seconds, warning of treacherous sea and rocks. There is a sense here that you are on a ship in the middle of the English Channel. An opposing wind backcombs the tide into huge crests, making you feel seasick as if the land is moving. I head north to the old lighthouse (now a beautiful private home) and into the cliffs and quarries, home to several peregrine falcons hunting along its edge. The stunning arc of Chesil Beach emerges – one of the most spectacular views on the south coast. Light rays race across its length like a time-lapse movie, their speed a clue to the strength of a freshening south-westerly. The sun punches a pyramid of light through the convulsing clouds, twisting and torturing the ground below. It is a celestial light show, intense, religious and powerful – a divine sun god arguing with creation, demanding attention, and reminding the planet Earth who is boss.

It is a thrilling walk to the quarry sculpture park, where the history of Portland stone is told. It is a brief stop before returning to the hostel, where I refuel and walk across the causeway to the banks of the East Fleet. A walk along Chesil Beach would be a challenge in the shingle, but that route, in hindsight, is preferable to the deep mud ditches around the rifle ranges at Charlestown. It is possible to walk along the 18 miles over an estimated 180 billion pebbles to West Bay, but there is no shelter, and it is closed when birds are breeding, or the firing range is in use. I know from experience that in bad weather stones can be picked up by crashing waves and become missiles, but the sheer monotony and effort to walk over shingle is soul-destroying. Fishermen knew this and developed plank-like slippers to walk it. I take the muddy path, and my boots sink above their cuffs in the gloopy mud. There is no easy route west.

Shelducks, shovelers and mute swans feed and shelter in the brackish waterways used to test Barnes Wallis's bouncing bomb in 1942. Birders have eyes peeled on a falcon harried by crows above the woodland. The path ascends on to the downs for a stunning ridge walk into Abbotsbury, guided by the sentinel Abbey of St Catherine's on Chapel Hill. I gingerly descend and navigate through bullocks to the farm, keeping them in a quizzical state with gentle tiptoe steps until I can reach the safety of a stile. A few minutes later, I am on a perfectly timed bus into Weymouth which links immediately to the Portland service to drop me outside the hostel.

My luck runs out the next morning, as the early bus to Weymouth station is late and I have to sprint for the connecting service, only to learn that it is for school kids only. I must wait until the next service, but the three-hour wait to start walking robs me of energy before the day has begun. A lane walk takes me to the coastline to follow a rough road behind the shingle to West Bexington, but then the path is endless shingle of a variety that slides a planted foot in any direction. New muscles I have not felt before activate to cope with a new walking style, sapping energy on every step for little apparent progress. A fingerpost suggests a winter or summer route. I select the former, which briefly replaces the shingle banks with thick, gloopy mud again. Then it is back to shingle and a new experience of walking like Herman from *The Munsters* in pebble-dashed one-ton boots into Burton Bradstock. I use a piece of driftwood to scrape away the setting concrete conglomerate mix. Beneath lies leather and Vibram soles that will eventually reveal themselves when I can find a deep enough puddle to wash them clean.

I won't take the foreshore, for the cliff falls here are real and dangerous. I have stayed on campsites in the area for over 30 years and can recall only a few landslips during that time, but recently there have been multiple falls, frightening in their scale. People have lost their lives along this beach, so it is up along the golf course to West Bay for lunch, following the roped-off path where cracks are starting to appear. I should have skipped the Cornish Bakery chain, for Rachel's is open, serving stunning pop-up seafood meals, even in this weather. You can't get a table at peak times in summer, but today it is quiet. It is lovely to chat with the young woman at the counter. She is vivacious, chirpy and bright and has an infectious smile as she leans with her elbows at the counter window, beaming happiness to anyone and everyone, reminding me of Spike Milligan's famous *Smiling is Infectious* poem.

The next climb to Eype is one I know, and these sections are at risk of collapsing too – a familiar abandoned timber-framed house is getting closer to the cliff edge each year. The climb to Thurstone Beacon announces another change in topography and contours along the Jurassic coastline into Lyme Bay. Having dropped down into Seatown, with its picturesque Anchor Inn, it is another climb to Golden Cap, arguably the highest point on the south coast (depending on how close to the coast you measure) at 191 metres. It is time for a breather.

Perhaps too much oxygen has lightened my head, for gazing around a 360-degree view, I wonder how I perceive this unlimited vista. We do not see things as *they* are; we see them as *we* are. How real is the scene I am observing? How do others see it? Do I filter out different patterns and movement to my neighbours? At this scale my visual neural pathways are overloaded by this complexity, triggering a sense of awe. I descend without effort, floating on this natural high, in a flow state, a joyous mood that takes me to Stonebarrow Lane and Charmouth. The combination of physical effort, an open mind and the scale of this epic journey is humbling. I am within the landscape now and I begin to understand the enormity of what I am trying to do, and I ask myself why. The answer will come from an inner voice, now speaking clearly to me – I am alive and able to ask such a perplexing question now the distractions of a modern world have gone.

I can see the tide is out, and checking the timetables to be safe, I walk into Lyme Regis along the beach and shoreline ledges. There are many fossickers, re-enacting Mary Anning's passion for palaeontology, hoping to unearth a plesiosaur or pterosaur, but more likely an ammonite. The cliffs are slipping into the sea, as would the town if it were not for recent civil engineering works, nailing the cliff face to stable ground and deflecting winter storms from a soft undercliff. This is a 'hold the line' coast, costly to protect, yet costly to lose, unlike the earlier 'managed retreat' shore at Charmouth and 'do-nothing' wilderness at Stonebarrow cliffs. All three categorisations of a shoreline management strategy are in one view, all with the same geology but a different economic context.

To the west, the Undercliff provides frightening evidence of what is at stake. Huge landslides have created a netherworld subtropical jungle landscape, rich in flora and fauna in a mythical pixie-world paradise, somehow displaced in geological time. To enter at dawn is to begin a seven-mile meditation through a fascinating habitat, unlike any coastal path in England or Wales. The same trepidation that preceded my aborted entry into Bonchurch returns, but then turns to delight as I step carefully over the gothic tree roots and chaotic rock. The birdsong is different, deer are on the path ahead, unwilling to venture into the woodland, and slow-worms rest on the rocks, waiting for the sun to penetrate a thick canopy of trees and bush.

How does my body know to place one foot in front of another? I'm not looking at my feet as I walk. I seem to be able to preconceive six or seven steps ahead. My mind has already placed my feet on the ground without my knowledge. This spatial awareness has developed over years of walking on different terrains. A part of my brain is evolving as my fitness improves, making my steps effortless and swift and enhancing my experience. I reach Goat Island, an orphaned plateau and home to species untroubled by modern agriculture, its terrain cleaved from the mainland. My adapted human form made short work of this difficult terrain compared to the efforts I recall 15 years earlier. I notice and acknowledge the change and feel grateful for my new abilities.

Normal flat track resumes as I descend into Seaton and then the wonderfully named Beer, with its iconic row of coastal cottages bathing in the morning light. I awake from my Undercliff dream and stop for brunch, studying the map for the next goal. Here, I read the word 'combe' all the way west, a word to fill any South West Coast Path walker with dread. At the first such test, I freewheel recklessly into Branscombe, where my pace shudders to a halt as if I have forgotten to change into a lower gear. The ascent is brutal, warranting a stop to refill with water, where car-bound visitors sensibly stay in the car park and cafe boundaries, trapped by geology. The westerly winds build, so I sweat up the climbs in the lee and then freeze as I reach the summit to face the gale, hastily putting on a windproof that moments later will be removed again as this cycle repeats. I take a breath and stop to chat with Anna, a National Trust and RSPB ecologist who is out for a day walk, ignoring the weather forecast like me.

'The Undercliff is a highlight. I am unsure what deer I saw, and the trees are full of birdsong I didn't recognise,' I say.

'Probably roe deer and dawn chorus thrushes,' she explains.

'Have you seen any falcons?'

'Yes, almost daily, but no cetaceans yet; it may be too early in the season.'

'Yes, it will be, but stop to look at the vegetable market gardens at Weston Plats; they are amazing. Perhaps rest on the beach to see the cliff geology too.'

That rest is welcome, but the escapee garden seeds that will colour the path have yet to flower fully; spring has only just started. I disrobe before another combe ascent and descend to sunbathe in the lee of a rock on the shore. The wind is increasing in strength as the day unfolds, uncompromising and unyielding in its intensity. Barely have I recovered, and another combe, and then another. You reach a summit, see a level path ahead and rejoice at the thought of easier terrain. Then you walk 10 steps to see a sliver of missing Devon coastline, eroded over millennia by a simple stream – a thin slice stolen from a landscape cake, teasing you to earn your progress.

At the hotel in Sidmouth I finally clatter, exhausted, into reception and enter a very different world of received-pronunciation retirees, immaculately dressed for dinner. I am blanked as if I do not belong, my dishevelled appearance at odds with the dress code for the evening. At breakfast I tidy myself up (boots left in the room, and fresh socks), but it is difficult to engage in conversation. I listen in to the next table.

'Do you know Topsham? It is delightful. My sister Marjorie has a wonderful riverfront property,' a lady declares to the neighbouring table. 'Another pot of tea, waiter,' she shouts, waving her hand in his general direction. She then looks at who I assume to be her husband. 'Donald, don't play with your eggs benedict, and use a knife dear, please.' A comment that bounces off his balding head as he rolls his eyes in the style of Wallace's dog Gromit.

I am holding back my giggles as I pick through the buffet, eager to return to the path. It is a wonderful hotel, stuck in the 1960s – where you go to recall the good old days. I like it, as there are no complicated modern gadgets or technology to detract from the core comforts: a comfy bed in a silent room, nice hot showers, a tasty full English and a complex warren of creaking staircases and fire doors that would challenge the finest navigator.

I have a short day walk to Exmouth station and can slow my pace. A good friend will provide a bed for the night, which is handy as the Starcross to Exmouth Ferry is closed. Breathing easily and up to speed, I arrive at a viewpoint when six spaniel gun dogs appear: all brothers and sisters, out to explore the day. The owner follows, and we have a long post-pandemic chat, releasing the latent pressure from our fizzy bottles full of pent-up conversation. Many people I meet have missed social connections, as I have too. Walking alone, I am more approachable and if you ask a few open questions, the cork is popped and the conversation flows until you both realise that you are talking openly to a stranger, with raw emotions as strong as they might be with a close friend.

The path follows low red sandstone cliffs and loops around the Budleigh Salterton Otter Estuary Nature Reserve, which is an easy walk even though the overnight rain has reactivated the mud. I can hear the rifle range at Straight Point; the crack of single shots punctuates the natural white noise of wind and waves. Reaching the *Geoneedle* sculpture (the western extent of the Jurassic Coast) I can read Earth's history in its structure: deserts, seas, shifting rivers, dunes, organic formation, marine reptiles, crustaceans and dinosaurs – all now compressed into Cretaceous, Jurassic and Triassic rock over 250 million years, sampled and presented to me on a walk from Swanage to Exmouth.

After a very comfortable stay with my friends and too much wine I catch the train to Starcross. The weather is foul and set for the day. A full Force 7 hits the train carriage window as I alight at an exposed estuary-side station. Zipped and toggled up, with my vulnerable gear buried in waterproofing layers, I walk to Dawlish, not knowing how the day will end. It is high tide, and the waves break over the seawall to add salt to the wound. I retreat to a high-level road through town, diverted by many paths closed for engineering works at this time of year. One more combe and then the Teignmouth breakwater, where I can see idiots walking their dogs on the lower steps, at risk of being swept out to sea.

If the ferry isn't running, I'll walk across the nearby bridge, less than a mile inland, but my resolve weakens. With a nasty weather front and storm approaching, set for a week, I decide to bail out while drip-drying in a cafe. To cement the decision, I can see a sequence of river crossings ahead and can't devise a sensible strategy to deal with closed ferry services without messy walks up deep estuaries. A cheap super-off-peak senior railcard return ticket decides for me. I board the train 30 minutes later. As I dry, the carriage gets soaked at the aptly named Sprey Point as the train departs east. I squeeze in my earbuds and select a playlist for Paddington, not caring whether I fall asleep as the carriage rocks through the appalling weather. It'll clear in a few weeks as spring takes hold. My clothes might dry by then.

# 7
# TEIGNMOUTH TO PAR
## The tide rises and the tide falls

*'Solitude gives birth to the original in us, to beauty
unfamiliar and perilous – to poetry.'*
Thomas Mann

### Distance walked: 750 miles

Now Easter has passed, the ferries are back in action. I carried a tent from Chichester, and now it will earn its keep where hostels cannot be found. I am travelling with *Freya Bevan*, a Great Western Railways Class 800 Intercity locomotive to Penzance – a name I have noticed stencilled on the carriage for many a journey to the south west. I Google her name while waiting for the train to depart; the little girl was diagnosed with a brain tumour at 22 months of age. Her bravery and courage over the next seven years is humbling, putting my modest efforts in context. My brother died in his mid-50s of the same condition; a good friend has just had a heart attack, and another succumbed to alcoholism. I take a moment to be grateful for the experience ahead of me.

The Shaldon Ferry has had a lick of paint and looks resplendent in the mid-morning sunshine. This must be the prettiest passenger ferry on the coast of England. This one is No.4 – the fourth motorised vessel since 1903. It has a traditional castellated gunport decor in keeping with one of the oldest services in the country, whose history can be traced back to 1296, possibly to earlier Anglo-Saxon times. I have my £2 ready.

'How many South West Coast Path walkers this week?' I ask.

'You are the first heading west, one or two heading east. Are you planning to walk to Minehead?' the ferryman replies.

'Cromer, hopefully, I am walking around the coast of England.'

'Well, you are the first this year, and I can't remember anyone doing that last year.'

'Perhaps they use the bridge, as many walkers I know doing the whole thing have rules about using any motorised services,' I suggest.

I describe my bail-out in early March, and he confirms the ferry was not running due to weather and tide conditions. Today, the ferry gently slides on to the shingle, guided with the skill of someone who has done this a hundred, a thousand times before, inch perfect.

I resume walking with what I hope is an easy half-day to Torbay but have forgotten to tell my legs that Maidencombe, Watcombe, Oddicombe and Babbacombe lie ahead. It is a rude awakening, and time to put walking poles and triceps into gear to supplement the quads and calves rested for a few lazy weeks. Engaging 4x4 mode makes life easier on ascents and descents, and my poles are becoming natural extensions to my bipedal frame, strengthening my core, back and shoulders.

The ferryman will have new customers soon. I meet Sophie from Germany, now battle-hardened since starting from Minehead. Then Lucy and Steve from Cromer.

'Gosh, we drive home tomorrow, and it will take us seven hours, and you have walked all that!' says Lucy.

'We're walking the South West Coast Path in sections and have been doing that for a few years now,' Steve adds.

'Well, it is roughly the same distance again from Bournemouth to Cromer, much closer than you'd expect. It shows you how wiggly the coastline can be here.'

Wild garlic, bluebells and fresh foliage confirm the arrival of spring. Kestrels and buzzards are busy, preparing to breed. It is 12ºC with a cool easterly – perfect conditions for walking if only the terrain were flat. A birder quizzes me about possible sightings of cirl buntings, which the RSPB protects at Labrador Bay. Maybe a sighting of yellowhammers, but I am not quick enough to see the difference and curse again not bringing binoculars to save weight.

The sea reflections change as I turn into Tor Bay, past Thatcher Rock and East Shag, two isolated outcrops where gold has been found. Even a small change of direction alters the way light plays on the surface of the bay, reflected by a new wave pattern. The expensive fleet of yachts and motorboats in the marina, guarded by high fences and security gates, are in shocking contrast to the poverty and deprivation of the seaside town. The brightest lights somehow cast the darkest shadows. A man with a broad Scottish accent propels his ageing mother down Beacon Hill in a wheelchair. I can't keep up with them as they have a full-on argument about where to eat.

'I'm nae eating at 'Spoons agin son,' she screams.

'Shut yer geggy ma – I'm payin,' is his short and final reply.

Even a fan of Rab C. Nesbitt can only just about translate the accent, a Glaswegian stereotype I try to shake as I observe the rough sleepers and addicts who have gravitated in the side streets. Looking for something to eat, I realise the sales algorithms have perfectly matched demand, filling the mini markets with profitable cheap alcohol, ultra-processed snacks and energy drinks. The tatty diners, nightclubs and pub crawl architecture will rest until nightfall, as its decor does not sit well with a sunny afternoon. Compared to the stunning coastal scenery I have just walked through, I feel out of place. I hide in a soulless Premier Inn after a fruitless search for a quaint campsite or reasonable B&B. I hope my trail legs activate soon as I look forward to pitching a tent along the more remote sections of the path.

No matter how early I start walking, I cannot beat the wild swimmers to the shoreline. They bob up and down in bobble hats as if the air is colder than the water. I admire them – it is a gorgeous day that is not to be wasted. Ticking off a couple of number 103 huts along the popular beaches, my legs ease out the pains of yesterday's exertion. The air intake and oil temperature of my bodily engine are optimal after about five miles, signalling to my mind that I can use full revs on climbs. It will not take long to reach Brixham, but I come across a pit stop that can't be missed – Fishcombe Cove Café. I am drawn helplessly off the path by a fresh coffee tractor-beam aroma and to the serving hatch.

This is a wonderful social hub – on old surfboard, repurposed as a blackboard, lists sunset yoga with Nicola (sold out), story time with Josephine, and a seal and jellyfish talk. The resident robins hop from table to table in search of crumbs, each skilled in charm and known by name, having claimed their crumb-rich territory in a windless cove. As I rest, I can't help reflecting on the social mix along the path. At one moment, worrying deprivation, then a relaxed hippy bohemia, followed by the comfortable middle classes with status anxieties. Walking the path you experience every dimension of society, rich and poor, narrow-minded and wide. You must set aside your prejudices and open your eyes and ears to understand their perspective of their worlds and what the coast means to them. After all these conversations I can't help wondering if we have a common unconscious love of this littoral boundary, born of our shared humanity and condition, and underpinned by a deep-seated connection to nature and the sea.

I'm in a good mood as I depart, drifting towards Berry Head with the sun rising in the sky and warming the local 'Pride in Brixham' volunteers cleaning the cast iron benches and pretty mosaics depicting seaside scenes. I stop at a kiosk for a seafood roll, which is expensive but beautifully prepared and wrapped, and something to look forward to later. The local parking warden is smiling and seems to be enjoying his job.

'How far are you walking today?' he asks.

'Probably 20 miles, but I prefer to measure the time I walk rather than distance, so a good eight hours with stops. I can see your Fitbit watch; how many do you do daily?' I ask.

'Probably 20 miles, too. Keeps you fit issuing tickets,' he laughs.

The usual conversation about the South West Coast Path and England Coast Path, and my start from Cromer, follows until I move along and meet John, a 92-year-old army historian who gives out leaflets telling the story of Operation Tiger: the tragic events around Slapton Sands in April 1944. It is a story I know, but he was alive then and a first-hand witness.

'I used to play football with the GIs,' he tells me. 'They were lovely chaps, smartly dressed, and full of spirit. It affected me deeply when I heard of the disaster in the 1980s. More men lost their lives rehearsing for D-Day than on Utah Beach. It was kept secret for all those years.'

'Is the tank still there on the beach, the one dredged from the bay by a fisherman?' I ask.

'Yes, Ken Small was determined to have a memorial; take a moment when you get there.'

We chatted for ages, and it was a lovely encounter with someone who wanted to share his grief, his story, something he wants us all to remember. I stop for a moment at Berry Head to reflect and eat the purchased roll, whose aroma drives the seagulls crazy. The rugged coastline will be the norm for a few weeks, and memories of flat promenades in the east have faded. Yet I find the change in tempo is less weary, rotating my muscle use compared to the monotonous pavement pounding. I follow the steam train's whistles into Kingswear, blown for touristic effect rather than requirement, and join a queue for the ferry to Dartmouth. Not wishing to linger, I weave my way out through endless parcel delivery and construction vans, squeezing down streets designed for horses and carts. A happy day ends at a comfy campsite in Stoke Fleming – the coastal scenery improving with each mile as I walk deeper into Devon.

Early morning wrens flitter their tails in the tree branches as I walk towards Blackpool Sands. Their chatter, rattle and piercing song weaves a tuneful thread in the still morning air – all the spring birds are singing their post-dawn songs and alarms as I disturb them in the hedgerows and trees. I'm meeting five to ten South West Coast Path walkers a day now. The first, an Australian, is overloaded with gear and seemingly unaware of the path ahead, making it up as he goes; then there is an eco-warrior visiting projects on her way to John o' Groats; then a couple walking the South West Coast Path in stages, and so on, a broad spectrum of countries, ages and backgrounds. You meet more people walking clockwise, as the guides are written for the opposite direction. My crude survey of long-distance thru-hikers suggests that 50% are women, 30% are retired couples and only 20% are in my cohort: men who walk alone. I am not sure why that is. Maybe it correlates to those who have the time for such long trips?

But none are so determined to finish the South West Coast Path as a lesser stag beetle slowly walking with me. I kneel to measure his (or her, I can't tell) pace and then spend the next few miles working out numbers to keep my brain occupied. That's 100 centimetres in 40 seconds, er, a kilometre is 40,000 seconds, hmmmm, maybe 1,000 minutes. Let's check that again: 28 hours is four days per kilometre roughly; assume eight hours a day walking, that's not right. Shall I get a pen from my pack, as my brain is hurting? That's 2,000 days to do the South West Coast Path, which seems reasonable, but he (or she – need to look that up) will only live for one or two years, so its offspring must complete the journey. So that's five-odd years, or approximately three lifetimes of walking. Blimey. Well, at least it demonstrates that anybody can complete this iconic National Trail with determination and purpose.

Somehow, I have not fallen off the cliff, distracted by my mental arithmetic. The wind dies as I turn Start Point, the gentle easterly now a tailwind along a stunning section of rock cliffs, coves and headlands. I remember Gammon Head in a storm, but it is now serene, innocent and harmless compared to the frightening tempest I saw in 2007. I take the busy ferry across the harbour to Salcombe, looking for something to eat and find a quirky vegan cafe. The Estuary Club is run by August (he is named after the month), who holds weekly meetings to discuss quantum mechanics at this self-declared time-traveller venue. So, I recount my beetle story, and he ponders the sanity of this weird coastal walker who has entered his premises while he polishes the cappuccino cups.

'All routes lead home,' he declares, popping out to the kitchen to prepare a Buddha Bowl salad – a perfectly considered and philosophical answer. I would love to stay in this place, but the rooms are £125 for the night, and I have managed to find a B&B for a quarter of that up a back alley in the heights of the town, which is preferable to the rowdy streets of Salcombe, full of bored posh kids at night. Over 50% of properties are second homes here, and more construction plagues the road out of town to Bolt Head, attracting those interested in capital growth and yields and disregarding the impact on local communities – the extrinsic incomer displacing a fading intrinsic culture. I can't help reflecting on the monetisation of a natural landscape at the expense of those who call this beautiful port home.

It is a relief to wind through a rough coastal path and return to the seascapes at Bolt Head. The wind is slight, and a silence rings in my ears. Great northern divers are cooing in the bay; their long eerie cry drifts with great beauty in the gentle eastern breeze – captivating, romantic and mysterious. They prepare to leave for their breeding grounds while passerines flit excitedly between the gorse bushes. Stonechats swing on the highest twigs, their chirps like the clatter of two stones knocked together. Yellowhammers and chiffchaffs, less bold, fill the air with their song. A symphony of warning calls unfolds as I progress along the narrow path, fading as I pass.

Hope Cove is alive with visitors enjoying an alfresco brunch, yet the reminder of a second-home economy is stated explicitly on the side of service vans parked outside the cottages. 'Taking care of your home' (I read 'asset'), starts a conversation in my head that continues with an aggie vibe of private property 'no parking' signs. Golf courses confirming privilege are emphatic: 'no camping,' 'beware of golf balls' and 'police will be called' signs, which makes me wonder what people have done to upset the club committee.

The coastline is stunning, and property ownership rights detract from what should be available to anyone on this public path. The warden at the Bantham Estate car park has seen these changes over the years. I ask him about crossing the River Avon, and he suggests I wade, but directs me to the boathouse after I declare my love of passenger ferries. I meet Rick, who wipes his greased hands on my arrival after working on an engine, to take my fare. He expertly navigates the shingle and sandy channels in the shallow draft craft, tilting the modest outboard motor in the shallows to glide on to the opposite beach, perfectly coaxing engine thrust to balance river flow, wind and momentum to the direction he wants to go.

'What do you recommend at Erme?' I ask, referring to the next estuary with no ferry.

'You should be able to cross tomorrow plus or minus two hours of low tide,' he checks his timetable booklet, always carried, it seems, in his top pocket. 'Low tide is at quarter to one. The rivers are low, as we have had little rain, so no problem, but a little cold maybe.'

I am grateful for the lift, but I could have waded if I had known where to cross. I stay on the beach and eat what is left in my pack. The campsite is above me and I am in no rush. I sit and watch the whimbrel and little egrets. In the sun trap I slip off my boots and socks and lie on the beach, a few feet from the incoming tide. I rest, imagining the imperceptible movement of the Earth and the moon as they exert their gravitational force on the colossal oceans and seas. The estuary fills, and my meditation breaks as the water touches my heels. I sense these worlds, and the tides respond, as they have done before the beginning of life on Earth, before the concept of time. A poem by the American poet Henry Wadsworth Longfellow captures the transitory nature of a lone coastal traveller:

*The tide rises, the tide falls,*
*The twilight darkens, the curlew calls;*

## TEIGNMOUTH TO PAR

*Along the sea-sands damp and brown*
*The traveller hastens towards the town,*
  *And the tide rises, the tide falls.*

*Darkness settles on roof and walls,*
*But the sea, the sea in the darkness calls;*
*The little waves, with their soft, white hands,*
*Efface the footprints in the sands,*
  *And the tide rises, the tide falls.*

*The morning breaks; the steeds in their stalls*
*Stamp and neigh, as the hostler calls;*
*The day returns, but nevermore*
*Returns the traveller to the shore,*
  *And the tide rises, the tide falls.*

Henry Wadsworth Longfellow,<br>*The Tide Rises, The Tide Falls* (1879)

Looking at my smartphone, I have options: A) a cosy campsite with a farmyard pop-up cafe at £9 a night, or B) the hotel on Burgh Island at £488 a night (minimum two-night stay, plus meals). The latter budget would keep me comfortable for a month or two, and it doesn't even have a good sea view. The next morning's pop-up cafe is superb: a latte made with the dedication of a young lad keen to add barista to his CV and freshly baked croissants from the farm cottage Aga carried in a gingham cloth-covered tray by his girlfriend. The site is full of cool dudes in VW T4 campervans here for a gathering, so the previous afternoon's social scene was chatty as we enjoyed the elevated views of Bigbury Bay and a serene sunset. We shared adventures and hacks for quirky ageing vans, vowing to keep them running in the face of endless complex technological developments that reduce reliability – a good engineer should make things as simple as possible, durable, not complex. 'Keep them running, they will go on for ages,' we chime with enthusiasm.

My goal is Plymouth, but that depends on river crossings so I leave without a fixed plan and will just let the day be what it will be. The Nisa local doesn't sell single apples, which is a pet peeve of mine, but it has other calories to sustain me. At Erme, the sign says you can cross in one hour around low tide, but I am three hours early. I have a Mexican stand-off with a chap on the opposite bank who wants to cross too, so I throw caution to the wind, take my boots and socks off, and wade in – using poles for stability. The water touches my crotch, but the flow is steady, and the water is deliciously refreshing and cool. I emerge nonchalantly beside my *compadre* with a casual and nonchalant 'Mornin', which triggers him to remove his boots and not delay his crossing, which he starts in earnest before realising he is a foot shorter than me. His 'package' is well and truly soaked (judging by the yelps I hear as I put my boots back on).

The cliff paths are blue and yellow with bluebells and gorse, a rugged terrain where you'd expect solitude between the river wading and ferry points, yet the path is busy with holiday walkers on circular routes searching for secluded coves. I turn inland at Gara Point and trek through the woodland to another ferry. Conversation flows freely with a captain who loves his job.

'What's the best pub in Plymouth? My mate says The Dolphin is great; lovely pictures by Beryl Cook,' is my conversation opener.

'Was my favourite, but the Proper Job was off last time. Try The Fisherman's Arms; that's good. Nice pint of Bass.'

'Or maybe both?' I suggest.

'Ah, but that would lead to a pub crawl, very dangerous,' he replies.

My good friend, Tony, lives locally and I will meet him later. He has given me the inside secrets of the town.

I won't take any more ferries after Wembury today and walk on to the coastal defences that guard Plymouth Sound. The pubs will wait, and I'll remain sober, staying somewhere cheaper in Hooe, which has a couple of fuss-free takeaways. I step over the 'Welcome to Plymouth – please wipe your feet' stone, which my mate jokes is placed the wrong way around.

I walk around Hooe Lake and through Turnchapel to reach the ferry at the Mount Batten pierhead. The roads are named after T. E. Lawrence in recognition of the great man's service as a humble aircraftsman with the nearby RAF Flying Boat Squadron (under the assumed name of T. E. Shaw). He was discharged in February 1935, only to succumb to motorcycle accident injuries on 19th May a few months later.

## TEIGNMOUTH TO PAR

*All men dream: but not equally. Those who dream by night in the dusty recesses of their minds wake in the day to find that it was vanity: but the dreamers of the day are dangerous men, for they may act their dreams with open eyes, to make it possible.*
T. E. Lawrence, *Seven Pillars of Wisdom*,<br>first published in 1926

The ferry is a solar-powered marvel. I expect a 'chugg, chugg, chugg' to the marina pier, but there is a silent purr instead. Enough for conversation with the departing sea kayak fishermen on the slipways, rods standing tall with lures ready. Guided by South West Coast Path markers, unique to the city, I make gentle progress around The Hoe, with its refurbished Tinside Lido outdoor seawater pool – an Art Deco masterpiece. You could spend a day reading about the history of this harbour, but I am eager to catch the Cremyll Ferry and up the pace around Royal William Yard (home of the South West Coast Path Association). I miss it by a minute and seek shelter in the nearby cafe for a late breakfast.

Half an hour later, I step off the ferry. I am in Cornwall and search for the clock I remember. It has been lovingly restored. 'Dost thou love life – then do not squander time' and 'Time and Tide – Tarry for None' written in the clockface. This must be one of the most delightful timepieces I have seen on my walk. I hold those statements as I walk into the grounds of Mount Edgcumbe Gardens and follow the shoreline into the woods. Milton's Temple marks the entrance, but something does not look right. It is only then I realise that a photographer is taking a picture of his completely naked girlfriend posing inside the structure. We look at each other – I in disbelief, her trying to maintain the pose. I take one more step, and the illusion shatters. She dresses quickly like a disturbed bird that froze in the bushes and then flees. You don't see that often; I can't quite believe it myself.

The bakery in Kingsand has pasties, and seeing as I am now in Cornwall (just passing the old sign for the former border) it is time to add them to my diet, for they are the perfect meal for a walker. A drizzle has started, but not heavy enough to warrant a waterproof jacket, the beads drying at the same rate as they land on my base layer. I hike out to Rame Head and shelter there before heading west with my back again to the easterly wind. My boots pick up the damp rain from the grass and slowly soak, but the road walk to Tregantle Ranges dries them. It is one of those days when you can't be bothered to stop and put on your jacket, knowing you will be too hot, versus getting wet and drying off as you walk. I am not about to stop, for there are cows, with calves and bulls, in the fields. It is a relief to pirouette through the last gate into Portwrinkle for a cup of tea at a cafe. I am served a lump of something disgusting, possibly cake. The gallery of dog pictures suggests it may have been intended for them.

The drizzle has turned to rain, and I walk alone towards Looe, the paths cleared of other walkers. The campsite at Millendreath looks like a place to stop. I knock on the door and am met by a delightful lady who has recently lost her husband. Our conversation is steady, her bereavement still raw. She is determined to carry on, not knowing what else to do. I can hear in her voice an emerging determination to navigate her future. After a moment's silence and reflection, she says I can pitch anywhere I like.

I walk in to find two lightweight backpackers just starting a meal. I introduce myself, start to shiver after talking too much, so put up my tent and layer up and join them on the picnic table. Gary and Mark are walking the South West Coast Path anticlockwise. They met by chance a few weeks ago and now seem the best of friends. They both dreamt of walking this path, and the pandemic galvanised their resolve. We chat for hours, adding more layers to our clothing, eating freeze-dried food and drinking endless mugs of tea. Gear notes, routes, clothing and experiences are compared until the sun sets, and we have no choice but to retire to our tents and sleeping bags as the temperature drops. The conversation continues between the tent walls until we all drift off to sleep.

I'm up and packed, ready to go in 30 minutes, about my average time. If you travel with less, you pack less; if you know your system and repeat it, it becomes muscle memory, and you can almost do it in the dark. In heavy rain, I will emerge ready to walk with only the tent left to pack, its wet carcass going into a waterproof bag and packed on the top of my backpack. Colour-coded dry bags help, as does the discipline of keeping everything in the right place. I say my goodbyes and wish them luck, then drop down to Looe for breakfast and lunch shopping, all completed at a bakery. I feel great as I take the lane to the coast and return to a glorious path. I say goodbye to 'one-eyed' Nelson the seal, whose sculpture looks out over the channel entrance, a much-loved character who reminds us of the need to cherish the rich marine environment. Polperro fishing village leaves no doubt that I have arrived in Cornwall, for it is as picturesque and romantic as any – a brief blip of humanity until I reach the path again and the seascape view opens once more.

Yachts are trying to race along the coast. There is no wind, yet some are progressing. The whole strategy of the race can be seen clearly from the cliff, with the faster vessels sailing inshore through a hint of breeze betrayed by ripples on the water's surface while others remain bolt upright in the doldrums. Their positions barely alter over the next hour as I reach Polruan, where a bigger ferry is needed, for the crowds are out in force. Fowey opposite has also been infected by the investment property virus spreading from the east as roads improve access. The only cure is a national economic downturn when investment retreats – a volatile economic cycle that impacts the outer edges of the south-west. I am lucky to get a table at a cafe, and people-watch until the meal arrives. Galleries and trendy shops are busy with day-trippers, something I can't remember from 15 years ago. A new *Rook with a Book* artwork, inspired by Daphne Du Maurier's writings, stands near the ferry point. It is quite scary, of a size which would peck small children from the pavement, were it to become animated.

I only have one more headland to walk and admire. The Gribbin Head daymark is recently repainted and resplendent, with bold red and white stripes visible for miles. 'Ban second homes' graffiti adorns a few gates – other sentiments are much ruder and more explicit. I wander into Par expecting an easy late afternoon, but I have one last mini-combe tester through Polkerris. I wiggle around the holiday park and walk to the Royal Inn, perhaps the best option for the area, a lovely railway station-side pub with a deep bath, which fits my frame for a change.

# 8
# PAR TO ST IVES
# Turn right at Land's End

*'The world reveals itself to those who travel on foot.'*
Werner Herzog

## Distance walked: 885 miles

Walking in the shoulder months finds the right balance of accommodation and camping in Cornwall. Prices for hotels, B&Bs and pubs in the summer months (if you can find one) are ridiculous, and winter means a fruitless search for off-season accommodation, or wild camping (if you are stealthy and brave enough). I always prefer to camp first, then hostels, then B&Bs or hotels – mixing it up but keeping costs low. The South West Coast Path and the England Coast Path need a network of simple and affordable overnight stays spaced at sensible distances to make the path accessible to everyone for multi-day hikes. Youth hostels are ideal, yet the YHA has closed many beautiful premises. It is encouraging to see new independents taking up the challenge with quirky, interesting stays that do not conform to any homogenous brand. My target tonight is YHA Boswinger, about 18 miles further west.

Walking between the clay works, the pop-up party land of Carlyon Bay, and the golf course, I am keen to get going in search of remote coastline. I am thwarted by a closed pathway into Charlestown, which I ignore as it is an unresolved right-of-way dispute (the path is perfectly serviceable), and then around Duporth where the path has collapsed, and the council must negotiate new routes. Eventually, the daily exercise programme returns: the familiar peak heart-rate intervals are separated by recovery periods matched to ascent, descent and level paths. Walking out to Black Head Fort, I sit for a while looking to the Gribbin daymark and a fading sequence of headlands eastwards. My mind perceives past distance to be less than future distance, as if I fear the challenge ahead without considering fully what I have already achieved, as if some inner voice demands a rest and tries to trick me.

There is another diversion around Pentewan Sands on to the main road when I should have contemplated a walk along the beach and a scramble up the cliff, but I behave and ease into Mevagissey along the formal route. The She Sells cafe is perfect. I hide inside and enjoy a bowl of tomato and spinach soup. Most clients are outside in the sunshine with ice creams; the owners are inside discussing council regulation compliance of their competitors. The politics of the fishing village seem surreal when I recall the 1980s, when I first visited. The B&B at the end of a lane had a dome-shaped bed made of straw, and the cured bacon was cut from a hanging leg in the shed. The pubs were warm, welcoming and friendly, and the walk back to our beds in the pitch-dark sky was a challenge after a few pints. I have changed, and so has the village, a combination that makes for an unrecognisable memory after 40 years.

It is a long hike, passing hidden bays and inaccessible beaches, to Gorran Haven for provisions. A dual-masted tall ship has a full rig, making slow progress in a slight breeze. The ribbons of still water meander in the bay, forming patterns that suggest the wind doesn't know how to blow. I am ahead of schedule and rest at Dodman Point Cross, knees to my chest, my head in the cradle of my interlocked fingers, gazing out to sea. Nothing is moving. It is utterly quiet, the soft tinnitus in my head the only perceived sound, until I hear the familiar call of the great northern divers in the bay – a head-spinning haunting voice of birds preparing to migrate north to Greenland. It must be one of the most beautiful sounds in nature. I take a drink from my flask and notice a paradox between the transparent water and the opaque wind-brushed sea, reflecting uncountable hues, tones and textures. What world lies beneath the surface, and what spirits observe us through this secret mirror? An atomic gossamer between primal elements, between two realms of our world.

Turning to face inland, I can see the hostel in the rising hills, along a twisting lane that drops to Hemmick Beach. I arrive with perfect timing for the warden to open the doors, and sign up for the evening meal. I am joined by a chattering gathering of cyclists and walkers, where the conversation flows easily – many are ex-Duke of Edinburgh Award (DoE) or Outward Bound instructors drawn to the area for their leisure, which is surely the highest endorsement. I retire to the dorm early and dream away the day's efforts, finding my sleep comes easily after my head nestles into the pillow.

Waking before dawn, I can't help but leave early to savour the sunrise. I am a lark, not an owl, encouraged by the knowledge that setting off before light will often be the day's high point. I am not disappointed, for a temperature inversion has filled the valleys with an early mist, giving the impression the sea has flowed into the landscape. A three-windowed lookout hut, built for the guests of Caerhays Castle, creates a landscape triptych. The colour blends from an orange gold to deep blue as you scan each panoramic frame from left to right. The path is deserted as the morning unfolds into a still-clear day. I am now in shorts and a T-shirt base layer, my limbs wearing a thru-hiker colouring, the piebald tan lines like long-distance hiker tattoos on neck, arms, hands, nose and calves.

Portloe is quiet too, untouched by modern commerce, its fishing crabbers hauled up the concrete slipway, bearing registrations from Penzance, Falmouth and Fowey. It is getting warm. I contemplate posting some clothing home to lighten the pack, but my boots still earn their keep, for I fall awkwardly on a descent overgrown with weeds, my foot sighting hidden. Poles save the day again, bending almost to breaking point to arrest a more serious sprain.

Yet, for much of the day, I simply follow the bare earth path as it weaves in parallel to the coastline, taking a route as old as the days of smugglers and coastguards. Every turn and cove is named, with lost meanings: Hartriza Point, Lemoria Rock, and Caragloose Point. The names evoke a Cornish language akin to Welsh – a Brittonic dialect once spoken before English displaced it to extinction in the 18th century. It reminds me of the couplet 'By Tre, Pol, Pen – shall we know all Cornishmen.'

There are ponies along the path, which do a good job of keeping the grass cropped. The tall ship has finally overtaken me and anchored at Portscatho, but I have no rest until St Anthony Lighthouse and the entrance to Falmouth Harbour, a port with a rich maritime history. It is my home for the night after I first cross to St Mawes on the Place Ferry and then the Falmouth service half an hour later. I am lucky, as yesterday's low tide means the Percuil River service was cancelled, which would have meant an unpleasant road walk. It is a critical crossing that warrants some research before arrival. I do not know how the fastest known time (FKT) runners factor these crossings into their logistics and the rules that govern such races or competitions, as the delay or diversions can be significant.

My glasses broke in the fall, and they teach me a lesson: pack them in a solid case instead of the Shetland wool sleeve I have used for years. Boots the Chemist has simple, cheap, unfashionable but functional reading glasses which will work if I squint one eye. I wander towards my booked B&B and hear a loud market trader call, offering half-price pasties near closing time, which solves my need to search for food later and allows me to collapse in the simple room early. I open my journal, hold my pen, and force my mind to write, actively processing my day's thoughts, reflecting and learning. Where did I walk, who did I meet, what did I see – how did it feel?

The breakfast is excellent, and more than offsets the accommodation fee. This is the 50th day of walking since I started in Cromer, which is insane progress when I consider I am halfway along the South West Coast Path, which took 37 days to complete in 2007. This popular National Trail will account for a 24% of the England Coast Path's total distance, but that doesn't seem right when you open a map of the British Isles. It must be the rugged coves and headlands that make a difference. The Cornish coast is the longest in England, after Essex, both counties with complex footpath topologies that compress crow-flying distance. It is an entertaining rabbit hole to dive down, calculating the length of the UK coastline, for the closer you look, the longer it becomes. As a footpath, England should be 2,700 miles; Wales is 870 miles. Scotland is a very complex measurement if you factor in the archipelagos of Shetland, Orkney and the Hebridean Islands – and not forgetting Northern Ireland. Together they would add another 4,000 plus walkable miles or so, depending on your route, as it could be much further than that. I'll round it up to 8,000 miles, which many coastal walkers record if they attempt the entire British Isles. So much depends on how you tackle western Scotland.

The new national pastime of wild swimming endures, for the bays are filled with post-pandemic wetsuited paddlers pulling their fluorescent floats across the bay. The swimming styles vary. You can float on your back like an alien abductee, attempting a sort of back butterfly, or try a gentle

Victorian breaststroke, with head high to keep your hat dry, and then the advanced ultra-endurance front crawlers, smashing the waves with their arms as if to overcome the elasticity of their wetsuits. It is a broad church and a religion which sees an ever-growing congregation.

The seals have been evicted and sit on the rocks, bemused at various human bodily forms. I am tempted to join them, but I want to cross the Helford River early. I know I am close when I reach the National Trust preserved village at Durgan. I hand over £6 at the ferry hut, which seems expensive until the ferryman recites the house prices.

'See that big house over there?' he says. 'You could buy that for £115,000 not long ago; now it's worth millions. None of the young'uns can afford to live here anymore, and you try booking your car for a service; they just can't get the mechanics. I don't know what the world is coming to...' he continues non-stop until we reach the opposite shore. It is a frustration I will hear many times, underpinned by the high cost of finding a home.

I am happy to have crossed another estuary, but one more remains around the corner: Gillan Creek, which I was told is easily passable three hours either side of low tide. I can't find the stepping stones, so perhaps this is why I find myself wading up to my armpits with my backpack held high in my sockless boots on the rocky riverbed. I receive applause from a family as I emerge soaked but clean, with only a thought of emptying my Meindl boots of water before continuing. In hindsight, I'd walk an additional one mile around the creek, but I am a seasoned river crosser now, and I love cold water soothing my aching muscles. My boots dry out soon enough for another diversion around a broken bridge at Parbean Cove, where the value of the closure signs seems to exceed the cost of a new bridge. I stop at Porthallow for lunch, where the cafe's owner has sent his staff home as it's so quiet. He serves a tuna baguette and relays the story of this coastal fishing village, once home to a prolific mackerel and pilchard industry.

'The tuna has sent the mackerel deep. There used to be huge shoals in summer offshore, but now they are hard to find... monkfish, monkfish. You could be eating any slow-growing bottom-dredged rubbish nowadays... of course, your tuna came from a tin, probably from Thailand, but the real thing can be found offshore now. Changing sea temperatures, I reckon.'

'A busy fishing port then?' I interject.

'Yes, yes, huers would watch from Black Head and cry "Hevva! Hevva!" (they are here) when they spotted the tell-tale bubble patterns in the water. They then directed the lurkers and seiners fishing boats to the shoals by semaphore. If you look, their names are still carved in the rocks on the headland, as they filled idle moments waiting for the fish.'

It seems odd that his business is down on such a gorgeous day, so I mention the cafe to several walkers heading west. Two women, highly organised, have every overnight stay booked from Minehead to Bournemouth; another woman wild camping only, inspired by others but discouraged by locals; and lastly, Neil, who is heading to Hebden Bridge of all places, in memory of his mother who died of Covid-19. He is walking, like many, for a charity, in this case the Woodland Trust. We have plenty to discuss, and it would be great to join him if we were going in the same direction. He mentions the Fat Apples Café inland, where he has just finished an unforgettable lunch (and where you can camp, too).

Inland again to Porthoustock – away from the coast, but at least you are entertained by the comedic signs the locals have created. Skeletons hold placards saying, 'dehydrated coastal path walker' and others play on the plight of exhausted backpackers. For some reason, the coastal path avoids Porthkerris. It is a rough walk inland, passing huge gunnera rhubarb-like plants choking other flora along the stream paths. The coast returns for the final flat but rough track into Coverack. The old lifeboat station is now a chippy and easily receives my award for the best takeaway since Cromer. The cod, covered in a crisp beer batter, melts in my mouth, the chips are perfect in size with just the right number of crispy scraps to finish. It is a steep, slow climb to the YHA, and my legs as usual are stiff and complaining. I have a dorm where I can make a mess, spreading all my gear for a full audit. The views are spectacular, and the warden assures me I will not have guests. The bliss of a solo dorm night, where I can pretend it is my own bedroom.

I have no fixed plan for the following day, waking up for a late breakfast. My unconscious mind is calling for a rest. My conscious mind wants to get going, and the lie-in doesn't feel right as I should have 10 miles under my belt by now. I slink out of the hostel and on to the path and immediately meet David, Paul and Nicky, a group of IT guys out for a week. They have brought Bowie with them, a young spaniel that explores every possibility along the paths. He has a GPS tracker fitted to his collar.

'His stats are amazing; he walks 40 to 50 miles daily, three times what we do. It is probably more. He doesn't seem to mind at all.'

I walk between them, exchanging life stories and experiences of the path. Today is more talk than walk, and I welcome the social interaction. The path is busy; a young chap with a leg injury is hobbling along, and others are looking for basking sharks, seals and maybe something more exotic. The usual peregrines and buzzards patrol the high skies, and bushes on the paths are now alive with flittering passerines. It is not a day for isolation, but to engage with others. But not, perhaps, in the manner of the YouTuber crew ahead, filming pieces of some imagined long-distance hiker clothed in the latest gear – repeating clichéd phrases to the camera. She spots all my gear and namedrops for a minute or two, for she is a well-connected ambassador for outdoor brands.

I consider having a canine companion, but I worry about a soggy mutt laying claim to my dry sleeping bag, or refusal at B&Bs and hotels that often will not allow dogs, so limiting my options. More than this, I am not confident I could navigate the encounters with nervous cattle in the fields. Yet, borrowing Bowie for an afternoon would be a joy, to experience the responsibilities and companionship for a short time. I am told I am a cat-person personality, but I think I prefer dogs, although my wife would say my shadow self is more wolf – a lone wolf – off on epic treks whenever the moon is out.

Before we know it, lost in conversation, we have passed the lifeboat station and reached Lizard Point. Nicky buys me an ice cream, and we chat to the National Trust warden, who is delighted to share his knowledge of the area.

'A minke whale this morning excited us, so keep your eyes open. The choughs are on full display towards Kynance Cove. Listen for their "che-ooow, che-ooow" call and watch their aerobatic flying skills,' the warden enthuses.

My walking companions have further to go, but I cut back inland at Caerthillian Cove to Lizard village early. As I climb the gully, I step over a stile and face the path again. Ahead of me is a bright yellow bird, looking tired, metres away on a branch. I freeze instinctively. It is a golden oriel – a thrilling and rare encounter. I double-check my smartphone guidebook and talk to locals, who confirm the possibility. It is the right time of year, and this area has a very active birdwatching community that never misses a wayward migrating bird. It is a popular local hobby.

On entering the village, I notice that Ann's Pasties empire is expanding with new entrepreneurial vigour. I can now buy branded clothing, have a beer or a gin cocktail, or order catering for a wedding. The pasties are delicious, still made by hand to a recipe passed down through generations and untouched by any brand-jacking corporation. I buy two and ask for directions to the campsite.

Not only does the Lizard have the best pasties, but also the best quirky campsite. Henry's is a wonder, with little unique pitches hidden in a semi-hippy garden paradise, full of character where the vibe is relaxed. The exotic plants shelter backpackers and birds alike if you can find your pitch in the maze of paths. A normal rule of thumb says that a good campsite is inversely proportional to the number of instructional 'no' signs. Here, you are expected to use common sense, chill out and watch the sunset – its position on this gorgeous peninsula is perfect.

An early departure is rewarded with a mystical sea mist cloaking Kynance Cove, clearing out to sea as the sun illuminates the cliff layers: yellow lichen, sheep-cropped grass, sun-bleached serpentinite and tide-marked rocks with their black skirts. A buzzard is an early riser, too, with enormous light under-colour and complex feather patterns – a mature adult. A chattering of choughs plays over the cliffs, their unmistakable red bills and playful calls in keeping with their antics, wings folded to dive like a brick, then soaring again with a comedic wink. There is so much to see and learn, more than I expected. I meet Paul, who has been on the path for five weeks, studying the flora and fauna. He is a walking encyclopaedia.

'Yes, quite likely to have seen a golden oriel on Lizard,' he says. 'Watch out for the tiny purple orchids ahead, doing quite well in the gorse.'

'There are slow-worms around. I've seen a few, but no adders,' I reply.

'They are about. Don't tread on one. Actually, don't tread on anything.'

We exchange contact details. It would be fantastic to walk with Paul for a day or two to learn more about the coastal natural environment. While I am usually observant, greater knowledge would improve my journey.

I must consider taking days to walk shorter distances with binoculars, which enrich your experience and make a huge difference to what you can see, once you get used to them.

I am making good progress along the coast and can afford a rest after crossing the shingle at Loe Bar. It's time to sunbathe. I force myself to rest for an hour and stare at the sea, contemplating a swim. It's May, it can't be that cold. Easing in, I tolerate an estimated 10 degrees as I swim away from the shore, slip off my boxers and wrap them on my arm. I am not embarrassed – it is liberating and thrilling. The chilling sensation as I breaststroke into the waves resets my body's core temperature, wiping away the accumulated heat of my walking day. Some deep part of an unconscious ancestry remains, for I feel alive in the water until the chill reminds me that the land is my home now. I tread water, replace my makeshift costume with a quick underwater skip and hop, and climb back on the shingle. Laying down, my skin absorbs the heat of the pebbles and the sun. My exposed skin tingles with delight, as my recovering heart rate pumps the decaying stress hormones around my body.

The ice cream in Portleven seems wrong after that dip, but I meet up with Bowie and the trio I walked with to Lizard and can return the favour. They depart as I plan to stay at the local campsite. As I walk into the adjacent pub, the barman says I must book using an online website, which is a challenge with the poor signal. When I finally select a pitch, it informs me that the site is fully booked, even though the field is empty. The locals can't help me as they are two or three pints into a session and care little for a coastal walker – their heads glued at a 20-degree angle to the sports coverage on the TV hanging from the wall. It is the wrong vibe so I walk on, catching up with the trio, who have met Danni, who is exhausted. I offer her a wine gum for encouragement, and we all walk into Praa Sands, where she meets her concerned friend.

I could walk on to Penzance and the YHA, but I decide to pitch in the field campsite above the surfing community, who are chilling in the seafront bars. I knock at the door. No website is needed, just a welcoming host who says I can pitch anywhere for £13 in cash. Water, toilets and showers are in the only building. My friends are there too, and Bowie checks that I'm ok (getting in extra miles) as the shadows lengthen, bringing a sharp fall in temperature that warrants an early night.

No matter how hard I try, my body clock alarm demands I wake up and walk. Peering out of the tent, I note another inversion filling the valley, and I get up to shower. I make the mistake of returning to my bag and promptly fall asleep – my circadian rhythms are out of step with my physical recovery needs. It is embarrassing to see David, Paul, Nicky and Bowie depart as I wake; my reputation for early starts is in tatters. It is not a problem as I only plan to reach Penzance YHA today.

I am on automatic pilot to Marazion after a full breakfast at Perran Sands, wasting time, for the hostel opens at 5pm. I dawdle along, tripping over rocks with my concentration disengaged but awakening when I meet Mal.

'You look like a South West Coast Path walker, and you're also doing it for charity?' The RNLI T-shirt is a dead giveaway.

'Yes, it's a long story, but I almost lost my life in a rip tide, and it was a RNLI RIB that saved me. This is my way of saying thank you,' he replies, genuine tears welling up in his eyes, the trauma raw and unprocessed.

Sometimes, I think the RNLI is overfunded, with new flashy lifeboat houses and up-to-date equipment gleaming in the sunlight. Yet, something about the service resonates with the donors: their bravery, their independence from government, their volunteers, and their relationship with the coastline. It is an admirable institution that encapsulates what it means to be an islander. It is baked into our collective psyche as a maritime nation, perhaps explaining its popularity and status.

St Michael's Mount dominates the coastal vista, its priory crowning this granite outcrop, a hint of the coming geology. It costs £24 to visit if it were open, which the signs say it is, but the internet says it is not. It could waste a few hours of my time, but instead, I decide to review my backpacking needs and head to Halfords to find gas canisters, which they do not have, so I dawdle into town to find a hardware store after stocking up with goodies at Tesco. I find a canister eventually (they were hard to get hold of during the pandemic) and can relax at The Quirky Bird Café and nurse the nettle welts on my legs, which still irritate after a shortcut from the campsite this morning. I normally shake this off easily, but the sheer volume of red and blotchy stings overwhelms my defences. A swim in the sea is a wonder cure, but I can't find the motivation to try until I see the Penzance Jubilee Pool, with a geothermal tidal pool. The *Scillonian III* is docked on Sunday for a weekly rest. The pool looks inviting, but I walk up the hill to the YHA, one of the larger hostels, and wait in the garden for it to open. Will I never learn, will I never take a moment to take care of myself, rather than battle through?

I have an exclusive dorm and time to clean everything in my pack and retire to the canteen as the washing machine hums. A busload of boisterous teenagers piles through the door, throwing their backpacks into the corridors, before they disperse to fight for a top bunk. I sleep well, but the competition for the breakfast buffet is fierce. It was a good move to get there early as the group clears the buffet trays clean like locusts, reminding me of my appetite at that age. My nickname at age 16 was 'pedal bin', the joke being that food scraps would be shovelled into my open mouth when someone stood on my foot. The kids are from the Isles of Scilly and are at the end of a week's expedition, and the excitement is palpable – they clearly make the most of their time on the mainland.

I weave through the back lanes to Newlyn, rejoining the path where I touched a fingerpost as a gesture of continuity the previous afternoon. The paintings alongside the wet fish halls depict contemporary scenes, yet the quayside will have witnessed prosperous times when one of the world's finest fleets operated from this harbour. The tidal observatory, a benchmark for the tides of Great Britain, is evidence of its stature. Known as Ordnance Datum Newlyn (ODN), it is the mean sea-level zero against which all other heights are measured – a simple brass bolt in a block of granite is the reference for every triangulation station (known as trig pillars) and mountain top in the country. Sea levels have risen by 21 centimetres since 1900, and the rate is accelerating. The medium-low emissions scenario measures sea-level rise in metres as we approach the year 2300. From another perspective, our mountains are getting shorter, but it is the impact on coastal communities that I find alarming. I am starting to overhear conversations about uninsurable properties due to flood risk and a resignation to stay put and enjoy it all before it is gone. This threat is a new narrative along the coastline, an inconceivable topic of conversation a decade ago.

I get lost in Mousehole's narrow streets, looking for a famous barometer the Meteorological Office gifted to the harbour authority in 2009. It lies securely protected by thick glass in a recess. It was originally loaned by

Admiral Fitzroy to the village in 1854 to collect data for storm warnings. This was the very year the Met Office was founded, now a sophisticated service based in Exeter with huge computing resources. The shipping forecast followed in 1859 and is the longest-running national forecasting service in the world. A sea area is named Fitzroy in his honour, the only one of the 31 surrounding the British Isles coastline and the western Atlantic named after an individual. The barometer still works, recording the ever-changing atmospheric pressure which drives our weather systems.

I regain the path and enter a world of granite. It is steep, rough and hard going through vegetation that has not been cleared. Foot placement needs concentration, and my poles arrest a few slips and twists again. Bluebells and wild garlic are in full bloom now, and the sweet aroma is sometimes overpowering. This coastline is rugged – the pink granite impervious to the ravages of the weather and water. The pretty fishing villages of Lamorna and Penberth are timeless, solid and unchanging compared to the industrial ports I have walked past. I can see the *Scillonian III* as it departs for St Mary's, bobbing nicely in the Atlantic swell, living up to its name as the 'big white stomach pump', its stability compromised by a shallow draft needed to enter the island's main port of Hugh Town.

I am happier on land, enjoying the coastline paths at the end of the world at the south-western tip of the British Isles. The campsite at Treen meets all my criteria: it is non-bookable and family-run, and has crazy artwork and quirky signs. It gets the basics right and has a wonderful campers' kitchen, which saves an aching back. I pitch and walk into Treen to visit one of the best pubs in Cornwall, The Logan Rock. It hasn't changed much since my memorable stay in 2007. I meet my good friend, Tony, an expert on Proper Job beer, who rode his motorcycle from Plymouth to meet me and stay over. We can't resist a pint, which renders me immobile, switching off my leg muscles with a powerful relaxant. It reminds me why I usually do not drink and walk, but Tony is very persuasive. We share another to fuel conversation about the area, which he knows very well. Like me, he is endlessly curious and adventurous, living every moment he can spare on his motorcycle, kayak or campervan with his wife, Heidi, and their mischievous border terriers.

I finish a breakfast apple, walking down a farm track to the cliff edge. It is one of those mornings when you sense a glorious day. The air is clear, warming nicely, and the panorama expands as the Atlantic Ocean comes into view. Porthcurno Beach has just been swept by the high tide, removing all footprints. A penetrating channel is evidence of a nasty rip tide that would catch the unwary. It is not a place I would choose to swim, but it is possible in the summer months when the seas ease and a lifeguard service operates. Cuboid pink granite blocks are stacked like Lego along the coast, reflecting a soft, warm light. The natural amphitheatre at Minack is preparing for an opera, play or concert but has yet to open. I push on to Gwennap Head, sensing I will turn a corner. The choughs are feeding close to the National Coastwatch Institution lookout hut, where the wardens are nursing a fresh cup of coffee before their day begins. I rest for a while to savour the view, sitting in a line with the two conical navigation marks. This headland has a better viewpoint than Land's End and is one of my favourite spots, offering quiet contemplation at the end of the world.

The Longships lighthouse is visible two miles offshore whenever I emerge on to an outcrop from the hidden *zawns*, a Cornish term for a gully, a word sound and shape that mirrors the rugged coastline. The sun now warms the back of my legs, the wind tickling different hairs on my neck and arms as my direction turns north. On arrival at Land's End, with its iconic signpost, the photographer in the booth is pleased to meet a walker who doesn't quibble at the cost or attempt a sneaky shot. After taking my picture, he invites me inside the booth to look at the wonderful history of photographs. Cyclists, walkers, horse riders and all manner of weird vehicles line the ceiling, including the famous naked ramblers, now with their private parts taped over after prudish complaints. All those images capture the hopes and dreams of a hundred journeys, each with a unique story to tell.

'Wasn't it the case that the same company ran the John o' Groats and Land's End photobooths, but the one north has now gone and lies rotting away in a field?' I ask.

'Yes, that's right. I have been doing this for 27 years,' Peter replies. 'Maybe it is time to retire. I am not sure what will happen when our contract comes up for renewal.'

'You must have met so many interesting characters, celebrities and eccentrics.'

'Mostly LEJOG'ers starting from the south-west, fresh-as-a-daisy compared to the weathered completers who have cycled or walked from Scotland.'

I have no desire to wander around the shops and cafes and yomp on to Sennen Cove, skipping along with a sense of achievement. A cafe I remember seems like a place for a second breakfast. It has an online ordering system, which defeats me after 30 minutes of Wi-Fi and website hacking. I give up, refusing to divulge my personal details just to order a sandwich. The staff are bored and disengaged, their jobs automated in the name of progress and corporate efficiency. Customers without a smartphone or contactless card are disenfranchised, unable to function in a world dominated by technology – a pervasive technology that, if it failed, would render us impotent. Was it Lenin who said the world is only three meals away from chaos?

The beach is bleached white, and the azure sea fades to a deep blue. Blink, and I could be in South Africa or the Caribbean. It is tempting to swim and sunbathe, but I drag my dew-soaked boots through the dune sands back on the cliff path. I search for campsites at Cape Cornwall and set a course for Morvah through a scarred mining landscape of loose rock. I consider an alternative site at Pendeen Watch, but it is basic, barely one notch above wild camping. I should have stayed, as the Morvah site is just a field, no longer a pandemic pop-up that met the heavy demand when flights were unavailable for continental holidays.

My contingency is to use the bus services and return to Botallack. I wait for the 15:43, but it never arrives. A closer inspection of the damp timetable reveals it is not operating for two days due to road works further east, which leaves me with the choice of wild camping or hitching. I can't remember the last time I stuck my thumb out – probably in the early 1980s, but I try, and the first car stops. A lovely lady is unconcerned with my damp pack, muddy boots and walking poles and gives me a lift.

'You look a bit soggy,' she says. 'You know the bus isn't running. Where are you off to?' she asks.

'I'm going to try the campsite after Botallack, if you're going that way.'

The site is a dream, and the host wonderful – a site I will return to next year. The clockwise bus takes me back to Morvah the following day in heavy rain, the roadworks now complete. I am perversely looking forward to a lonely, desolate walk around Zennor at a steady pace, for this is a tough section of the South West Coast Path. The coastal swell breaks heavily on the rocks, forming bubble baths of organic foam that glide up the cliff face. It is timeless, restless and ageless and envelops you in its natural power, reminding you to respect nature. You succumb to its force and feel humble – you cannot compete with it, reason with it, or master it. You must go with its flow, conserving your energy and using your skills to ride its emotions.

The sun comes out, and waterproofs can be packed away. Walkers come out too, mostly on circular walks from Zennor, sampling the wonders of this north-westerly coastline, which is not an orientation found often in England. North-facing beaches have that unique backlight that intensifies contrast and colours the sea and sky with alluring shades of blue and green. The day walkers are replaced with those who have set off from St Ives that morning: a few rugged thru-hikers, a professor studying the geology, a masochistic fell runner with a twisted ankle and a couple with every detail planned and written down in a waterproof map case. My relaxed pace restarts after many short conversations. The path is a social gathering, and everyone is open and friendly, wanting to share their joy and happiness at walking on such a glorious day.

St Ives Head comes into view, where I avoid the melee and hide in the further recesses of a restaurant. No seagull is going to steal my chips. Cars and people squeeze through the streets, making me anxious in these new surroundings. I retire early to a chic surfer hostel and relax in the common room. With her usual perfect timing, my wife has sent me a pretext promise of a Sunday roast, and I know domestic paperwork and duties have piled up. The reflex response is to check *trainline.com*. I find a cheap ticket in the morning, so bail out before the madness of summer arrives in the south-west. I will return later in the year, but for now I have run out of expedition credits and must address the balance. I am homesick too after walking a few weeks – a feeling that builds slowly each day and is only made worse with evening phone calls.

# 9
# ST IVES TO BUDE
## Walking in a washing machine

*'The biggest difference between time and money?
You always know how much money you have; you
never know how much time you have.'*

Anon

**Distance walked: 1,020 miles**

Somehow, events conspire to prevent a summer return to the England Coast Path, but a window of opportunity opens in November. I awake in St Ives to join a mix of bikepackers and backpackers gathering early in the communal hostel kitchen, as eager as I am to start the day before sunrise. We all have some miles to get in during the shorter days. They are all heading west; I shall head east. Most holidaymakers and tourists have gone, and the rich man's playground is quiet, leaving the locals to reconnect. Many cottages will remain unoccupied and unavailable for those who call this seaside town their home.

The glow from a cosy corner bus shelter that looks like someone's living room is the only warm light on a grey day. I wrap up for the morning drizzle and walk to Hayle through a dreary, colourless Carbis Bay. It is difficult to imagine that this spot was chosen for the 2021 G7 Summit, where the world's most powerful leaders gathered. I hope they left with a memory of the beauty of St Ives Bay, which has captivated artists for centuries. Each took a memento home – an oak wood twist pen carved from an old South West Coast Path fingerpost by a local craftsman from Ivybridge. I hope it gives them some direction and will be used to sign long-term treaties to protect our planet.

There is water pouring down the path, inundating a cottage garden. A contractor runs towards me, asking if I know the owner, as his road crew has just dug through a water main. It is another empty home as deserted as the paths and villages I walk through; the tell-tale sign of Master key boxes and drawn white blinds signify untold warm beds on a cold day. I order a pastie at yet another 'world's most famous pastie' shop, only to find I have lost my wallet. I empty my pockets and pack in frustration, imagining how I would recover with only a mobile phone. I panic and start to curse when it drops out of the rain cover. I missed the pocket when I stowed it earlier, and the flimsy fluorescent cover caught it in a fold. It is a stern lesson, so I distribute cash and cards between what I wear, my wallet and my backpack, and vow to install some banking payment apps on my phone. I am getting lazy and complacent, and no longer focused on the diligent preparation of earlier years. With my experience I should know better.

Outside Hayle, builders are eager to finish the developments at the harbour for next season and secure a sale – all investment opportunities for second homes. The path opens after walking through the mixing lorries towards Godrevy Point, along the low-tide line of Towans Beach – voted the best in Britain by a newspaper journalist who had visited over 500 as part of his research (sounds like a job for me). It is completely empty, with not a single dog walker in sight. My only companions are the tiny sanderlings dancing to the rhythm of the wave line. How does a little 50-gram bird with tiny legs outrun a 100-kilo backpacker with size 12 boots, reliably sensing each rogue wave as it washes deeper up the beach? I get a soaking, yet the birds scatter back to feed with their comical high cadence. I measure my lolloping steps with the sand my boot heels kick up, seeing how far I can flick the compressed wet bombs. It is desolate and wild. I am alone in my thoughts. My pace is my progress – an autonomous soul amusing myself with observations of nature and childish pleasures.

The north-easterly urges the swell to the shoreline, pushing the foam-laden surf up the beach – its energy absorbed gently, washing the dry sand without drama. You can read wave set theory in the patterns, a periodicity driven by complex mathematics that surfers sense after hours bobbing up and down in the swell. Fibonacci sequences, hidden bathymetry and wave caravans mix with the capricious nature of the sea. On average, the troughs and peaks group into 12 to 16 sets, explaining why every seventh wave will be the one to ride.

The lighthouse rock ahead is a different matter, for the immovable slate and siltstone gullies stand firm, measuring each swell and wave as the mass of water violently thumps into their unyielding forms. Huge foam geysers erupt into the air, the water aerated and blown by the wind across the rock face, at one moment black and then white. The seals haul out into a protected cove, squabbling with each other for a place to rest. Walkers have gathered to peer over the cliff face to see the pups, perfectly hidden in the pebble beach as their pure white Arctic fur fades to mottled grey, an evolved genetic characteristic of the Ice Age that would be camouflage if it were much colder.

The drama of the northern coastline to Portreath intensifies. The cast of wind, sea and waves are joined by rain-laden squalls and a cloudscape doing battle with the low-lying southern sun. It is an intense argument, but at least I time my soaking to the minute. A weather forecast is unnecessary, for I read the future by facing the wind and observing my fate. The sun breaks through and shines on the lead actors in the landscape: the cliffs, rock islands, beaches and approaching waves. Each has a fleeting focus of fame until they are extinguished backstage. Hell's Mouth and Deadman's Cove are well-known celebrities and warrant their descriptive names. This is the tempestuous story, a thrilling November seascape performance that will play out over the coming days. I break for an intermission, nursing a pastie in a soaked double paper bag under my waterproofs, as I sit crouched on the ground behind the lee of a stone wall.

November is the quietest month, the low season when hosts can rest, but not the sea. While the second-home ghetto villages and towns are deserted, they miss the second act of the meteorological production that starts on time as I reach the cliffs. The curtains are drawn to reveal ominous, brooding clouds unable to contain their cargo – gravity insisting that water must return to the earth. Fresh wind-cut rain cascades out of the deep black-and-white clouds; a turbulent maelstrom is heading my way, and I will soon be shoved into an industrial washing machine. I have no choice but to walk ahead as the cold taps screw open to the maximum to fill the tub for my Atlantic salty power wash. The greater black-backed gulls and choughs revel in the updrafts, enjoying every moment. It is thrilling to watch their nonchalant mastery of the air currents. A peregrine falcon weaponises a tailwind to terrorise witless birds dashing for the safety of a woodland or lee cliff. All these aviators are beautifully adapted to their environment. Subtle twists of a tail feather or wing tip, and keen sense of wind direction, are all they need to subdue the violent currents of air.

The cliffscape is scarred with mine workings, tailings, conical batcage capped shafts and forgotten steam power-engine towers – an iconic *Poldark* Cornish heritage now flushed clean with the sea air, where once suffocating blasting dust, coal, smoke and fumes would have billowed downwind. Nature is slowly reclaiming the mineral desert with heather and gorse. The path is wet but firm, ideal grip for an adrenaline-fuelled walker to reach Perranporth in good time. The No. 4 cafe is empty, but the chef is on top form – the hot soup and club sandwich are delicious, the heating high enough to dry my base layers as my core warms with each spoonful of a homemade tomato and roast pepper wonder.

I climb the sand dunes like a knight chess piece across the board, stepping left and right, forward and sometimes back. The low-tide route around Cotty's Point is out of the question as it fights the swell, landing successive blows against the immovable cliff face. Perran Beach is utterly deserted. The angry squalls, accompanied by rainbows and occasional lightning, throw abstract impressionist paint strokes on to a natural canvas of golden sand and pastel dunes. I am sailing on a broad reach, my backpack pushing me along the line of the breaking surf. I can steer by using my poles as rudders, adjusting my footing as the wind does its best to topple me. The high dune above me gives no clue to an exit, but at the very end of the beach an ascending cliff track reveals itself. I am now on firmer paths, momentarily, until I reach a sequence of secret beaches, laying down my boot prints again until the angry white hands of flushing waves wipe them away. Holywell, Polly Joke and Crantock beaches receive their winter clean, stripping the sand of summer playtimes, exploring every orifice, leaving no pebble unturned.

Newquay is in sight, the adventure sports culture announced by kite surfers streaking across the bay, lifting from power wakes to perform gybes, acrobatic twists and jumps that look like they might never land. They are immersed in the present, dancing with nature, flowing with its force – something that must trigger transcendent spiritual joy fuelled by an addictive cocktail of happy hormones. I arrive at the wooden bridge at Penpol and cross the wooden slats revealed as the tide eases. One surfer is taking a shortcut home, flying downwind in the gully of the River Gannel, wrestling with the freedom the kite seeks. I am struck by the balance of forces. The kite will not fly without an anchor; the anchor will not move without the kite. In between, the lightest touch balances these forces through the controlling cords.

The summer-dude vibe in the hostel is missing, needing a bevy of sun-bleached surfers to bring it to life. In November it is deserted but cheap and comfortable. The staff are great but can disappear without notice if a perfect wave beckons. This hardcore skeleton staff are there for winter waves, giving the place a lived-in feel missing from other smaller coastal villages. The breakfast is functional but ideal for the walk to Watergate Bay, whose sands are hidden by parallel ribbons of surf rolling up to the high-water mark. Due to popular demand, nature prepares another matinee performance. Rainbows signify the transition from dramatic showers to romantic sunshine, and the audience of sea birds watches for free, static gliding in the breeze. I climb over a 'curzyway' stile (a Cornish herringbone-pattern slate wall) and stop to marvel at the scale of Bedruthan Steps, backlit by the morning sun. The sequence of calved rocks like black teeth snarling at the incessant sea, refusing to yield as they get their salty morning brush.

Corn buntings are thriving in the heathland, lifting into the air, blown as a cluster ball wherever the wind takes them. There is no shelter from the driving wind for these birds or walkers. I descend into Porthcothan, but it offers no joy or comfort – it is a closed theme park, devoid of life in winter. Walking on, the coves resemble top loading washing machines with their lids open, spewing a twisting vortex of organic bubble foam that decorates the gullies – a slapstick pie fight with inexhaustible ammunition. I will reach Treyarnon Bay early, with its YHA hostel which I have booked for tonight. I have enough time to walk to the freshly painted lighthouse at Trevose Head, which stands sentinel and proud, facing the Celtic Sea.

I head to Harlyn Bay, thinking of Bridget Riley's faceted colour paintings inspired by her time along this coastline. I appreciate how the disconcerting shimmers in her work reflect the complexity of nature's movement – the infinite atomic and quantum calculations, never repeated but connected, forming the patterns in our world. This is entropy in action – unrepeatable, irreversible, time as forward motion – so beautifully captured in her paintings.

## THE COAST IS OUR COMPASS

My dream-like contemplations are shattered as I reach the bus stop. A 'fuck your second homes' sticker is explicit, a sentiment endorsed by many. A local man laughs at me as I study the damp timetable, saying he hasn't seen a bus here in years. His face is a picture when a double-decker pops over the hill and opens its door before me. 'Single to Constantine Bay, please.'

The hostel is fantastic, as I remember it from 2007. The meal is wholesome, the staff wonderful, and again, the joy of a single-occupancy dorm. The sea-view double-glazed windows muffle the breaking surf, an ideal soundtrack to lull me into a REM dream world and deep sleep. I could lie in, but the day demands an early start, and I will not wait for a mid-morning bus. Returning to Harlyn Bridge is only a mile until I can mix it up again with the coastal paths to Stepper Point. The golden-hour low-morning light textures the stubble fields, and every detail of the terrain and vegetation is revealed, as are huge sinkholes that pepper the cliff fields. This season's lambs are now robust and wearing decent coats, feeding still to fatten further. I march on, leaving the shelter of the stone daymark, to Padstow, eager to cross the estuary. I wave at the ferry, just departing, and the captain thankfully returns, a blessing for a walker eager to reach Port Isaac for the sporadic bus service to Wadebridge. Accommodation options in Rock, Polzeath and Port Quin are ridiculously expensive, that is if you can find anything available.

It is a weekend, and the beaches and paths are busy with well-to-do second homers. This area remains active all year around, now buoyant as a retreat for urbanites. A wood-fired sea sauna shipping container is doing good business, and the owner is happily taking money off the clients, who have a perverse passion for mixing sand and sweat. For a moment, I consider it. A means to warm my chilled bones, but the door opens to disgorge a swarm of screaming women running to the sea, the tone of their cries increasing an octave or two as they reach the water. I dare not venture in there, so climb to Pentire Point for a pastie and flask of tea. Port Quin and Port Isaac follow, now more famous as TV locations than fishing ports. The streets are deserted, like a film set without actors or extras. I climb to the bus stop next to a closed cafe, expecting to wait for a good hour. By chance, a taxi drops someone off, and I jump in with Mike, who takes me to the hotel in Wadebridge. We hit it off immediately. He is a kite surfer and adventurer, filling idle time working the routes in the area in his Vauxhall Zafira diesel taxi.

He opens the conversation. 'We get a lot of walkers and runners in summer; we're non-stop doing baggage transfers, but not at this time of year.'

'I met a couple walking the South West Coast Path who estimated they will spend £6,000 on accommodation! That is why I am walking off-season,' I reply. He ponders that thought.

'Well, at £2.50 a mile, it will be cheaper to hire a taxi.' We both laugh loudly at the absurdity of that calculation, but it puts the cost of long-distance walking into perspective. No wonder people wild camp.

He picks me up the next day, offering a compelling round-trip deal as if I have any choice, for there are no buses on a Sunday. It is good to get back on the path, even though a Met Office yellow wind warning hints of a dramatic day ahead. Strong westerlies are forecast, gusting over 45mph, which should be alright to Boscastle, though I should take heed and review again. I meet a volunteer looking for a stranded seal pup that someone had reported at Port Gaverne. I say I haven't seen any from the cliffs, and then we both promptly walk right into one, perfectly camouflaged. The volunteer checks its respiration. It doesn't look good. Her colleague is coming from the Seal Sanctuary near Gweek, which is a fair drive. I can do little to help. She will wait and observe its fate.

The paths get gnarly, and the going is strenuous, but I am hardened to the task and lean in. The rain holds off along exposed remote sections of the path. Steady and sure will win the day, a rhythm I maintain until Tintagel. Trebarwith Strand and Tregardock Beach have been swallowed by surf and tide, which are useless to anyone as the waves wash past the mean high-water levels. The white surf merges with the white crests of waveforms out to sea – one image that blends landfall with the ocean swell. The wave pattern indicates a Force 6 or 7, and if I remember my Beaufort Scale correctly, the winds are building to Gale Force.

A peregrine narrowly misses a kittiwake, which emits a bloodcurdling death scream as it twists away, instantly breaking my pace and head-down-path-focused posture. Tintangel and its rock island and beautiful Gallos sculpture of King Arthur is closed, for it is unsafe for mere mortals to cross the bridge. I eat for necessity in an empty cafe, purely to fuel another yomp into Boscastle, where I am relieved to see the village sleeping quietly in the lee wind, the residents tucked away in the comfort of their homes. I am grateful for an open shop to augment my freeze-dried contingency meal and energy bars for tomorrow. It is going to be another tough one.

My host left a grab bag for breakfast, and I leave early to get into the day. Yesterday's forecast has eased from the 70–80 mph gusts to 50–60 mph offshore, and I hope the landmass will offer some shelter. There is a coastal bus service from Crackington Haven, so I'll review the forecast at lunchtime if I need to escape. As I ascend above the YHA, the village, still sore from the catastrophic 2004 flood, is bathed in darkness. I have just stayed in the building that withstood the torrent, whose roof was used to winch survivors into Sea King helicopters. Hedges and stone walls provide good protection, and the sea state is calm in the lee of the gale, but on entering the combes the capricious wind will come from any direction. The eddies are violent and unpredictable, threatening to knock you off balance. The waterfalls now flow vertically upwards, exploiting the undergaps in my hard-shell waterproofs. I am soon soaked: my crotch, arms and torso feel the cold as it seeps through the base layers. This power storm reaches the body parts other storms can't reach, but I remain warm if I keep moving.

The climbs are brutal, and the descents are slippery. My poles are essential to steady my way. I must be careful not to trip over them, for the wind picks them up when not placed in the ground and they swing across my feet. I ascend High Cliff, which earns its name. It is exposed at 223 metres, introducing me to the full force of the gale. Rivers form down the paths, ignoring the drainage gullies so carefully built by the rangers, further eroding the paths with brutal efficiency. These waters flow as I flow, each shedding potential energy to reach equilibrium. The cafe is in sight and thankfully open. I step inside, gripping the door tightly as it threatens to slam, and close it to a world of calm, warmth, silence and sanity. I feel embarrassed to sit on the nice chairs in my sodden clothing. Little puddles form beneath my feet, but the staff don't mind as they have seen it all before.

'What would you like to drink?' my saviour asks.

'Several mugs of tea and a full English, please. I hope you don't mind the mess I am making.'

'You're fine; we have a mop.'

'I remember how good this cafe was in 2007. Not much has changed. I'm happy you are open today. You don't know how important this stop is for me.'

'Yes, we're open every day except Christmas from nine-ish to five-ish. Not much has changed, and the founders you would have met then left to live in New Zealand. But it is still in the family.'

The only other customers are a group of South Africans reminiscing about their homeland, dressed in shorts, flip-flops and T-shirts. I do a double-take. They look like they have just finished a game of beach volleyball in glorious sunshine, knowing nothing of winter clothing, and this weather is amusing to them. I wonder if I am hallucinating.

'Aww, Storms River pushes up a bigger swell than this. I miss the sunshine, not sure when we can return. Besides, I like Cornwall a lot,' the nearest to me says. We engage in a few words which confirms they are real people, as they ask me about the path.

'You might want to think about waterproofs and sturdy boots. It's quite dangerous in places, and exposed,' I suggest, suspecting they would walk through it without concern. 'Skin's waterproof,' the least clothed among them replies.

Their conversation warms me up. As I eat, my mind tells me to keep going, now that I know my fuel tank is full. The banter resets my expectations of bad weather, and the contingency bus does not arrive for an hour.

I pack up and re-shell, paying attention to every detail of clothing. Cords are adjusted, zips checked and gloves inverted after peeling them off wet earlier. I open the hermetic seal and step outside. The rain has stopped, but not the wind or the changeable nature of the sky. I set off quickly to reach operating temperature, activating my newly found reserves and benefiting from a 100-metre climb to the headland. In the classic South West Coast Path style, this is followed by a similar descent to another waterfall. I run across this gap in a vain attempt to avoid another soaking, but somehow, the water has reached my nether regions again.

My only photograph, so far, is of a perfect full English breakfast, for my phone is sealed in a food zip bag. I didn't have time to photograph the scary descents, the expansive sea views or the racing clouds as my mind was preoccupied with safety. The winds give no quarter, and it requires concentration to stay upright. The combe at Scrade exemplifies the day: a waterfall turned firehose, a rocky river descent into a maelstrom of foam-drifting footballs, slippery ascents and water-soaked paths for further entertainment. The hardy sea birds laugh at me, and the smaller birds likewise giggle from the safety of the valley woodlands. I reach the road at Millook, for a moment of reprieve is welcome before another ascent into the waterpark. Soon, Bude comes into view, battling against a storm surf pushing deep into the bay, threatening the shoreline, keeping everyone indoors.

The paths level out and become safer over open ground as they turn from dune channels to firm grass, then pavements and roads. The last section over Efford Down offers a terrifying view of the coastal battering. I aim for Compass Point beacon to shelter, peer out the windows, and take a final picture. The low sun is wrapped in clouds, seen only as an occasional spotlight to highlight Bude's seaside architecture until its canvas is washed again with rods of rain. Faced with this onslaught the sandstone coast is eroding, the underlying bedrock noticeably different from the steeper cliffs further south, the familiar weaker orange and brown biscuit colours warm when the sun has time to spare.

The Brendon Arms is a welcome sight, the bar warm, and my room ideal. Its history proudly recalls 1845, when George Brendon established the Bude Haven Philanthropic Society (also known as The Death Club, which gave a death benefit of £6 to members for a 6d/quarter fee) at The Falcon Hotel. Now renamed, it can trace a lineage in the Brendon family for 150 years, and it shows. It is welcoming, with a pleasant buzz at the bar from customers like me, sheltering from the storm.

The forecast worsens, and my ambitions wash away as I try to make it across the car park to the coast path the next morning. I can barely stay upright. Every fibre in my body says bail out. Maybe it is the knowledge of the tough Hartland Quay section ahead, but it is time to end my walking season. I have long learned to listen to common sense and not to exceed my limits, a wisdom born from experience. The path will be there next year, and I prefer Type 1 (enjoyed at the time) to the Type 2 fun (enjoyed afterwards) experience of the last few days. Type 3 fun (not enjoyed during or afterwards) will teach you a valuable lesson, and that line would be crossed if I continue, causing permanent damage to my ego. I have been there before.

# 10
# BUDE TO MINEHEAD
## Ocean backpacker

*'It is in our heart that the life of nature's spectacle
exists – to see it, one must feel it.'*
Jean-Jacques Rousseau

### Distance walked: 1,140 miles

*Freya Bevan* again takes me west to Exeter to connect with a very pleasant service to Okehampton Station and a No. 6 bus to Bude. The local community loves the Dartmoor Line, campaigning successfully to keep trains running and restoring the station buildings to pre-Beeching glory. The ticket office is perfectly preserved, with teak furniture, rotating date ink stamps, ashtrays, pipes and cardboard tickets. Old maps show the line's former status as a main route to Plymouth – it is a time warp taking you back 60 years, a pleasant, reassuring feeling and a nice place to wait until the double-decker rolls me through the Devonshire countryside into Cornwall. I have a front-row seat four metres above the ground, a fare-capped £2 cinematic A-road movie to Bude Bay.

The bedroom is familiar, the breakfast faultless, and I now have no excuse not to head north through the toughest section of the South West Coast Path across the county border to a YHA hostel. It is not far, but the map contours are dense and frequent, and that word combe (or coombe) appears again. I'll take it easy, a gentle introduction to my journey to the Severn Bridge. I touch the *Bude Light 2000*, a conical needle of rock commissioned for the millennium, a lodestone on my journey, the end of my last section and the beginning of a new day. The car park is now tranquil, and I choke up with joy as I ascend from First Cove. I am back walking the England Coast Path, connecting again to inner and outer worlds.

Out on the calm sea a kayaker makes good progress, overtaking me as I head north. Walker numbers diminish as Bude fades into the distance and the not-so-secret GCHQ satellite station comes into view. Kestrels, buzzards and peregrines patrol their territories, and choughs feed in the fields. My avian friends will enjoy a relaxing day after the trials of winter. Dippers are in the streams, so I kneel to watch them dive and resurface, twerking the water from their feathers and cleaning their white chests with their bills. Spring is in motion: breeding, growing and flourishing – a planetary annual regeneration.

The offshore breeze keeps my core temperature in check. The conditions are perfect for walking: clear skies, cool winds and dry paths. My winter fitness regime pays dividends as I breathe easily out of the first testing climb at Duckpool. The views are extensive, and the visibility is exquisite as I reach Hawker's Hut and bury myself inside. Looking out to sea through the door frame, I wonder what thoughts, inspiration and ideas were conceived here when poets and writers frequented this romantic shelter: Reverend Hawker may have shared an opium pipe or two with Charles Dickens and Alfred Tennyson within its timber structure.

I have plenty of time to visit Morwenstow, but the cafe is busy, so I explore the churchyard and return to the path through the fields. 'The way is easy, for those with no preference' is a phrase etched into a bench near Bude – a statement that mirrors my ambling, lazy pace: 14 miles in six hours, often stopping to stare and lie back in the dry grass, inspecting every curiosity, reading every sign.

I cross the county line into Devon and enter Ronald Duncan's writing hut, his retreat and the birthplace of his poem *Man*. It is an epic in five parts charting the unfolding of the universe and the emergence of mankind – an ambitious Jungian odyssey, his writing processing his own emotional crisis. I couldn't think of a better place to contemplate the birth of consciousness. I rest outside, looking for inspiration, but it is too early in the walk. It will come later, fed by a book I am reading about Albert Camus. Words with similar angst resonate like a tuning fork on my heartstrings:

> *And here are trees and I know their gnarled surface, water and I feel its taste. These scents of grass and stars at night, certain*

*evenings when the heart relaxes – how shall I negate this world whose power and strength I feel? Yet all the knowledge on earth will give me nothing to assure me that this world is mine. You describe it to me and you teach me to classify it. You enumerate its laws and in my thirst for knowledge I admit that they are true. You take apart its mechanism and my hope increases. … What need had I of so many efforts? The soft lines of these hills and the hand of evening on this troubled heart teach me much more.'*
Albert Camus, *The Myth of Sisyphus*, 1942

There have been sufficient recent rains to keep the waterfalls flowing, each stream finding a path to the sea over the rock striations and ledges. The folding geology is perpendicular to the shoreline, etched east and west by river and sea, rain and wave. The rocks bear testament to millions of years of nature's work, undermining the highest hill, exploiting any weakness, fault or flaw, forming combes and gullies. Manmade leats that once powered water mills are redundant, now disguised by vegetation yet still carrying the flow. I head inland over grassland cut short by the gentler mastication of cattle. The lane leads to Elmscott Youth Hostel, a building rescued by the Goaman family from the YHA and now independent. The warden and I spend time talking, processing our respective days, and ending up in conversations about other hostels we know, the decline of the YHA, and a vote for a favourite. We chime together for Pwll Deri, Pembrokeshire, one of the finest coastal hostels in Britain.

After a day of dreaming and not thinking straight, I casually book a hotel in Bideford, disregarding the challenge of reaching it. This complacency is the result of relaxing too much and overestimating my abilities. I cheerily head north to Hartland Quay, imagining those few miles are a hop and a skip before turning eastwards, but they are not. The views are breathtaking in the early light, and the waterfall at Speke's Mill is like a scene from an exotic holiday brochure or Sunday paper advertorial. To the east, the inland parish church of St Nectan stands alone in a valley, poking its head above a cloud inversion. This backlit country picture scene merges into the low cloud – smeared together by a painter's damp thumb. The sea is calm to the west, and the conditions are perfect for seeing cetaceans. I pause and survey the coastline at Hartland

Point, imagining feeding Atlantic dolphins or harbour porpoises in the tidal flow… but nothing. My avian friends chuckle at me, for they know where they hide.

It is a weekend, and the paths get busier with runners, walkers and birders fanning out from the car parks. I meet my first South West Coast Path hikers, who started from Minehead earlier in the week. I will chat with four or five a day as they set off at the ideal time of year. But it signals that my days on this National Trail will end soon. I should savour every moment but must keep pace and get some miles done. The open rocky coastland becomes woodland at Mouth Mill, which hides the approaching combes in a world of hardy trees. An alternative route sign guides me around closed paths and cliff falls obscured by vegetation. The *Angels Wings* shelter comes into view just as the rains start, perfect to rest a moment and unpack waterproofs. The afternoon's clouds have hijacked the early morning sun. I splash my way into Clovelly, only to be interrogated by a German couple – tourists who mistake me for a guide.

'How long does it take to walk to the harbour?' the female tourist asks first.

'Do you mind taking our picture?' her companion follows. I oblige.

'No, sorry, can you get the background in, please?' she now demands.

'Can you recommend somewhere for lunch?' he adds. It is becoming a constant stream of uni-directional conversation.

I need to start charging for this, as my desire to be polite is about to be overtaken by a curt comment, but the rain ends the conversation. I retire to the visitor centre for soup and a roll. It is deserted, save for an elderly couple sipping tea and looking into space – it looks as if their relationship is empty, for it seems they have nothing to say to each other. Watching them is depressing, a warning of the effort needed to sustain a marriage. A ray of sunshine might help, but I pack up, clatter down the hall, and march back on to the path, offering them a smile as I leave.

The path is now a track known as Hobby Drive, sheltered under the trees, keeping to the contours and looping around the gullies and streams. It was an old horse and cart road before the days of the automobile. The moss, lichen and ferns thrive in the damp air, and the branch-framed views of the Bristol Channel only hint at the anger in the wind and rain. Bluebells, wild garlic and primrose flourish here. It's a perfect place to be, a sheltered path, silent and meditative – soft aromas and subdued weather making progress pleasant.

It doesn't last long, for the path becomes energy-sapping, tough and awkward. I can see lowlands ahead, the estuary mouth at Bideford Bay, and the sands beneath the dunes. I slip for the first time since Land's End, my poles arresting injury once again. It's a sign my boots need replacing, as their Vibram block pattern is worn at the heels and edge. The cliffs relinquish their height slowly through the woodland. This is a haven for wildlife, the slopes inaccessible to humans and so protected from their interference. My legs welcome the flatter accessible tracks into Westwood Ho!, ideal for a wheelchair and lightly shod tourist. I visualise a warm fish and chip restaurant but finding one where I can sit takes time.

I am unable to finish the soggy chips and leave to progress alone around Northam Burrows, for the weather has washed the paths of walkers. I am getting cold, and nibble on an emergency Snickers bar to keep me going through the quayside streets of Appledore. The bleak paths behind shipyards lead again to a river where Tarka the otter once swam. As I reach Bideford, drenched local rowers look forlorn as they wait for their coxswain call. A fisherman does his best to relight a cigarette under his heavy waterproofs and resumes his gaze to the rod tip, feeding a line in the incoming tide. I turn to cross the bridge and fall into a hotel. I am damp, cold and exhausted after a solid 30 miles. I can barely move after a meal and a deep hot bath. As I watch one of David Attenborough's nature documentaries, his soothing voice hypnotises me to sleep.

The Royal Hotel was once the headquarters for the Combined Operations Experimental Establishment, a group of high-ranking officers from each service who developed strategies for allied landings during World War II. The breakfast room would have heard conversations and decisions of the utmost secrecy, and the legacy of Royal Marine logistics and training will be evident as I walk along the banks of the River Torridge and River Taw into Barnstaple. I can take it easy now, knowing there is a mind-numbing, foot-bleeding cycle track to follow for 16 miles to Braunton – an abrasive surface that will surely finish off my boots' rubber soles.

After Instow, a short grass seawall track is welcome. The estuary is filled with shelducks, and the hedgerows are alive with goldfinches. During an otherwise boring march into Barnstaple for lunch I hear a cuckoo, a highlight of the day, its call replaced by a church bell, which draws me into town. Oh, I wish I had a bicycle, my feet demand, as I cross Taw Bridge and head towards the older Long Bridge upstream, where I find a Wimpy, thankfully open on Sunday. The TV is on, and I can watch the London Marathon. My new son-in-law is due to appear on screen at any moment, but the commentators seem more concerned with celebrity matters than genuine runners. His time is two hours and 41 minutes – an outstanding achievement. I admire his athleticism, yet he thinks my sequential 20-mile days are unreal. He should know, having competed in many ultras, notably the nearby Tsunami Ultra 24 from Bude to Clovelly and back – a brutal run of 75 miles within 24 hours.

Heading west, I stop to double-take at the sight of a woman running towards me, topless. She has had a double mastectomy and cares little for her appearance, running to live life to the fullest, owning her circumstances. What courage, what verve – a stunning avowal to do your thing in the face of adversity – I am utterly inspired. 'Go for it!' I shout to myself after she has passed, for how could you not offer encouragement? The only other track users are sedate cyclists, who ring their bells as they approach. I walk out with the tide into Braunton to knock at the door of another cheap, anonymous hotel appropriate for a day of anonymous, lonely walking.

I download the Merlin bird identification smartphone app overnight, not expecting much. That morning, I walk down the lanes into Braunton Burrows and give it a go. The dawn chorus is at a peak, and the app immediately identifies a song thrush and Cetti's warbler. I couldn't ask for a better A-list birdsong performance, for their duet is incredibly uplifting and joyful. There are deer, too, feeding in the clearings with the rabbits, now reduced in numbers, giving their name to the landscape. Before myxomatosis, they overran the golf course and military playground unchecked, peppering the sandy soil with burrows, tracks and pellet scatterings.

The upmarket holiday ghetto of Saunton cares little for coastal walkers, and the developers are obsessed with securing private views of Saunton Sands that stretch out to the south. The path weaves to the flick of a surveyor's pen and disposes its users on the rough path above the road to double back around the £10-million *Grand Designs* lighthouse-inspired folly that looks destined to fall into the sea. The TV show documented a failed marriage and spiralling costs, contrasting with a personal dream – the perfect televisual emotional narrative that had little to do with architecture. It is empty, cold, and devoid of life, waiting for a new owner to enjoy a small section of a stunning coastal perspective I have enjoyed for 67 days. The path follows the property boundary and then turns to Croyde Sands, where I meet Alex, a young lad who has packed his life into a 30-kilo backpack and has set off for Bournemouth. He has a fishing rod, too much clothing and pots and pans hanging from straps, but no social media ambitions. He is burdened in one regard but free in another. He doesn't care; he is relaxed and will let his walk unfold, learning as he goes, not seeking validation for what he does. I am sure he will be a different man when he reaches South Haven Point and will have a new circle of friends.

My competitive edge surfaces when leaving Croyde Bay for Baggy Point as I egg a walker along the path. His pace increases, as does mine. He doesn't look back to acknowledge the race, and this continues until he stops at the viewpoint. I notice the incoming storm, lightning flashing from brooding dark clouds with a daunting vertical development. I keep my pace fast, for this is not just some passing rain cloud – it is carrying a real punch. I reach a cafe at the southern end of Morte Bay and settle in for an egg roll and cappuccino. The soft, wet egg explodes over my base layer as I bite into the crusty roll, precisely as a huge crack of thunder announces a deluge. The corrugated plastic roof barely contains the weight of water leaking on to the tables as the occupant diners flee. The sound is deafening and frightening. I stay and put waterproofs on, trying to clean the yellow glue from my chest with soggy napkins as a channel of water pours from the ceiling. Rain turns to hail, and the noise is insane. The roof could collapse as the hailstones get larger with each thunderclap. The beach turns bright white, covered in ice marbles, some as big as gobstoppers. The dogs cower under the tables, and the owners consider joining them as they shield their heads with handbags and newspapers. I sense it easing and leave to walk along the two-mile beach into Woolacombe. The thunder fades inland as I crunch through the ice hail beneath my feet. I squish the hailstones like an excited kid in wellies as they diminish in number in the warm air and emerging sunshine. I have had a lucky escape

– I can't imagine what would have happened had I been on the headland. That mock race saved me.

The trail into Ilfracombe reintroduces the rocky cliff topology: intricate slate and sedimentary bedrock, angled and twisted in a myriad of forms, unwilling to be polished or smoothed by the rolling swell. I arrive in the town, guided by the beautiful ceramic tiles – a white acorn on a blue square – towards the harbour. I am eager to see Damien Hirst's *Verity*, a 20-metre bronze sculpture of a naked half-flayed woman holding a sword to the sky, with the scales of justice behind her back, standing on thick legal books. I sit and try to interpret the work but leave none the wiser, other than understanding the commerciality of a provocative, in-your-face artistic style. It makes a great lightning conductor and a head for gulls to crap on. It will be removed in 10 years.

I have booked into Ocean Backpackers, a welcome independent hostel, which is perfect. A fellow guest, Jimmy, relays a story about the beach at Crosby, where the Blitz rubble was dumped – another beach of broken dreams I will walk past in a few weeks. We all discuss our adventure experiences over mugs of tea or tins of beer, our legs draped over the sofas. The common room is clean, comfortable and convivial. It is a traditional hostel where you can raid the unwanted food cupboard, strip your bedsheets before you leave, and mix with a wide diversity of characters.

I begin walking after a bowl of porridge and before Ilfracombe wakes. The streets are empty, other than the fluorescent-jacketed bin men, road repair gangs and fishermen walking the pavements – clearing rubbish, filling potholes and landing buckets of dogfish. The only sound is the beep-beep-beep of reversing trucks or bin lorries, with their spinning amber lights carving shadows in the early morning light. I climb out to a viewpoint to see the white town buildings, lit by the rising sun and lying in the protected embrace of the surrounding hills, sheltering it from winter south-westerlies. The path keeps company with the A399, only exploring headlands and coves when the opportunity arises, until it conveys me into Combe Martin for lunch. The bread is freshly baked, and the exotically filled rolls will delight my tastebuds later.

I ascend from sea level to Great Hangman which, at 318 metres, must be the highest point on the England Coast Path. Golden Cap in Devon is a mere 191 metres, and Boulby in Yorkshire is nearly 213 metres, so I rack my brains to think of anything higher. The chalk cliffs in the east do not even come close. Wales has Bwlch yr Eifl (350 metres) behind Garn Fôr (444 metres), and I am sure Scotland has something to offer. I will waste an afternoon studying maps to find the answer one day, but the commanding views of the Bristol Channel are spectacular.

It is a long slog to the summit, but I am feeling good. I offload my pack and break out my flask. The chickpea baguette I bought an hour ago falls apart like a cluster bomb, covering my clothes with turmeric spots. My waterproof will need a good Nikwax later, for I now resemble a leopard, with stubborn egg and spice stains all along my sleeves that even the strongest downpour will fail to remove. As I eat, my eyes trace the Welsh coast, the Gower, Port Talbot Steel Works, and Aberthaw Power Station, but neither of the Severn Bridges, although I sense them coming soon. That estuary view must wait as I descend to Heddon's Mouth, a brutal path of shifting stones, with the inevitable climb out back on to what I affectionately call Exmoor-on-Sea. The terrain is now rugged moorland, reminding me of Scotland. Heather-covered sandstone spurs dip precipitously into the flat sea and walking this mountain-sea boundary is dramatic, life-affirming and exhilarating. This joy ebbs as I enter woodland and the Valley of Rocks, the eerie Devonian rock towers guarding the entrance to Lynton. I am staying at its namesake hotel, a Victorian Grade II gothic glory, spooky, untouched and decaying. It is surely haunted, but I sleep a deep sleep, untroubled by sheeted ghouls.

I have a day to reach Minehead and the end of the South West Coast Path. I have walked from Swanage in 34 days, three days faster than in 2007. I have no explanation for my pace, 14 years later, other than a new, relaxed style of walking and my experience. I follow the final contour-hugging tracks through the woodland cliff escarpments. It is easy-going where civil engineers have tamed the terrain, but tough when you leave the track. The moorland geology persists, rising to almost 300 metres, followed by long treks through the wooded cliffs. Desolate Farm is aptly named, an accurate reflection of the remoteness of this walk. The church at Culbone is a gem, almost 1,000 years old and the smallest parish church in England. It was named after St Beuno, a Welshman who sailed across the Bristol Channel, and seats just 30 people. Continuing, I lose myself in thought, stopping only to chat with the steady stream of South West Coast Path walkers heading west. Their boots and gear are clean and shiny, and they have complexions yet to grow rosy and tanned. They seem pleased to have collected their first passport stamps for the newly printed booklets from the South West Coast Path Association. The pedantic walker will seek to collect all 130 stamps, and this guidebook will tempt visits to the participating businesses along the way.

The cafe in Porlock Weir is one stamp point and my last option for food before the stupidly steep ascent of Bossington Hill after walking serenely through the flat marshland fields above Porlock. I then take the tougher, rugged route nearer the cliffs, to Minehead. There is subsidence in places, requiring concentration and frequent stops to rest on my poles and admire the stunning views.

Soon, the terrain will be almost flat to the Scottish border, so I saviour the last glorious sunny days along one of the best coastal paths in the world. I descend, satisfied, through the woodlands to the South West Coast Path start/end sculpture. I ask the first person I see to take my picture with this public artwork. Known as the *Iron Giant,* it was inspired by a design by Sarah Ward, drawn while a pupil at a nearby college. The smile on my face says it all, for since Poole, I have walked another quarter of the England Coast Path. I turn and amble into town, observing the West Somerset Coast Path fingerposts that will guide me tomorrow. Steel scallop-shell waymarks are inlaid into the pavement. I wonder which pilgrimage route they represent, for I can find no information board to help me. I take them to represent my spiritual journey around the coast of England but later discover that they have been co-opted to guide you around the Minehead Maritime Mile Trail, which promotes the town's heritage.

# 11
# MINEHEAD TO CHEPSTOW
## Where's Wally?

*'Because in the end, you won't remember the time you spent working in the office or mowing the lawn. Climb that goddamn mountain.'*
Jack Kerouac

### Distance walked: 1,270 miles

A Cetti's warbler shrieks in my ear as I leave the Premier Inn at Minehead, admonishing me for being late. The alarm snaps me out of my slumber, a delightful surprise to start the day in an urban environment. The walking should be easier now, for I cannot see a single hill or cliff along the coastline, just the remnants of a submarine forest around the shingle and mud platforms of Blue Anchor Bay. Holiday villages and golf courses are behind me, and nature returns. The River Avill flood-relief channel is a calm haven for insects until a gulp of swallows feasts on them. I marvel at their agility between the concrete walls, twisting, turning, carving, looping through the air – gorging on the bounty in a frenzy of flight. It makes me feel peckish, as this morning's cheap porridge pot failed to satisfy. The Driftwood Cafe offers a solution, and I join the locals for a bacon butty in a room buzzing with gossip and conversation as their day starts.

The England Coast Path fingerposts for this section to Brean Down have been in place since 2016. The route has adopted most of the West Somerset Coast Path, which retains its identity with reassuring ammonite waymarks. I am not expecting any navigational challenges and ease into a gentle pace to time my arrival into Watchet, for I have arranged to meet the coast path officer who manages the path until the River Axe.

'It's wonderful that the England Coast Path is open in Somerset, but can you help me with the route past Brean?' I ask her.

'You shouldn't have any problems to Sand Bay, but they're still working on a route to Clevedon. I can put you in touch with the path managers to Gloucester if you like. You should pop into the East Quay art centre as the path almost runs through it. There's lots to see,' she adds.

We discuss the plans for a forthcoming festival and the Somerset art community that thrives in the area, with many members spending time capturing the beauty of the coastline. In addition to the paintings on display in the art centre, I notice Poetry Pin waymarks on the fingerposts. If you scan these into an app you can read local poetry on your smartphone in the geo-tagged location you walk through. This local visual and written art stimulates thought and reflection for many and gives a community insight to this transitory walker in their landscape.

A day later, I get more detailed path information from Sand Bay and plot a route around the River Yeo using lanes and cycleways; it is messy, and I expect problems as this is a dynamic landscape where a locked sluice gate or closed path or bridge can greatly impact timings. The usual philosophy of keep-the-sea-to-the-left rule will work for a while, and then estuaries will play tricks with my internal compass, confusing my mind as the sun's angle changes and the wind chills a different shoulder.

The geology has changed dramatically; not only have the hills gone, but the path underfoot is muddy, and the flora is mostly brambles instead of ferns and heather. I can see new birds feeding in the mudflats and beach sands. I am grateful for a low tide, for at high tide the path would be unusable at Helwell Bay and then again at St Audrie's Bay, leaving no option but to wait or walk deep inland. I hope the path planners find solutions, for coastal erosion eats away at the obvious paths and creates greater route challenges in future. Today, a waterfall cascades over the cliff, requiring me to step away and divert on to the rock ledge that looks like it has been poorly laid by an apprentice plasterer with a rough piece of wood. These wave-cut Jurassic sea platforms are full of ammonite, reptiles, shellfish and some of the oldest submerged fossilised forests in the UK.

Back on the cliff path, a Lynx helicopter is on manoeuvres over the Lilstock Royal Navy Quadrant Hut gunnery observation tower. I am not sure if it will strafe me as it approaches, so I wave. It arcs overhead, hugs the fields inland and disappears behind woodland, only to reappear without warning. I sense the pilot has chosen me as a dummy target, and it is quite frightening to imagine how helpless you would be if this were real. The silence returns, and the eastern view fills with a colossal project: Hinkley Point C Nuclear Power Station. I have never seen so many cranes, including the enormous yellow 250-metre-tall Sarens SGC-250 'Big Carl', the world's largest – able to lift an astonishing 5,000 metric tonnes. It pivots and dips as I approach, changing angles and throwing shapes in the skyline. It dwarfs all the others, busily twisting and turning like an inverted millipede struggling to right itself. This is the largest civil engineering project in the UK and undoubtedly the largest construction site I have seen on my trip. This mega-project cost and project overruns beggar belief – the original plan (2017) foresaw a cost of £18 billion and an opening date of 2025, but this has ballooned to £46 billion and 2031 – causing much discussion between the UK government and EDF, the French Company responsible for construction.

A local farmer and ex-Marine is out walking his dog. We stop to chat about my walk around the coast, the construction project and the pleasure he gets from walking this same route almost every day, in any weather. Like me, he describes walking as a defiant act, symbolically rejecting modernity for the simple pleasures that feed the soul. As I walk on, I reflect on progress as a synonym for time. Scientific and technical developments rob us of our past, social networks are replacing meaningful interactions, and automation disengages us and displaces our skills. Walking is an antidote, taking us back in time, reminding us that we do not evolve as fast as the world around us. It reminds us of the pleasure of working with your hands, of solving problems with trusted friends, and directly experiencing life and the environment. These precious few minutes of conversation in the shadow of atomic energy technology make me wonder if such progress threatens our wellbeing as we enter a transformative digital age.

As I reach the outskirts of the power station boundary, a fence blocks the path, forcing me to follow the alternate route inland to Shurton – which is fine as this is my accommodation for the night. Before doing so, I sit and study the enormous industry beside me. A pair of PWR (Pressurised Water Reactors) will generate 3.26 gigawatts of electricity over a 60-year period. This capacity would easily have powered the whole of the UK in 1920 and will substantially contribute to our energy mix when finished. I hope they have robust flood plans, for this installation sits along the

Bristol Channel, which experienced catastrophic floods on 30th January 1607 when the perfect storm struck, a deadly combination of spring high tides, a low-pressure surge, strong winds and a narrowing estuary. Current models assume 10-metre-high surges, and I am sitting on a seawall 10 metres above the high-water mark. If you factor in rising sea levels and the dynamic nature of the world's second highest tide ranges, I hope we can trust risk models from organisations that forecast overspend of more than £28 billion and deliver a project six years late as future generations depend on greater certainty. Some experts believe that a tsunami struck in 1607, and we all know what happened at Fukushima, in 2011.

I don't sleep well, having surreal nightmares about drowning that haunt me in the morning as I walk around the site. I am guided by health and safety notices across roads and gates, keeping a distance from the fleet of inbound buses and lorries. Almost 9,000 people work here and are housed in accommodation nearby. The security guard looks at me perplexed, as if someone has decided to walk to work, but he helps me with directions when I explain my journey on the England Coast Path. I point to the new fingerpost above his head, which he hasn't noticed before. He will not have seen many coastal walkers this week.

To reach the sea again, I walk alongside Wick Moor at five metres above mean sea level, suggesting the sea would surely encircle the facility if flooded. It makes me nervous, but the birds don't seem to care or even know what lies in their midst – they are chirping away in the reeds. The fence sign reads 'licensed nuclear site', which makes me wonder about this double-speak, for where will I find an unlicensed one?

At Stolford, I can think of nature again with my back to the struggling multibillion-pound industry. The reeds and wildflowers reintroduce meditative sound and colour. Egrets and plovers are picking at the shoreline, and skylarks are ascending and singing. I become more deeply immersed in her embrace as I enter the Somerset Wetlands National Nature Reserve at Steart – a wild, remote sliver of marsh and fractal-probed mudflats. Communities have fished these tidal zones since the Bronze Age, using a traditional mud-horse sled to slide across the flats and carry their catch. The last mud-horse fishermen, Brendan Sellick, passed away recently, ending a unique way of life that had existed for over 3,000 years. Brendan's son and companion, Adrian, tried to keep it going, but it is a lonely place to be in fog and mist. Archaeologists occasionally uncover a preserved example of the typical wooden chest-height sledge, evidence of a simple living in sharp contrast to the modern technology rising to the west.

The Wildfowl and Wetlands Trust (WWT) manages the Steart Peninsula, a new reserve created to respond to rising sea levels. It has the twofold benefit of maintaining critical salt marsh habitats and acting as a carbon sink. This organisation was founded in 1946 by Sir Peter Scott from his base at Slimbridge, further along the estuary. It spawned the formation of the World Wildlife Fund (WWF), whose panda symbol he first sketched in 1961, and which sits on a wall in his study. As Sir David Attenborough declared, 'If there is one place that can be regarded as a birthplace of worldwide conservation, it is surely here at Slimbridge and through the work of Peter Scott.'

Where water and land meet, magic happens. A place where our life itself came to be, in the interstitial tidal zones. What efforts could be more urgent than protecting these landscapes? We all unconsciously feel the importance of these coastal zones. We feel it, even though we can't fully explain it. This must be why coastal walking is so joyful, as it explores our very existence on the littoral boundary between the sea and the land.

I climb the bird observation tower for a better view of the River Parrett and gaze over the complexity of the water channels and marshland formations. I can see Brean Down, almost touch it, it seems so close. A strengthening wind whistles through the wood slats, and opening a binocular window would be foolish. I rest in solitude, studying the sun-faded bird species panels, munching on an energy bar: grey heron, little egret, shelduck, shoveler, scaup, gadwall, oystercatcher and knot – a rich list of species that will call this place home for a few months during their migrations.

Walking again, the signs of Somerset agriculture can be discerned in the farmyards. Many apple blossom colours burst from the orchards, complementing the rampant hawthorn blossom – all having an exceptional year. The perfume is overwhelming, hinting at fruit varieties unseen in a supermarket. A path now connects birdwatching hides and open-air viewpoints for an enthusiast to hide and watch. I make a mental note to return with a bicycle, binoculars and lunch to spend a short winter day exploring the area along the new cycleways that link these observation points.

I walk into Combwich, hoping for a cafe before the long seawall path into Bridgwater, but its only pub has closed doors. It is a painful walk, the cut grass hiding tractor tread tracks that easily twist an ankle. The River Parrett Trail meanders into the town and is deserted. The mud river view remains unchanged for miles. The tide is out, and the drained contours of the ugly silt channels are deep, exposed and alien. Seeing a walker on the opposite bank, where I will be tomorrow, is disheartening as it will take hours to reach that point. The path becomes concrete quayside as I arrive in a town troubled by alcoholics, drug addicts and the homeless, carrying their possessions in carrier bags and army surplus backpacks. I don't think I have felt so unsafe since leaving Cromer – it is a big surprise. The atmosphere is threatening, and the contrast with my exposure to the coastal beauty since Bude is quite shocking, taking a moment for me to adjust to.

I am staying in an anonymous hotel, the cheapest I can find, but the only option on this long estuarial walk. Endless franchise cafes and fast-food outlets line the streets, and I struggle to find somewhere I fancy until Piggy's Sandwich Bar makes me stop, open-mouthed. It looks inviting. The meal is excellent and the coffee is perfect, served by smiling staff to happy customers. I contemplate dessert when the owner's friend pops in with a tray of *pastéis de nata*, or Portuguese custard tarts made maybe an hour ago – how food can lift the spirit. My assessment of Bridgwater is reset.

My evening consists of overheard foul language and racing cars, exhausts popping and tyres screeching. I am considering the wisdom of staying in towns, when options are limited. Perhaps a seawall wild camp would have been better. I leave at dawn, the litter pickers and rotating sweepers clearing the streets of fast-food packaging, cans and bottles. I find a superstore and choose something for lunch, balancing taste, calories and weight. I can't think beyond bananas, malt loaf and a meal deal stuffed into the external pockets of my backpack – a lazy, cheap option that will get me to Burnham-on-Sea.

The river scene returns, with the tide out again and mudflats exposed. The wind has eased, and the birds are relaxed, feeding. Whimbrels are gathering in good numbers. Marsh harriers patrol the hedgerows and treeline inland. It is quiet, and the incessant wind noise from the past two days has gone. The vast transmission towers provide scale to the mist-laden landscape, fading out to the power station and the cities. Stert Island emerges in the mist as it clears, eerie and mystical, its existence dream-like and unexpected. Birds call and then appear, gliding low, using the ground effect over the water to reach their destinations. After eight miles, I meet only one birdwatcher and no day walkers. I haven't met a long-distance coastal hiker since Minehead – this new section of the England Coast Path has yet to be discovered. I am sure it will, as it is enchanting and serene.

Crossing the New Clyce Bridge, I arrive in Burnham-on-Sea and select the first chippy. It is fuss-free, functional and full. I reflect on my diet. I am losing weight, but my energy levels are high. I eat less than I would at home but crave home cooking. Freeze-dried meals have been a godsend after my Eastbourne experience with varieties delicious and filling. Today's diners are polishing off massive plates of chips, burgers, sausages, fish, sauces, bread and fizzy drinks, and almost everyone appears overweight and sedentary. Something is wrong. While this meal is healthy, almost every small shop I find is packed with ultra-processed foods, high in sugar, salt and saturated fats. Access to good quality food is a challenge and leaves me with limited options. People get addicted to the taste and consume more than they need, hoodwinked by persuasive marketing campaigns. This is food made for profit and not health. I leave to breathe the air again, overlooking a decorated seawall.

Svetlana Kondakova Muir, an Edinburgh-based public artist, created *Burnham-on-Sea-Life (Mudflat)* in 2022. It is a glass and ceramic mosaic mural triptych of the unique habitat found on the shoreline. The work is one of the best I have come across, freshly installed and intricate in detail, with rich and expressive colours and textures. Like the Steart information boards, the tide-in and tide-out panels add sea gooseberry, shrimp, crab, snail, cockle, ray, jellyfish, eel, ragworm, urchin, krill and Arctic barrel-bubble – incredibly diverse sea life. I wonder how many people stop to read its wonders to understand what lies at their feet.

I drop to the beach, passing the white wooden nine-legged lighthouse, which still provides a navigational aid to vessels entering the River Parrett and is the perfect foreground interest for photographers capturing a sunset. The National Cycle Network Route 33 runs along the beach. Signs advise me to remain on firm sand, but I ignore them and get stuck in the mud, engaging reverse gear to extricate myself. My boots are filthy, and gain weight as I walk through the sand. I have six miles to wear that off, as this must be one of the longest beaches in the south-west. I look at my watch and measure my pace on the flat, firm sands, heading towards Brean Down in the distance.

Cars are parked along the tideline, facing the sea. The owners have brought enough gear to build a small village. Tents, shelters, barbecues and windbreaks probably take half a day to erect and will take another half to dismantle – you wonder if this is the sole purpose of their visit. A warden patrols the beach in her Toyota Hilux, making sure things don't get out of hand, and stops with me to look at a perplexing scene. Two schools have decided to hold a 50-a-side beach rugby match, with everyone dressed as *Where's Wally*. The melee of red-and-white-striped T-shirts, bobble hats and googly glasses disguises who plays for which team, and players seem to change sides without warning. I can't tell what rules apply, as it is difficult to follow. It is chaotic, eccentric and wonderful.

I reach the National Trust cafe in under two hours and stop for a snack. I ponder why only three-quarters of the sandwich is in the pack when you expect the chef to cut four quadrants. If this is shrinkflation, then it is getting creative. Short-changed, I climb on to Brean Down. My legs revel in the ascent, now conditioned by the South West Coast Path combes. I wonder when they will see a climb next. I rest on the headland, overrun with yellow cowslips, and study the huge beach to the south. A large pattern fills the sands, created by raking intricate patterns, in a design to be viewed from above. It is an ephemeral artwork that will be washed away by high tide in a few hours. The islands of Steep Holm and Flat Holm sit in the channel, limestone outcrops pointing to Wales. They are the 19th-century defensive platforms guarding the mouth of the Severn Estuary and the ports at Bristol, Avonmouth, Cardiff and Newport. I could stay here all day as there is little wind, and the sun is out. I wake, having nodded off, and descend, walking over a huge white arrow, which I later learn gave direction for the bombing range I passed two days ago. The River Axe estuary coast path to the campsite will be closed from mid-

July to protect the redshanks, the 'sentinels of the marsh', who roost along the banks in summer. Now it is open, and I can walk directly along the uncut grass seawall riverbank to a huge campsite.

It takes a while to find the reception. I walk in disbelief through acres of caravans, motorhomes and tents, all set up for the bank holiday weekend. Awnings shelter sofas, TVs, kitchen units, carpets and tables. One room has a row of three ceramic ducks on the wall, a classical family set from the 1970s. Many pitches would shame the proudest homeowner, for they have brought their Home Sweet Home with them. One man has a lawnmower and is tending to the grass on his temporary estate, marked precisely by boundary stakes in the ground. I am an unusual sight in this company. The receptionist is astounded that I have walked 24 miles from Bridgwater, carrying a 15-kilo pack with my worldly possessions: a shelter (Terra Nova tent), a kitchen (MSR stove), my wardrobe (one change of clothes) and a bed (Thermarest mat and sleeping bag) for a night's stay in the field.

Travelling light, I value every possession, even more so if they have multiple uses. I have trimmed my needs to the bare minimum and no longer want or desire the things I can do without. If I take this lesson home and consume less, I can lower my earnings and therefore pay less tax, subverting a growth model that underpins a capitalist system. I hope one day I will have something that those seeking money, status and power will never have. I will have enough, and be satisfied, valuing things you cannot buy, valuing the slow ways and the old ways, before progress changed all that.

I wake at 6am having slept well, and I am packed and ready in half an hour, walking out across Bleadon Levels to Uphill, through the sluice-gated pils to the marina cafe I hope is open for breakfast. I'm too early, and walk on, looking in wonder at the partially ruined Norman church of St Nicholas standing above the limestone promontory ridgeline, the terminus of the Mendip Hills that extend to Frome. It would have been a frightening place to witness the 1607 floods that inundated the Somerset Levels. Over 2,000 people lost their lives, many unable to swim.

I find a cafe later, opening its doors during a surprisingly quiet Saturday in Weston-super-Mare. I check the map and work out a makeshift route to Clevedon. The official England Coast Path ends at Sand

Bay, and I must find a route using narrow lanes, cycleways and muddy paths, hoping critical bridges on the map are open. The rain-washed motorway hums a deeply unpleasant drone, a demotivating sound in the lonely fields until I hear the distinct whistle of a steam train. To my delight, at this precise moment the *Flying Scotsman 60103* passes under the rail bridge I ascend. It is a schoolboy thrill, triggering an involuntary wave as it approaches. The sweet coal-perfumed clouds linger, and the whistles fade. It is a welcome treat during the long, boring road tramp to the outskirts of Clevedon.

The weather is grim, overcast and colourless – a Brizzle-drizzle easing up the channel, set for the day, ready to pour on Bristol. Marine Lake contains a solitary swimmer sticking to a training schedule. Woolly hats have been knitted for the railing posts, preparing for King Charles III's coronation in a few weeks' time. Exiting the town, the path enters an overgrown, lonely world hugging the shoreline. The mist is getting thicker, and a fog horn starts, emitting a deep tone call at 20-second intervals. It is the only sound in the muffled atmosphere, until a slow-moving cargo ship passes, its Doppler-effect chugging tone slowly fading north to south, along the estuary.

Electric bluebells, fresh and intense in the dew, somehow generate their own incandescent light and guide me north. I approach Portishead, and the Café Lido is a good stop for tea. It is only a mile to another cheap, branded shopping-estate hotel, but it has everything I need. I caught a chill in the refrigerated supermarket aisles, so I strip off damp clothing and hang it to dry in the room while I sit in a short bathtub, with my knees held against my chest, searching in vain for the minuscule bar of soap in the murky water. I demolish my evening meal, write my journal and study the route to Wales.

Cycle paths are the day's theme and will rescue me from a succession of closed paths and urban routes through Avonmouth docklands. Civil engineers are building new power distribution lines using a lovely new T-shaped earring design. The work means closed roads and diverted paths. I ignore signs, and in turn, I am ignored by the workmen, who are more concerned with vehicular incursions than lone walkers. I sense they know my plight and the irritation a lengthy diversion would mean. Soon, I am walking around the security fence of the dockland car parks, where I can see acres of new vans and cars – thousands of them, many unreviewed next year's models. The vans are ready-painted with commercial logos. Cars and vans of all colours are parked in massive arrays, every variant represented, and their pre-registration identity is scribbled in white marker on the windscreens. Over half a million vehicles pass through this Bristol port a year. The scale is bewildering, giving a sense of the material and energy impact that motor vehicles have on our planet. Sit on any motorway bridge for 10 minutes and wonder where all these people are going. The sheer numbers do not register when you drive in their flow, in your comfortable steel bubble.

I climb up to the motorway ramparts that lead to the footway across the River Avon, the culverts and tunnels gleaming with exotic graffiti. This vast bridge, built to clear shipping to Bristol, carries the M5 motorway. The walk induces vertigo, and I feel queasy and unsafe, so I walk away from the railings. Solar-powered Samaritan telephone booths will connect you directly to a volunteer, as this bridge is located near dense population areas, it will have witnessed too many suicides. I can't imagine the desperation that leads someone to end their lives in such an inhospitable place and on a path that has given me such joy. If only they could walk that path, too.

On the north bank, I turn east at an urban farm that connects people to nature. Allotments claim small pockets of land, tended with care, new crops emerging from the tilled rows. Walking through the detritus of burnt-out vehicles, fly-tipping and trash, I squeeze by two solid concrete blocks, backpack aloft, to cross the motorway. This cycle route has been blocked to prevent abuse, and my journey would be severely disrupted if I could not make it through. I smell the sea in the estuary but must first pass through a wonder world of logistics: warehouses, articulated lorries and speeding delivery vans. The path to the Severn Way is blocked, so I must walk along the road and endure overgrown and unkempt verges. At last, I reach Severn Beach and Shirley's Cafe – a haven which couldn't be more perfect for a weary walker, fed up with a landscape designed purely for the internal combustion engine.

As my map suggests, I walk under the new Prince of Wales Bridge, expecting a clear path to the Severn Bridge, but substantial flood defence works block the route. The signage and severe fencing tell you to turn around; the route along Northwick Oaze is shut, and a simple two-mile walk to the Severn Road Bridge is blocked. A local resident tending her borders is as angry as I am.

'I don't see why they block all the paths. It won't be until 2027 or longer before they have finished,' she says. 'If you want to get to the bridge, you'll have to do some road walking. Turn left at the pub and follow the cycle track.'

This is a £18 million priority sea defence project that should protect 17 kilometres of coastline and several thousand homes. It will create 80 hectares of wetland habitat, so the WWT will approve when it is finished. For me, it is a painful walk along the B4055 and A403, with ceaseless delivery vans and juggernauts lifting dust into my eyes. I expect relief at Cake Pill Gout, but that is blocked too. I have a dangerous mile, without a footpath or verge, to reach Aust and the path to the motorway service station and lockable Severn Bridge footpath gate. There should have been an easier route, but apparently no one could tap into their budgets for a few directional signs. I relax, pacing across the suspension bridge, flying 50 metres above the River Severn, with stunning views and a close-up of the engineering that went into connecting England to Wales. It opened in 1966. Before then, you would take a ferry that would be lucky to transport 200 vehicles a day, compared to the tens of thousands that cross both bridges now.

It is perhaps my worst day on the path. I should have considered walking along the river to Slimbridge along the Severn Way, for the map shows fascinating tidal reservoirs and former ports. I would also have passed two nuclear installations at Oldbury and Berkeley, both decommissioned for now but earmarked as possible locations for prototype Small Modular Reactors. However, I wanted to walk the bridge and connect to the Wales Coast Path I completed in 2019, a route that is 870-plus miles to Chester, where I will resume my England Coast Path journey. I look forward to the murals under the motorway bridge, which inspired me four years earlier. A piece entitled *Young and Old, as Ancient Stones and Shipwrecks* has gone, painted over by another. As I walk through, the artwork evolves, and the tunnel is busy with artists. They shake their spray cans; the metal mixing ball rattle reverberates in the enclosed space. The work is stunning, complex, expressive and celebrates Chepstow.

## THE COAST IS OUR COMPASS

I collapse my walking poles and dress for the long train journey home, connecting minute-perfect through Newport, Reading and Slough. I put in my earbuds, listening to rhythmic sounds that rock with the train's motion, and I fall into a dream world, my legs knowing a rest is coming, having done an excellent job carrying me from Bude.

# 12
# CHESTER TO FLEETWOOD
## Another Place

*'If a man knows not to which port he sails, no wind is favourable.'*
Seneca

### Distance: 1,370 miles

It is a good decision to swap my heavy boots for trail shoes, for there will be endless cycle paths and promenades for weeks ahead. I decide to travel light, leaving my tent, sleeping bag and stove behind and relying on affordable accommodation, public transport connections and a stack of freeze-dried meals. If I walk fast enough, I will need fewer days in this new urban environment.

I head north from Chester station on the National Cycle Network Route 5 into the Wirral – a 100-square-mile oblong bounded by the River Dee and River Mersey. A beautifully painted millennium milepost, 3¾ miles from Chester, marks an hour's walking, so my pace is good. I am lighter, and my legs swing easily with less weight to move. The rest reinvigorated me, and my fitness developed nicely as I carried a full load across Cornwall, Devon and Somerset.

Sealand Church and the Welsh border hint at the former shape of the Dee Estuary, which is now home to a huge Toyota factory, steel works and paper mill. What was once open water has been reclaimed or silted to form new habitats for nesting birds. RSPB Burton Mere sits beside a firing range, protecting them from man's interference. The cycle path that was once the shoreline is now four kilometres from the sea, a landscape of salt marsh and wetlands probed by deltas of salt channels, flushed twice a day. I see several harriers patrolling the marshes, their lazy and long wing beats a few metres above the ground; eyes tuned to movement until they drop on to their prey.

The Nos. 56, 568 and 89 cycle paths combine to form a superb coastal network around the peninsula, traffic-free and easy-going. It does not take long to reach Parkgate and my first hotel. I am early and sit on the seawall opposite two ice cream shops, trying to decide which one to choose. Nicholls wins. Its 1930s decor draws me in with a promise of a spiral vanilla cone expertly twirled for over 85 years.

The village was the major seaport during the Industrial Revolution, a leading embarkation point for Ireland, and a preferred passenger destination to Holyhead or Liverpool. It grew as the port of Chester silted up until a new 10-mile channel was dredged to Connah's Quay. This terraforming changed the silting flow and patterns, filling Parkgate's shoreline. Its fate was sealed as colonising grasses matted the sands and mud together, securing their foundations. After a brief period as a beach resort, it is now an orphaned architectural gem with many distinctive features: beautiful black-and-white buildings, recognisable coastal cottages and historic pubs. Discerning its former glory on a modern Ordnance Survey map would be difficult, but the seawall and quayside remain. It is a wonderful example of how engineers can change coastlines, which lead to unintended consequences for communities elsewhere.

I follow the old railway line to West Kirby, which is still marked by abandoned station platforms and buildings, some of which are now cafes for cyclists and walkers. The jays are lively and chatter loudly in the trees, like a police escort along the track, until the views open, giving a sense of the scale of the wetlands and huge estuarial sands. It is raining heavily in Wales. In one biblical moment the storm clouds part and the sun illuminates the Point of Ayr lighthouse, freshly painted. I am lucky to remain dry but risk a soaking around the exposed Marine Lake narrow seawall path, as roadworks have blocked the main street. I get closer to Hilbre Island as I turn right towards Hoylake. Crossing to visit this unusual landform is tempting, but the tide is turning. My route continues along Mockbeggar Wharf, where the wading birds are out on the shoreline, unseen, some two miles away. The outline of the massive Burbo Bank wind turbine arrays seems near, their scale a dangerous illusion, as if you could walk to them in less than an hour.

Endless coloured memorial benches, which the Wirral's 'Older People's Parliament' activist group maintain, tell endless stories of loss.

This community group gives a voice to residents over the age of 50 who are passionate about maintaining public gardens, paths and spaces. I sit and research options for lunch, then walk along the promenade looking for clues. I ask myself, is it a chain? Does it look busy? Are the staff smiling? The Seaside Cafe in Wallasey meets my criteria: a no-nonsense bread and butter, fish and chips, stainless teapot and mini-milk jug wonder with a 'don't mess with us, we know what we are doing' service vibe and a smiling, happy community buzz. It is a place to rest, people-watch, overhear conversation and relax before I turn right along the River Mersey.

The Port of Liverpool, which Parkgate's port challenged for passengers in its day, announces the imminent arrival of a city. Cranes, Irish Sea ferries, container ships and coastal steamers are navigating to their berths, guided by the New Brighton Lighthouse beyond Fort Perch Rock. Breakwaters catch silt to tame a shifting shoreline and protect the channel and slipways. I aim for the imposing ventilation tower landmark above the Mersey Tunnel, idling along the Millennium Trail historic quayside to the ferry from Birkenhead to Liverpool, reading the information boards and counting unusual distance markers.

I catch *Snowdrop*, the famous ferry painted with the *Everybody Razzle Dazzle* design by Sir Peter Blake. It is outrageously coloured and inspired by the World War I ship-dazzle patterns used to confuse an enemy. The docklands are alive with music and dance, for the annual *Eurovision* has come to Liverpool and is in full-on dressed-up party mode on the opposite shore. It takes a while to weave through the gaiety without getting swept up in the dancing. I escape to the suburbs and the only hotel I can find. It is a Tripadvisor one-star warehouse-cum-hostel with only the basics: no staff, kettle, mirrors, TV, soap or Wi-Fi – just a wonky bed shoved into the corner of a poky room, with one light switch by the door. Even the toilet roll has been rationed.

Sometimes, walking through a city can be as rewarding and surprising as a remote trail. Instead of a busy A road, I choose the Leeds and Liverpool Canal north, passing through an industrial landscape that hints at the great wealth this port generated in the 19th century. Modern commercial developments can't quite wipe away all this evidence of a vibrant past. Street corners retain their Victorian public houses –

defiant social hubs that echo a strong community, not unlike the joyous optimism that oozed from every pore in the *Eurovision* crowds. This city knows how to party.

The canal avoids the busy A5306 and the official path until I reach the container ports and docklands to turn towards Crosby Beach. Alongside the path, near Seaforth, a huge mural depicts an earlier time: trams, bathing machines, gaslights and the RMS *Titanic*, in memory of the many officers and crew who lived nearby. The work should be extended to include the Marconi maritime radio stations, training the pioneers of seabound radio who would learn how to tap out the S-O-S signal (three dots, three dashes, and three dots, repeated), a cry for help they hoped they would never send, but were used on the fateful night of 15th April 1912.

The tide is out as I reach the shoreline and *Another Place*, the stunning art installation by Sir Antony Gormley: one hundred 650-kilo cast-iron replicas of his bodily form, looking out to the sea along two miles of beach. Each form is the same, yet different, encrusted with weed or bird droppings. Some are far away, some nearby, some are submerged in water or buried in sand, while others are sunburnt, encrusted or occasionally smartly dressed in T-shirts or woolly hats. This diverse community of iron men defiantly faces sea and storm, technology and nature, and sun and moon – melancholic, reflective, vulnerable and passive. As you walk between them you become one of them, feeling what they feel and learning from their ageless wisdom. Their expressions are subtly different, each reacting to their plight in their own way having succumbed to the elements differently, their lives etched with an iron-flecked patina. It is an incredibly moving experience – a metaphor for existence and a universal desire to connect with the world as they contemplate the universe, time and tide inside their enduring forms.

As you pass the last statue, you enter another beach of broken dreams: the Blitz debris from the bombings of Liverpool in the early 1940s and the same beach Jimmy alerted me to in Ilfracombe. Each piece of ceramic, brick, glass or stone was once a part of the city where 4,000 people lost their lives. Architectural clues can be found, inscriptions can be partially read, and former lives can be pieced together. It mirrors the debris banks near Coalhouse Fort, which I passed near Tilbury, the last evidence of sustained bombing campaigns on two city ports during World War II.

## CHESTER TO FLEETWOOD

Only hours old, a brand-new King Charles III England Coast Path fingerpost directs me along an easy section into Formby. On 1st May 2023, the government changed the name from the England Coast Path. It is a bit of a mouthful, making me wonder how many signposts must be replaced. There needs to be consistency, as I have seen haphazard signage since Cromer: stickers, circular plastic discs, steel signs, painted roads and engraved wooden fingerposts. Some feature the National Trail acorn symbol (sometimes upside down), while others write the name against an arrow that occasionally points true. They all suffer abuse from vandals and weather, and their condition is deteriorating rapidly compared to the enduring black and white acorn steel plaques used in the past for the National Trail waymarks. Now a carpenter somewhere must be scratching their head, wondering how to fit 30 characters and five spaces on to a narrow board.

The Wales Coast Path (thankfully not the Prince of Wales Coast Path) has consistent, beautiful and colourful shell marks, some of which are embedded into the pavement stones and are always present. The King Charles III England Coast Path should have taken a little more time to consider its brand and integrate it into the family of National Trails. If done well, waymarks enhance the sense of identity and belonging, so improving the walking experience. Waymarks are friends; they reassure and give a sense of progress. They are touchstones around the coastline, accessible to those who walk two miles, 20 miles or 2,000 miles – reminding us of the connected network of paths that lead through our intriguing, beautiful and valuable natural and urban landscapes.

Yet, the sheer audacity of establishing a coastal path around England and Wales is to be applauded, for it is a thread that connects many issues: climate change, coastal erosion, habitat loss, avian flu, industrial vandalism, diversity loss, social deprivation, water quality and pollution. Many of these issues, and others, align with the concerns of our king and an increasingly vocal and diverse society that lives shoreside and inland. These phenomena have their roots in an existential human crisis: a playbook of capitalism, greater inequality, and the wholesale plunder of the natural world and its resources – all actions where nature's invoice remains unpaid, accumulating as a debt deferred for future generations. Getting out of your comfort bubble and walking the coastline exposes you to these factors, showing you first-hand how your place in society connects with these issues. This experience does not preach to you, but slowly seeps into your understanding of the world, if you take time to observe and wonder.

The dimension of time confirms this, as you read the history in what you see and study the many information boards. As I walk through Formby, I notice the Victorian houses, built to last forever, another sign of prosperity during the Industrial Revolution. The area has character, and contrasts with the backdrop of dune and heathland: a home for natterjack toads, northern dune tiger beetles and sand lizards in the acidic soils, washed of their seashell lime. The Sefton Coast is a precious habitat, where the heather mixes with the marram grasses into the Ainsdale dunes. Rare plants thrive, such as the white grass of Parnassus and the pink seaside centaury. It is a long, sandy walk to the outskirts of Southport, its beach growing towards the sea, orphaning the pleasure pier. I have time to walk its length, but it is closed. It needs 86 miles of new timber board to re-lay the decking, an unaffordable sum for Sefton Council. I wonder what the future holds for this 162-year-old structure as the coastline recedes further, making its purpose pointless other than as a poignant folly to a changing coastline.

I rest under the Trans Pennine Way wind sculpture as it rotates, the start/end point of a 215-mile cycle journey to Hornsea in the East Riding of Yorkshire. It is yet another coast-to-coast route that takes you across the grain of England, through urban, industrial and moorland environments to meet its twin sister, no doubt rotating at a similar rate in a complementary direction like quantum-entangled beacons. I navigate over the Marine Way suspension bridge to find an increasingly rare traditional B&B. Many have been acquired for social housing in an area with a declining economic outlook, impacted deeply by the pandemic. Yet, like Liverpool, it retains a strong and inclusive community identity that you can sense in the air and the conversations. The landlord is welcoming, full of local knowledge to impart. He is clearly proud of where he lives.

I leave early to walk along a cycle path, beginning my journey inland to Preston. The Great Bank and Horse Bank sands and marshlands are huge, giving a taster for what will come after Fleetwood around Morecambe Bay. I see Blackpool Tower and a navigation beacon flashing at irregular intervals 10 miles away. It is an intense white bolt of light on a sunny day, which seems illogical. Why is this needed during a day with excellent visibility? I'm intrigued, but finding the answer will take two days of walking.

The wetlands are home to avocets, shelducks, kestrels, buzzards, lapwings and much more. After Fiddler's Ferry, a seawall keeps me between managed industrialised fields and the marshland: one shaped by machine, the other by nature. I am isolated and alone, having not met a coastal walker since Minehead or, today, even a dog walker. My vision is unbalanced between these two worlds: fractal marsh creeks fade to the northern horizon, long lines of ploughed furrow zero to a vanishing point south – polarised landscape artforms that unnerve my binocular perception.

Hesketh Bank has an unexpected Booths supermarket, an opportunity to stock up on lunch to eat in the open after I cross the A59 bridge and walk past a pet food factory to rejoin the River Asland (or Douglas) riverbank on the Ribble Way. I can't find a bench to rest on, so I collapse on the grass, dropping off to sleep for 20 minutes after scoffing my ready-made sandwich. My stiff legs complain, but they soon loosen up, flowing with freshly digested energy. The high banks of the southern Ribble seawalls direct me quickly into the city centre, once Europe's largest inland dock. The spires of Preston Minster get taller than the electrical transmission towers across the river. It is only a mile to the hotel, through the shock of an urban rush hour after a long day's walk. Cars are impatient foreign objects, tooting at the pedestrians crossing the road to the station. The sheer number of humans overwhelms a lone walker more accustomed to solitude, until I close the door to the plain, white-walled hotel bedroom.

The chaos fades as I leave via the north bank in the morning. Arctic terns are fishing in the river. They lift and fall with each wing beat like elegant angels on puppet strings, dancing above the water's surface before plunging into the river to strike their prey. The cycle path offers the prospect of a quick exit but gets obliterated by a new bypass roadworks. I must climb a few fences and cross private fields to reach Clifton. My bare legs get stung by nettles on the uncleared, unused paths, but a traffic-free single-track lane soon guides me into the village. It is time to order a proper breakfast, a local construction of bacon, bread, butter and sauce.

'Bacon buttie, please, and a mug of tea,' I ask, my decision made after studying the options.

'Barm or bread, brown or ketchup?' asks Matt, chef, who has just walked from the kitchen to take my order.

'Errr – what's a barm?' He holds up a soft white roll. 'Ah, I see. That's a new name for me. I wonder how many names there are for a bread roll?' I start to memorise a few, and vocalise to Matt. 'Stotties in Carlisle, a cob down south, a muffin in London, morning rolls in Scotland ...' But he interrupts me.

'It's a barm round here, mate,' he declares as I add it to my list.

I cross a busy A road and walk back into the enveloping silence as I approach the estuary again. The marshland path is covered in flotsam and jetsam, suggesting an impassable route on a spring high tide. I reach Warton Aerodrome, the birthplace of many iconic British fighter jets: the English Electric Lightning and Canberra, SEPECAT Jaguar, Panavia Tornado, Eurofighter Typhoon and a personal favourite, which never saw service – the BAC TSR-2.

It is a muddy route around the security fences, with rubber tyre bridges and cattle-trodden mud at the stiles. I must make friends with dairy cows to reach a gate – their enormous tongues seek salt as I offer my hand as a gesture of peace. It is a relief to reach the seawall to Lytham through a final swing gate plastered with grumpy signs: 'no cycling', 'no dog fouling', 'dogs kill livestock', 'keep dogs under control', 'this is a public footpath only'. This farmer is obviously fed up with those without common sense and who need an explicit reminder. The route gets busier and firmer underfoot as I approach the Lytham Windmill and turn north. My estuary days are over until Lancaster.

It is a Saturday. Every promenade bench is occupied by couples with homemade sandwiches in Tupperware boxes and flasks of coffee, with a cup lid to share. The fast-food restaurants have queues, and my hopes of a cosy chippy with an indoor table are remote. I sit to study the options next to a sign with one of the best what3words addresses I have come across: ///*seagulls.shatters.argue*. I walk inland, searching for The Seafarers restaurant, its location gleaned from Google Maps. They have a table, the place buzzes with conversation, and people are smiling. I order a seafood basket and start people-watching as I wait.

It seems to be an Italian-run wonder, with three or four generations present. Grandfather is sitting in a prime spot, overseeing activities. His son (I assume) is busy taking orders, the kids are running about holding soggy chips in their hands and cannot settle, a baby is held sleeping in a mother's arms. This is a family business where they care about service and quality. I pick my way through a platter of prawns, cod, haddock and squid, fried in breadcrumbs or battered, served with sauces and skinny fries. The elderly couple next to me are so fully absorbed in their meal that they never speak once until, at the end, we smile and look at each other.

'I think this is possibly the best chippy in the UK,' we all declare with enthusiasm.

The polka-dot nettle welts are refusing to heal. Not a good look as I arrive in Blackpool walking alongside a long line of cars stuck in a traffic jam. They are overheating on the first warm sunny weekend of the year. Their engine fans whirr, or their starter motors revive idle engines automatically when they select first gear. The tramway terminus marks the start of an endless promenade and the hedonistic delights of this seaside town. I can slow the pace and mingle, stopping at the source of the intense light I wondered about in Southport. It is a slowly rotating mirror ball: 47,000 tiles glued to a six-metre-diameter globe. The sun is the light source, reflecting intense beams at a thousand different angles. Almost certainly, one will shine on Southport every few seconds. This huge, outrageous heliograph announces your arrival in Blackpool and is a taster for the brash, neon, in-your-face architecture to follow.

My senses are hijacked. Passengers scream with delight on the roller coaster and bodies are catapulted into the air on enormous rubber bands. You can while away your time in any number of amusement arcades, sea worlds, pirate islands or 10-pence bingo halls – all designed to extract your money in exchange for the promise of a thrill. This is daytime, and the place erupts at night. In the absence of the sun, the mirror ball will be lit by laser, casting a complex digital rainbow matrix over the buildings. A semi-religious light cross forms on these globes, a subtle talisman for this church of pleasure. The neon cathedral-like steel Blackpool Tower dominates the shoreline, reaching into the sky above all others. I thought Brighton was bonkers, but this is on a completely new level.

My night dreams hum with the bedroom foundations that resonate with the rhythm from nearby drum and bass nightclubs, spinning their audiences into euphoric trances. I wake early to witness the clean-up and early-morning trams, the artwork fresh and inspiring: cotton-bud steel sculptures, carpets of comedian names, waterwork nets and tide organs. I march double time to Fleetwood, for I would like to catch a train home today for a break. The road sweepers mow the promenade of evidence of nightly exuberance, and a few joggers ply the concrete. I wave at those I recognise, returning to their starting points.

A comical highlight of the day comes from a drunk on the path above.

'Fucking beef-packer,' he slurs at me. I laugh, for I have had worse from the opposite spectrum of society who voice their disapproval of any oddity that doesn't fit their world view. To some, I am a stray, leading a non-conformist existence. Yet, most conversations are great. Many people are genuinely interested in your journey and willing to share their knowledge of their home or holiday destination.

I arrive at Rossall Point National Coastwatch Institute lookout station, a meeting point for the Morecambe Bay Partnership Bay Lines and *Beach of Dreams* showcase project in a few weeks. My pace is a ridiculous eight miles in under two hours on the flat concrete promenade. The path through the houses to the bus stop is lined with garage sales being picked over by neighbours – a mass recycling, reuse, repair opportunity that buzzes with enthusiasm and chat. A bus returns me to Blackpool North station, and a rapid train carries me home via London. Earbuds in, the train oscillates to a trip-hop track that spins my mind, echoing Blackpool nights. I can reflect on my journey from Chester around the Wirral, along the Mersey, singing to *Eurovision*, skipping in the sand to Southport, the people of Preston and the madness of Blackpool to finally reach Fleetwood and stare at the enormity of Morecambe Bay.

# 13
# FLEETWOOD TO BARROW-IN-FURNESS
## Flying the flag

*'I hate who steals my solitude without, in exchange, offering me true company.'*
Friedrich Nietzsche

**Distance walked: 1,480 miles**

The sheer scale of Morecambe Bay doesn't register at first – it just looks like an awkward week of walking around the estuaries that drain the Dales and the Lakes into the Irish Sea. Looking at the map, I would have to make my own path to reach bridgeheads, knowing that crossing the sands requires the right tide conditions and a guide.

I join a group of walkers, artists, journalists and filmmakers supporting the Morecambe Bay Partnership project to walk the bay over the next week or so. It is unusual to be with others, and my expectations are low, but my eyes are opened when I spend half an hour with a local fisherman who has come along to see us off at Rossall Point Tower – an angular concrete peg building in the seawall, leaning into the sea, observing.

'What can you see?' the fisherman asks, pointing west.

'Well, the tide is coming in. That looks like Heysham power station, and that is Barrow-in-Furness.'

'Yes but look at the water.'

'Just looks flat today, with little wind and lovely blue skies.'

'Ah, but see that dark line? The water is flowing in a channel; it'll reverse soon, and another channel will open, flowing in another direction. The tide is weaving its way into the bay.' I could begin to see the shape of the incoming tide as it began its journey; it had a long way to go to reach the high-water line.

'What did you catch?' I ask.

'Shrimp mostly, but plaice, cod, ling and bass too – most things,' replies the fisherman. 'It's a very dangerous place: the sands change constantly, new channels form, quicksand is common, wind and tide construct games, and you need to know how to play,' he says with a warning tone.

It is a capricious landscape. I listen with fascination to a local who brings this seascape view to life, noticing things I would miss. It is as if he were a sea creature that had just emerged from the bay and was speaking to me about his world. I may know the land and see fields, forests, and mountains with many birds, plants, and insects. But he knows and has lived the sea and is tuned into this counterpart world: his knowledge of angling, sea fishing, tides, undersea obstacles, drift and weather opens my eyes and teaches me a healthy respect for its dangers.

As part of the Morecambe Bay Partnership project, 50 *Beach of Dreams* silk flags have been planted on the beach, each representing a personal story from the previous project on the Essex coastline – examples of what they hoped to achieve in the bay. These are the very same pennants mentioned by the people I met in Suffolk. They look beautiful: each flag flying with a personal message; together they're a collection of voices that speak to each other and to the observer – a metaphor for a community with something to say. This is how Ali Pretty conceptualised the project, inspired by the broken fragments on the Thames Estuary – offering hope for the future of our coastal communities. The plan over the coming weeks is to walk 120 miles, gather 120 stories around the bay and make 120 new silk flags – engaging anyone with something to say, letting them express their concerns and fears for the bay's future. I have joined them for a few days to walk to Arnside. It will be a different walking experience as we will meet people and listen – encouraging them to sign up and make a flag.

Art and walking go together; the interplay is a powerful friendship that stimulates your emotions and gets you thinking. Walking is an artistic expression on its own, but with visual, written or musical triggers it will multiply in power. Just before the NCI tower, the *Mythic Coast* installation keeps me wondering as I walk north. An ogre, his paddle, a shipwreck memorial, a giant shell – all make you stop to read and contemplate their presence in the landscape. This is the *Sea Swallow* – a particularly poignant artwork. It makes me think of rising sea levels and the power of a storm. Etched into a concrete seawall, a little girl faces a wave transforming into a stream of swallow birds, saying:

*Mary held out the shell,*
*Through her hands were shaking.*
*Still the tidal wave rose*
*Higher and higher.*

*The birds flew to the shore, free of wave tips:*
*When there's cobwebs in the sky,*
*It's a warning from the deep:*
*For down where sailors weep*
*The sea is rising high!*

It is a work conceived by Stephen Broadbent for the Wyre coastline, bringing to life the sea defence work, culminating in the Rossall Point Tower building. The story is told in a book, *The Sea Swallow*, a copy of which was given to 4,200 local schoolchildren. These works, and others I have seen in the past two years, have greatly impacted my relationship with the coast, stimulating thought, reflection and imagination – a philosophical context in a physical landscape. Incredibly, I am now part of a similar artistic endeavour as the Morecambe Bay Partnership charity kicks off the Bay Lines walk from Fleetwood.

We walk east to catch the ferry to Knott End-on-Sea, saving a walk around the Wyre Estuary for another day. It is easy to talk openly with our fellow walkers who have lived in the area. I am a transitory individual who will only see the path for a moment in time, but they have lived in this space for decades and have seen the changes: different weather and climate, new industries and different people. That experience connects them closely with their environment; they can tell stories you would otherwise miss, and they have a dimension of time that I do not.

Andy is a pilot for Glasson Dock and Heysham. We chat about the new Isle of Man ferry commissioning before it can enter the port, training their captains to navigate the vagaries of the bay. His knowledge of the interplay between tide, weather and the shifting bathymetry is crucial for safety, but like the fisherman I met earlier, he is of the sea, a life spent navigating these waters in all conditions. Nicola joins too and is our guide for the day. My eyes open to the diversity of flora as she describes wild carrots, hemlock, hawthorn and all manner of wildflowers I would normally ignore. I am in awe of her passion for the subject. It is thirsty walking and talking, yet we decline to stop at the Farm Yard Brew microbrewery, who pour perfect chilled glasses of hoppy ale, for we have a few more miles to go.

A lighthouse sits alone on Plover Scar to warn shipping of the hidden rock at the entrance to the River Lune. The nearby Cockersand Abbey ruins hint at the community that once lived on this isolated salt marsh headland, the past a forgotten country. Some of us carry on to Lancaster, pinballing along the cycle path after a quick visit to the Dalton Arms at Glasson Dock – our resolve weakened as our dreams of a pint tease our thirsts. Refreshed and emboldened, our pace quickens along the River Lune, but we arrive late in the evening. It has been an unusual day for me; I talked more than I walked, but the experience is relaxing and a change from my usual pattern of coastal walking. I am with others and not alone in my contemplations – less introspective, taking energy from those around me.

The high tide will cover the road through Lades Marsh in a few hours, so the group, with many new members, starts early to reach Sunderland Point. This sleepy village is an orphaned port, superseded by Glasson Dock in the mid-18th century, complementing the Port of Lancaster – once the fourth largest west-coast trading dock for goods circulating in the slave-trade triangle. Rum, sugar and mahogany arrived; textiles, manufactured goods and weapons departed. Our guide expands on this history and tells us an exciting story.

'During 1736, or thereabouts, a captain left his African cabin boy in the village while he conducted his business in Lancaster,' he begins. 'The boy, believing he had been abandoned in a strange land, refused to eat or drink and caught a fever. He died frightened, afraid of his fate, hiding in the rafters of this building.' The guide points to the door of Upsteps Cottage. 'A local farmer offered his land, where rabbits roamed, as a burial site, as he had not been christened and was therefore not eligible for the church graveyard. You can find him along this path,' he says as he points north.

Curious to explore further, I walk alone down the overgrown track across the fields as the group diverts to see other cottages and the quayside. Spookily, rabbits run from the field edge as I approach the shoreline and turn to find his grave. It reads, 'Here lies Poor SAMBO, a faithful NEGRO, who DIED on his arrival at SUNDERLAND' (capital letters preserved). The derogatory term remains inscribed on a 300-year-old brass plate donated by a chaplain from money raised for a formal gravestone. The plot is adorned with flowers and painted stones. He is fondly and rightly remembered:

> *Full sixty Years the angry Winter's Wave*
> *Has thundering dashed this bleak & barren Shore*
> *Since SAMBO's Head laid in this lonely GRAVE*
> *Lies still & ne'er will hear their turmoil more.*
> *Full many a Sandbird chirps upon the Sod*
> *And many a Moonlight Elfin round him trips*
> *Full many a Summer's Sunbeam warms the Clod*
> *And many a teeming Cloud upon him drips.*
> *But still he sleeps – till the awakening Sounds*
> *Of the Archangel's Trump new Life impart*
> *Then the GREAT JUDGE his Approbation founds*
> *Not on Man's COLOR but his WORTH of HEART.*
>                                  James Watson Scr.     H.Bell del. 1796

This poignant reminder is a treasure, reminding us of the cruelties of a past generation and an empire built on exploiting fellow humans and natural resources. Near the grave is a camera obscura, commissioned by Morecambe Bay Partnership and created by the land artist Chris Drury. The *Horizon Line Chamber* is a massive cairn shelter – an upturned stone hull. You enter and close the door behind you. The darkness envelops you, and then you notice an image appear.

The lens projects an inverted image on the wall. The sky becomes the sea, the sea becomes the sky, divided by the coastal marsh where cattle roam in from opposite directions. My visual frame is stolen and replaced with an unusual image of the littoral zone. I am taken to a place that brings together my coastal journey, here in the moment, all distractions removed. It is a moving experience that turns to dread as I sense in this image that the sea has dominion. It is ascendant, and a subtle warning of rising sea levels, as if biblical floods have come early.

Emerging into the sunlight, I find the group at the shingle point and retrace my steps along the beach. The nuclear power station draws us towards its form, as if gravity has shifted its axis to the mass contained within. We arrive at Heysham and ease our way into Morecambe and the promenade. Eric (Morecambe), the comedian and national treasure, has brought the sunshine; his statue in a signature static-skating pose draws queues for a photograph. All try to emulate the stance, but no one can match his comedic impact. Everyone is singing 'Bring me sunshine in your smile, bring me laughter, all the while,' his joyful, uplifting, hopeful lyrics.

Our day draws to a close. The Lake District fells are illuminated by the setting sun, each peak named in complementary warm tones on a cast iron sculpture relief on the promenade. This north-seaward perspective is new to me. These hills will soon cleave me from the backbone of England as I follow their western shores, but for now, I approach the southern flanks of the Lake District mountain range, encircling the catchments that feed the sands of the bay. The freshwater mixes with salt in channels that are flushed twice daily. Each tide holds a volume of water that would take 10 days to flow over Niagara Falls, yet fills the bay in six hours.

To time a walk to Hest Bank to meet a guide to walk across the bay is too much to ask. The conditions must be right, and you cannot contemplate a walk without expert local knowledge. The formal departure point is now at Arnside, our destination for the day. Michael Wilson, the King's Guide to the Kent Estuary, was appointed in 2007 as the 26th guide since 1548. I need to book a future date to do the route, for the experience must be wonderful. The three-mile cross-sand walk would save me a day, but I must navigate to Sampool Bridge. I will worry about the route details later as we weave around the salt marsh, listening to the cooing eider ducks 'aw-woo, aw-woo, aw-woo' -ing in the creeks.

We come to the *Praying Shell* memorial, a sculpture by Anthony Padgett that sits near Red Bank. It is a limestone cockleshell in human form, in deep contemplation, opening its heart to the tide in communion with the natural world – seeking solace, and perhaps forgiveness. It is a reminder of the day 23 undocumented Chinese migrant cockle pickers drowned in 2004. A human disaster. The consequence of modern-day slavery, lack of care and the unpredictability of the shifting sands.

After a pleasant lunch at RSPB Leighton Moss, the Lancashire Coastal Way guides us through Silverdale and over the crags to Arnside. It is a welcome climb, giving stunning views of the channels weaving between the sandbanks. We stop to hear the story of the Morecambe Bay Tragedy of 1894 when 34 passengers lost their lives after the *Matchless* pleasure boat capsized during a freak gust of wind. If you couldn't swim, you drowned. Only nine survived; it shook the community as the scale of the tragedy unfolded – the recovered bodies filling the makeshift morgues. The bay looks entirely innocent on a glorious day, which is perhaps its danger. This isn't a raging sea but a treacherous illusion that swallows its victims slowly

A week later, I am back at Arnside Station without the group, and with plenty of time to walk to Gretna in Scotland. A rail service that hugs the coast will ferry me to and from Barrow-in-Furness from any convenient station. This strategy means I can find cheap accommodation and travel light and fast as far as Maryport. I have booked three nights in Barrow-in-Furness (just called Barrow locally), a shipbuilding town at the end of the Furness peninsula, a cul-de-sac on England's western coastline and the northern extent of Morecambe Bay.

There are plans to add cycle paths to the rail bridges on the Kent and Leven viaducts, which would shorten the Bay Cycle Way and this walk. The National Cycle Network Routes 70 and 700 will be companions for a few days, as will a forgotten Cumbrian Coastal Way, its fingerposts rotting and often hidden. The path will fade to memory when the King Charles III England Coast Path is determined and approved. Until then, single-track lanes, dual carriageways and the A-roads' side paths are the only options to Levens, where I cross the River Kent and then the River Gilpin at Sampool Bridge.

I reach a seawall – the now common artificial embankments that protect the land from the sea, marshland now turned to productive fields for crops or cattle. You are exposed to wind and rain, walking a few metres above the landscape. There is no shelter or bench to rest on, no tree for shade, no rock or bush to hide behind. The endless wall extends into the distance, your only path, and monotonous walking until it diverts inland to Meathop, a small farming village offering a brief glimpse of Arnside.

The sun comes out at Grange-over-Sands, a former fishing port on the Cartmel Peninsula, transformed by the arrival of the railway into a Victorian seaside town. It is an ideal stop for a decent lunch which I can digest as I amble down the promenade that interweaves with the rail line. The lido is closed and fenced off but may one day be saved and offer an opportunity to bathe and gaze across the bay from its seawater pool – floating between the beauty of the fells, tidal marshes and sands of the bay. It is an Art Deco decadent delight in a perfect location and screaming 'help me' for restoration.

I can see Humphrey Head and can't wait to ascend this outcrop island for it is one of the best views in England. I shuffle around the marsh to the farm, taking care not to plunge into hidden culverts. It is a short climb through cattle to the viewpoint at 53 metres, which is enough to reveal a multi-layer mirage of shifting sinusoidal sand, sea and tidal channels that can be seen for nine miles to Heysham 1 and Heysham 2. These four AGRs (advanced gas-cooled reactors) shimmer in the haze, their unworldly energy somehow visible. Blackpool Tower stands 21 miles further, still calling you to investigate its delights. I rest alone, lying on the grass with my hands behind my head, contemplating this scene, accompanied by soaring swifts, whose soprano shrill entertains and thrills as they carve joyful arcs through the crystal blue sky.

I am joined by a retired outdoor leader who volunteers at the nearby centre. He is intrigued by the silk flag I carry, on loan from a storyteller I met on the walk. He bemoans the plight of the younger generations.

'It is a challenge to get them to just sit still for a moment,' he says. 'They're glued to their smartphones while ignoring all the wonder around them. These devices have hijacked their lives.'

'You should tell that story. The Morecambe Bay Partnership invites people to adopt a flag like this, create a design, and even paint and dye it at a workshop. You can share your concerns and meet the coastal community. Then you can carry it, like I am, and walk with them to weekly gatherings, where you can learn from others and perhaps act.'

I give him a card still in my pocket, hoping he will sign up. We walk off the outcrop to the lanes. I plod on to Flookburgh and turn south to the marshlands and a new seawall. A low afternoon light shimmers across an incoming tide; the inland grasses whisper their wisdom in response, and I join them in meditation for the final miles of a 28-mile day to Cark station. The coastal train west introduces Cartmel Sands, as the carriage crosses the viaduct, a shortcut for the estuary route that will take all morning to complete tomorrow.

My Barrow B&B is anonymous, unattended and empty but meets the fundamental requirement of comfort and quiet once I have decoded the door lock. Fully rested, I walk to the station and disembark at Cark half an hour later. I am resigned to a long road walk but see a CCW (Cumbrian Coastal Way) waymark inviting me into the fells. It takes me on a ridge route to Haverthwaite Bridge, where I can rejoin Cycle Route 70. It is great to be in the fells at How Barrow. The view at 170 metres is something I haven't experienced since Devon. I can see Cartmel and Greenodd Sands, coloured with the Silurian silt that drains from the Furness Fells, Lake Windermere and Coniston Water. Impossibly cute, Zwartbles sheep munch in the fields, their black bodies highlighted with white faces and paint-dipped tails and legs. I sing 'Zwarties' when I see them like I shout 'Belties' when I come across a field of Belted Galloway cattle; such is the delight to encounter them. I descend from Bigland Tarn through broken woodland and ease along the track to a footbridge that brings me to the village at Greenodd, where a lady tending her window plants stops me for a chat.

'Why the flag?' she asks.

'This is Henry's flag – Henry Fletcher. It represents his work as an artist when he built stone cairns in Iceland and copied the form at Thorpeness in Suffolk. He writes about it, too. I met him on a walk around Morecambe Bay as part of the Bay Lines project. I'm supposed to be drumming up interest for anyone who wants to tell their story about how they care for their bit of coastline'.

'How interesting,' she says as I write the Morecambe Bay Partnership website address on paper, having run out of cards.

'If you're walking to Ulverston, it's a pity it's not low tide, as you can pick out a route to Canal Foot around the shoreline. It's a lovely walk, full of birds in the winter, serene and silent, passable with care.'

Individually they are subversive, undeniable, expressive and thoughtful stitches – hand-woven, silk batik, naturally dyed pennants –

artistic forms that fly beautifully in the breeze. They communicate with the unconscious; they are a call to action, individual talismanic symbols that multiply in power when you see several hundred together. In a few weeks, some 500 will fly near Allonby, 500 undeniable individual stories floating in the breeze. I hope to time my arrival to help.

I enjoy walking along the high-tide hedgerow lane route to Ulverston Canal Lock – the headwater of a canal that once connected sea trade with the market town. Even though it is raining, the birds entertain, playing hide and seek and following me like robins. The road reaches the estuary at Plumpton Bight and follows the meandering channel to the lock gate. The remains of *Nance* lie inland, a half-deck, or nobby fishing vessel, designed to catch sprawns (pink shrimps), brown prawns and flatfish, and her 34-foot wooden skeleton is a reminder of days before the modern industries of the area. It has a simple form that is very distant from vessels built down the road in Barrow. It is an early incarnation of the most complex engineering structures ever built in this country: submersible weapons of war that can spend months undetected in the oceans of the world.

The tide is rising, and the shoreline anglers are out in force to snare the unwary that come in with the flood tide to feed. I follow the high-water mark along the shingle; progress is slow as the pebbles shift, and I pick my way between the weeds. Occasionally, the path weaves between the trees inland but it is tough going. Old, rusting tractors, whose condition looks terminal, are still used to haul catches from the bay, their hulks taking on a sea-battered texture of the salty sands, one day to become part of the minerals on the shoreline. I stop to eat, waiting for the ebbing tide to drain in the channels and reveal an easier sand route. It takes a while, and I can't wait that long. So I splash through the shallows with increasing abandon, soaking my shoes. I am guided by a navigation needle standing 20 metres high in the salt marsh. It is the only surviving example of 13 beacons built around Barrow and signals my approach to the docks.

My feet dry quickly on the road to Roa Island and the lifeboat station, housed on the end of a tidal cotton-bud breakwater that leads to the strategically important Piel Island, a monastic outpost that guards the harbour. I don't have time to catch the ferry to visit the Ship Inn but return to walk the five miles into Barrow, past dockland and reservoir to the suburbs and my B&B. I'm exhausted. It's a 70,000-plus-step day, 11 hours of walking, probably amounting to 33 miles. I barely have the energy to shop, eat and shower before sleeping deeply, despite the appalling and frankly disturbing holographic pictures of Hollywood starlets that haunt my room.

Before leaving Barrow, I travel pack-free and speed-walk around Walney Island for the day, safe in the knowledge that the King Charles III England Coast Path is fully open. I'm feeling remarkably fit considering yesterday's exertions. I walk down to the town, past Wetherspoon's, which is full at 7am with regulars holding pints of half-drained lager. I follow the 700 cycle route across Devonshire Dock, hoping to glimpse Britain's latest nuclear deterrent. It is empty, yet behind those warehouse doors lie £2 billion Astute Class attack submarines, nearing completion. Nearby lies an £8 billion, 17,200-tonne, Dreadnought Class ballistic nuclear missile submarine that will carry 12 Trident 2 D5 nuclear missiles, each of those carrying four W76 warheads with a yield of 100 kilotonnes, each of those six times the power of the device that exploded above Hiroshima on 6th August 1945. Each vessel will have 400 times the destructive power carried by the B-29 *Enola Gay* on that fateful day, or 4,000 times if loaded with eight W88 475 kilotonne warheads the missile can carry – the precise capabilities are secret, if somewhat academic. These calculated yields are beyond comprehension, technical specifications on paper that don't communicate their power. The few surviving Japanese hibakusha of those events 80 years ago are dying. They are the last first-account witnesses who can attest to the power and horror of atomic weapons. If the world experiences a full thermo-nuclear exchange, we will have no need of memory, and will no longer treasure time – for the living will envy the dead.

Maybe I should pop back to Wetherspoon's and think about that, but my path starts around Walney Island, which I choose to walk clockwise. The path waymarks consist of painted marks along the quiet roads, lined by sections that have bloomed into spectacular wildflower verges: poppies, dandelions, cowslips, daisies and more than I can name. It's as if someone had poured a bag of birdseed on the roadside. I follow the King Charles III England Coast Path fingerpost away from the lighthouse, which I plan to walk to another day with binoculars to see the birdlife in the ponds and marshes. Cumbria County Council opened its purse to establish story boxes on posts. You press a button, and a voice describes the history and ecology of the scene before you. Meanwhile, you scan a QR code link for YouTube drone footage of the shoreline to accompany the voice. It is a nice installation to while away the moments as you snack on an energy bar.

The coastline is eroding in the face of storms from the Irish Sea. Huge wind farms dominate the western skyline, converting wind energy to electrical current. This same wind energy creates the waves that have no difficulty converting shoreline fields to shingle in a storm. An orphaned fence line measures what winter brought earlier in the year. This coast is exposed, yet the island protects the industry of Barrow. It is a spring high tide, so walking around the northern headland is impossible. The alternative route takes you through the inland dunes, lakes and marshes overlooking North Walney National Nature Reserve.

I rest in an uncut meadow, letting the beetles and bugs explore my exposed arms, legs and face. The underlying vegetation seeks purchase through my clothing, and the grasses gently needle or brush my skin – an endless tickling sensation of nature communicating with me. I absorb her message and sink deeper into her embrace, drifting off to sleep for half an hour in a deep, timeless dream. I wake naturally, rested and somehow wiser for the experience of connecting with the Earth and her creatures. If the attachments we seek in family are absent, we can always rely on a connection to nature. It is important we are close to it, and it is important that we protect it – for it is the foundation of our existence and will always be there for us, if we protect it.

The tide has covered the path, but an inland route is available to Jubilee Bridge. The water level shuffles the abandoned boats to turn them over to rot in another position. Tidewater flows into their shells, and rust and diluted decay floats out. Shimmering rainbows of diesel and oil leak endlessly from their pores. They are forlorn, forgotten victims of a lack of interest and expensive maintenance schedules – their owners long since abandoning them for other pastimes. I cross to Barrow, fill my pack at the supermarket with goodies and return to my holograms. Wetherspoon's is heaving with customers still. I wonder how many have been there since morning, yet to make peace with the weaponry under construction a mile from their table.

# 14
# BARROW-IN-FURNESS TO GRETNA
## Cockcroft's Folly

*'In all chaos there is a cosmos, in all disorder a secret order.'*
Carl Jung

**Distance walked: 1,610 miles**

A no-nonsense 'Baguette Me Not' sandwich bar is busy with shipyard workers ordering subbie sandwiches before they build their own composite metal submarines. This trail-angel (help that appears in time of need, as if by magic) takeaway appears as I begin to lose hope of a decent lunch; the tuna mayo monster probably has enough calories to get me to Gretna alone and fits perfectly in an outside pocket, triple wrapped.

As I head north, the Kimberly-Clark paper hygiene factory is steaming away, preparing for another pandemic toilet-roll panic-buying frenzy. I leave the industry of Barrow behind, walking around a waste management plant back to nature. The indistinct path to Lowsy Point leads to a lost world of wooden huts, ideal accommodation for a witness protection programme. It is remote, leading to a path that opens onto a glorious beach and the dunes of Sandscale Rabbit Warren. There are no footprints after the tide swept the beach this morning as I am the first to walk north. I come across a ringed plover egg and back away from the dry shoreline. Their superb camouflage defeats predators and clumsy blind walkers like me, and the wet sand seems a good bet to avoid them. I turn east to view the majestic vista of the Lakeland fells, lit by reflected light from the estuarial sands.

It's a beautiful sight, but trouble is brewing, for persistent property developers seek to monetise this natural wonder. The National Trust,

Friends of the Lake District, RSPB, Wildlife and Wetland Trusts and many concerned individuals have a compelling case to protect this landscape from the development of 233 lodge holiday homes. These remote, sensitive dune-land estuaries are irreplaceable and critical for wildlife. The developer's spreadsheets will focus on yields and profit but will not account for the total environmental cost and the debt owed to future generations. Wildfowl and reptiles, plovers, knots, pintails, redshanks and natterjack toads all living in this habitat they call home will be at risk. It is one of the most striking reveals for a coastal walker as you turn the headland and gaze up the Duddon Estuary. The view is unique – a perspective of the Lakes viewable from a northern shoreline, lit by the arc of a southern sun, revealing texture and detail in the landscape. It is heart-achingly beautiful and must be protected.

I walk under the long-abandoned slag pier at Askam and hope the path will take me to the bridgehead. The Ordnance Survey map has red-dotted footpath routes arcing in all directions, but you would be a fool to follow them across treacherous sand and shifting salt marshes and channels. People are walking in this scene, fishing, cockling, but they know what they are doing. The Dunnerholme Golf Club has put in friendly signposts for walkers, and I can see white-headed posts in the distance, so a path exists. I must be careful not to get trapped by a rail line and the way is uncertain. I need not worry, for I meet Graham, who walks up to meet me. His collie dog sits at my feet, having corralled a stray in the flock.

'Hello, are you walking far?' Graham asks.

'Yes, around the coast of England,' I reply. 'I started this section from Arnside last week. Do you know a route to Millom, as the England Coast Path isn't marked until they finalise their plans?'

'Oh, yes, yes – just follow my posts,' he smiles as he points north. 'On reaching the rail line, walk to Kirkby and pop over the bridge; Pam's Café is excellent… Oh, wait a moment, she isn't open on Fridays.'

'What's with the flag?' he asks.

I tell him the story about Morecambe Bay, and we drop into an easy conversation about my journey, but more importantly, he has a fascinating story to tell.

'During the pandemic, everyone wanted to get outside,' he says. 'But the path through the marsh was a bit dodgy. So, we got some posts and painted them with white tops to show the way. We even built a bridge across a small creek. There was no need to tell the council; they couldn't help then, and we had our walk to think about. It's a public path, just a bit overgrown and little used. Many people use it now, and we have formed a little walking group.' He starts to smile with pride. 'Molly here has been a wonder. I wouldn't have made it without her. She gets me out walking every day.'

'That's wonderful,' I reply.

There are tears in our eyes. He doesn't speak to many people, and I haven't spoken to many either, but we have connected. An unspoken bond has formed, a common love of walking and the outdoors. His experience during the lonely months has rejuvenated the local community; it is a small-scale victory. We have witnessed each other and how our lives have changed because of walking. We don't have to explain it; we feel it – kindred spirits talking in the marshlands. The coast is our compass and has shown the way for both of us.

Graham clips a lead to Molly and walks south; I follow the white-tipped posts north, passing an empty and closed Pam's Café. The route to Duddon Bridge is awkward and messy, a collection of paths, single-track lanes and dangerous A road until I can relax again on a familiar seawall. The King Charles III England Coast Path is open from Green Road Station until Allonby, so I can relax and put the map away. I reach the town and then skirt around the Hodbarrow Lagoon on a seawall built to protect the mines from flooding, and now it is a haven for wild birds and pleasure craft. Little terns are fishing along the shore. These beautiful, delicate birds are quick and nimble, thumping into the water's surface to stun their prey. They are gathering with other terns in the safety of the sandbank opposite, filling the air with earnest twitter. I could turn east to my accommodation, but I have some miles left in my legs, and the sun is out. It is warm, calm and even balmy. A vanilla ice cream cone from a pop-up van is the perfect pick-me-up treat before I head west around Haverigg Point.

I walk along the beach and leave civilisation again. Before turning inland, I check the train times and realise I can afford a nap instead of waiting on a station bench. I remove my shoes and socks and lie on the beach. The air refreshes my toes. My steaming socks dry downwind, and my back folds into the valley I have dug in the shingle with my hands.

## THE COAST IS OUR COMPASS

The warm pebbles hold me as I close my eyes. My senses relax one by one, switching off as if I am drifting off to sleep. Only my stereoscopic hearing remains to follow the gently breaking waves as they peel down the shoreline from right to left, creating a pleasurable synasthetic hallucination as the sea reveals her time-bottled secrets from the depths in treble and bass tones. I must be tired, sedated by the endorphins pulsing through my veins.

The train arrives, and five minutes later I am back at Millom, searching for a stained-glass window that Graham told me to see at St George's Church. Thankfully, the heavy, wooden, unlocked door opens and I latch it closed behind me. It is an empty, silent sanctuary for a weary walker. I leave my pack and poles at the doorway, remove my cap and explore to find the magnificent Nicholson window on the north wall. The late sun casts a rainbow shadow into the church through the glass mosaic. It is a memorial to Norman Nicholson, a local poet, born in 1914. He lived in the town, writing and walking the coastline. Every panel reflects his work, his words etched into sections of the glass – showing samples of his poetry, beautifully interpreted in images by the artist Christine Boyce:

> *When the sea's to the west*
> *The evenings are one dazzle –*
> *You can find no sign of water.*
> *Sun upflows the horizon;*
> *Waves of shine*
> *Heave, crest, fracture.*
> *Explode on the shore;*
> *The wide day burns.*
> *In the incandescent mantle of the air.*
> Norman Nicholson, extract from *Sea to the West* (1981)

I had seen this image and felt those words an hour earlier as I lay on the beach before walking to Silecroft Station. It is a perfect end to a day. I walk past his house in St George's Terrace to my accommodation and spend an evening reading his poetry on my phone, finally succumbing to the rest I need.

The following morning counterposes the late afternoon dazzle of the Irish Sea, with celestial sunbeams radiating through the clouds from the heavens over the fells. Black Combe casts a backlit shadow from its peak at 600 metres. The vivid, radiant display is uplifting and spiritual, enhanced by the onshore sea breeze blowing waveforms across the barley fields. Movement in the sky, mountains and fields captivates me; their contrasting patterns paint a moving picture. It is Bridget Riley artwork in action again. I am rewarded by an early start and can immerse myself in the stunning outdoor art gallery that surrounds me.

The beach is empty, for this is a long, lonely section isolated by the West Coast rail line. Dead guillemots are now frequent, and the pernicious avian flu is devastating this year's seabird population. The beauty of these birds at close range is overwhelming: remarkably intricate feather textures and intense colours. If more people could witness this juxtaposition with death, they might be motivated to act – for what would life be, without birds?

The tide is receding, and I am anxious about the lack of bridges ahead. Even though the King Charles III England Coast Path is declared open along this section, Natural England is calling it too early, for the expensive critical bridges are missing at the River Esk and River Irt, even though the path reaches their banks. These gaps are noted at Selker Bay, with a suggestion that you catch a bus or train. But I take a chance and walk the three miles to Eskmeals Viaduct to ford the river, past severely eroded sea banks that force me on to the beach. I am glad the tide is ebbing. I meet a local man as I descend to the river's edge.

'Safe to cross?' I ask.

'Yes, you'll have no problem,' he answers. 'It's low tide in an hour, and the river level is very low. We haven't had much rain.' I am reminded of the impact of rain on river levels on the estuaries, not just the tides. 'Just follow the line to that bank; it's shingle, not mud, and you'll be fine.' He points to the opposite shore.

It turns out to be a trivial, refreshing crossing, but I suspect I have near-perfect conditions that, on another day, could be lethal. The opposite bank is muddy, but there are convenient ponds in the samphire beds where I can clean my feet and put my shoes back on. The walk into Ravenglass is easier, across drying mudbanks. This former fishing port was once a Roman stronghold, the largest on the Cumbrian coastline, and its bathhouse still stands inland. Nowadays, the main business appears to be second homes and beach cleaning, for a local man has made it a life's work to collect the flotsam and jetsam from the shoreline. Dave has boxes of plastic rubbish on display, all sorted and categorised. A box contains a thousand cigarette lighters, another cotton reels and hard hats, then more bottle tops and inhaler carcasses. His garden hides floats, rope, fishing gear, small boats and larger items – all on display to highlight what happens when litter is discarded thoughtlessly.

As I leave the village, a footpath bridge bolted to the rail line takes me across the River Mite, but the River Irt needs to be forded. Signs leading to the riverbank say 'private land', even though the OS map indicates a route with public access. It is a far more difficult crossing, requiring you to get your feet wet and climb slippery, muddy banks to reach the opposite shore. The alternative packhorse bridge inland is probably easier and safer, and I should have taken that. My feet dry quickly, and I feel comfortable and presentable enough to enter a cafe at Seascale, a mecca for locally made ice cream. I am in time for tea and a toastie, and luckily, I slot on to a table vacated by a couple who have just finished their meal.

Looking at the map, I see that St Bees would be a stretch goal for the day, but several railway stations are available if I get too tired. It is time to walk past Sellafield (formerly Windscale), the most ominous nuclear facility in the country. Once arable fields, these were cleared in 1942 for a high-explosive factory, and then, with the coming of the nuclear age, it became the centre for plutonium production. It is a frightening industrial complex that, over the past 75 years, has processed and stored nuclear materials for energy generation and weaponry. Calder Hall power station delivered the first nuclear energy to a public grid in 1956, the first in the world. The plutonium by-product was used as the first weapons-grade materials for testing programmes and a growing stockpile of missiles and bombs with colourful names like Yellow Sun, Red Beard and Blue Steel. Unfortunately, many unforeseen or unaccounted-for decommissioning costs will continue for centuries – a legacy that outlives the society that responded to the Cold War. Nuclear power in all its forms is an inevitable part of our energy and security needs in the future, but have we released the genie from the bottle and made wishes without understanding the long-term consequences? It is a subject that fascinates me, as my father witnessed the Grapple Z detonations on Christmas Island, in the South Pacific, in 1958.

The second nuclear accident in the world occurred at the site on 10th October 1957 (the first was in Russia, a few days earlier), when a fire released iodine-131, caesium-137 and xenon-133 contaminants into the atmosphere. If it were not for the physicist John Cockcroft's insistence on fitting a scrubber (filter) on the chimney stack, the Lake District and much of western Europe would have been exposed to significant fallout, for the filter caught 95% of the radioactive materials – a fact kept secret until 1988. Even with the filter, it is considered the fourth worst nuclear accident in history. Only Chernobyl, Fukushima and Kyshtym rank higher (in that order) using the International Nuclear and Radiological Event Scale (INES). Cockcroft's Folly, as it was called by those who thought it unnecessary, was not such a folly after all. The PR gurus changed the multi-function nuclear site's name in 1981 in a vain attempt to consign the bad name of Windscale to history.

These facts make me shiver as I walk past the security fencing, looking at the waste transportation trains and carriages collecting the country's nuclear waste for processing. Not from the chilling sea breeze but from the sense of an insidious, invisible death sitting in water tanks or concrete blocks, decaying against a half-life curve with an x-axis measure in decades and often centuries. This innocent coastline holds a secret that could end our existence on this precious planet, for Sellafield is one of the most dangerous locations in the world. I walk away, slipping under the rail line through a tunnel into an isolated and forgotten community of ramshackle huts and shacks built from driftwood and scrap. It is a hideaway where you can light a fire, drink excessively and smoke without bother. I feel like I have entered a post-apocalyptic movie set, a scene from *Mad Max*, where a self-reliant, off-grid life is the future. This is where my mind wanders after the experience of walking past the scary consequences of technological development.

I catch the train to Whitehaven, only to realise my hotel, with the same name, is in Workington, and now the trains for the day are cancelled (duh). I have no choice but to take a taxi, but even the driver struggles to find a route as major road works have closed the A595. The correct

Waverley Hotel, one of many on the coastline, was named after the famous paddle steamer PS *Waverley*, which still tours this coastline. There is another in Maryport. I will visit them all and stay in two.

When I return to St Bees, the train disgorges several other backpackers, which is unusual, as I have seen very few long-distance walkers since Minehead. They're all setting off on Wainwright's Coast to Coast walk, their boots clean and waterproofs crease-free. All have enthusiastic, fresh faces, yet to be tested by the Lakeland fells and weather. I walk alongside a few, and we chat.

'Where are you off to?' I ask.

'Robin Hood's Bay. Should take a couple of weeks. What about you?'

'Same, I guess, but I'll take a little longer. I'm walking the new King Charles III England Coast Path. I've been going for 88 days, starting in Cromer. I've probably done about 1,800 miles so far.'

'Gosh, a path fit for a King. How will you get to the east coast?'

'I'll take a train to Berwick, or maybe I'll walk along Hadrian's Wall and the Pennine Way. I aim to reach Scotland in a few days. I'll decide then.'

The route is very popular, more so than most established National Trails. There are plans to add it to the list in 2026, which will be welcome unless they rename it 'Rishi Sunak's Coast to Coast Way', for it runs through his constituency. Alfred Wainwright's influence is considerable, his 1973 guidebook inspiring thousands to walk the route. It has become a brand and a commercial offering for many walking companies, even though there are many coast-to-coast routes, such as the Southern Upland Way in Scotland. Perhaps his name should be used instead of some politician. I personally dislike naming paths after people, but Wainwright and John Muir deserve to have their names honoured.

The headland reminds me of the South West Coast Path. I have been walking almost at sea level since Minehead and miss the elevation and seascape vistas. The coastline weaves out to the horizon; I sense the Galloway Hills in the distance and can see the working towns of Whitehaven and Workington interrupting the cliff line, their positions betrayed by onshore wind farms. Sculptures, murals and information boards mark the industrial heritage, a reminder of the 19th century Industrial Revolution powered by non-nuclear or non-renewable energy. The coalmine and steelwork pairing produced the raw materials that fuelled and built an empire. Steel was poured from Henry Bessemer's converters to become rail tracks and was exported worldwide. A storyboard tells of a Desert Rat tank sergeant who could read the production code of a Libyan rail line during World War II – triggering homesickness – for he lived in this Cumbrian community.

My five-hour walk from St Bees to Workington took 27 minutes, in reverse, by train this morning. Now, I head north around the back of football grounds and cross the bridge into another wind farm. The scything blades carve ultrasonic arcs in the sky. It doesn't take long to reach Maryport after a brief excursion to help a farmer shepherd a wayward calf into a field, his quad bike and dog working furiously to catch the frightened animal. I stand safely behind the gate to hold it open as the calf walks in to relax and resume feeding next to its admonishing mother. I arrive at the third Waverley Hotel, which is untouched by time, a traditional bar, restaurant and hotel. The locals are sipping pints, discussing the philosophical problems of the day.

'Eh, lad. What do you think? Do you have hot pie and cold custard or hot custard and cold pie?' I am asked, an opening welcome gambit to join them in conversation.

'Err, I like hot pie and hot custard.'

'There, Jack, I told you so!' he declares as if a bet had been placed and he won. I could have stayed with their conversation all night, and it is tempting, but my legs are seizing up, and a deep bath awaits.

Breakfast the next day is traditional, and the experience is unfussed, warm, and untroubled by technology or corporate continuous improvement – as a result, it is relaxing and friendly. The staff are engaged with their work, not replaced with the procedure and process demanded by a corporate time and motion expert.

Maryport's history bleeds through every building. I have missed the annual fair, but the bunting is still aloft, and the town is buzzing. The port was once a Roman supply base for the western extremities of Hadrian's Wall, a substantial fort that protected against attacks across the Solway Firth. The *Alauna Aura* sculpture by the quayside depicts this changing history, as do handcrafted tiles along the harbour walls. The seawall takes me north to the golf course and into Allonby. Here, I find Natural

England staff holding a discovery day to celebrate the opening of the King Charles III England Coast Path from Green Road Station. The *Beach of Dreams* project has their 500 pennants on display, Roman re-enactments are in progress and wildlife telescopes have been set to view the shore. Arts and crafts stalls display their wares in the courtyard of Twentymans Farm, which sells delicious ice cream and has an amazing, automated milkshake dispenser.

It is my luck that the trail officer is around, as are many others with intimate knowledge of the Solway Firth and the route to Gretna. I am pleased to hear that new paths have been built, but signs have not yet been installed. Many fingerposts even have plastic covers awaiting the official launch date. I spend a few hours chatting with people who care about this coastline, and they are very interested in hearing about my journey and the flags on display. It is a happy coincidence, and I stay as long as I dare before I drop down to the beach at low tide and lose myself along a seven-mile section to Silloth.

The beach is utterly deserted. There is not a soul, not a dog walker, no one. The cloudscape and views across the open expanse of sand to the Scottish hills are sublime. A tailwind pushes me gently along. I walk without effort, as if on a sky elevator. The drying sand lifts and drifts into streaks, converging to a focal point. It's a gentle motion that mirrors precisely the golden silk pennant I have wedged in my pack, its silk tail wrapping around my face as the sand wraps around my legs – the wind and I winding our way north.

I stop to find a lee spot behind the sea kale, lie back and stare at the sky. The fractal clouds balloon into new shapes and forms, drifting across my field of view. The sun emerges from the cloud to warm my face and fill my closed eyes with a radiant light. I sit and absorb her energy, second guessing when the next cloud will arrive, without opening my eyes. It makes me feel of this universe – the recipient of a light beam that has travelled for eight minutes and 93 million miles and comes to rest on a supine walker on a lonely beach in north-west England.

I amble further, coming across a driftwood shelter, a perfect *Local Hero*-like structure where you could spend a night under the dark skies. I am approaching Silloth and refer to my map to turn inland to meet a path through the golf course that will bring me back to civilisation. I can take my time because the hotel is nearby, and I am early. A VW campervan-themed cafe is a perfect place to have an early meal. Gary, the host, has got the VW bug bad, having a collection of T1s, T2s, T4s and more. I show him a picture of my 23-year-old VW California, and the conversation doesn't stop for an hour at the expense of other customers seeking to buy postcards or order tea.

'Have the meal on me,' he insists, refusing point-blank to accept my contactless card. 'You're the first England Coast Path walker we have seen, and a VW fanatic too.'

'I shall return and bring my van,' I promise, for we could chat for hours.

I am sure that is the longest beach I have walked on the King Charles III England Coast Path; Burnham-on-Sea was six miles, and this afternoon was more. I start to think of the longest beach section and how it would be measured. Chesil Beach, in Dorset, is 18 miles of shingle hell to walk. But which is the longest single continuous walkable sand beach between the mean high and low water without getting your feet too wet? I keep that thought, for I suspect the Yorkshire or Lincolnshire coast may break the record… or maybe it is Bournemouth? It occupies my mind as I head towards Bowness-on-Solway, across a marshland with indistinct paths and critical bridges, teeming with herds of cattle that I steer around with caution until I reach the herding pens and exit gate, guarded by thick, gloopy, hoof-cleaved mud. Now, it is a simple long road walk to Bowness, with a tempting, overgrown alternative Cumbrian Coastal Way route along former rail lines.

Little toads are frisky and leap from the roadside, keen to get somewhere wetter. The marshlands reach out for a mile into Moricambe mudflats – remote and inaccessible to humans and teeming with wildlife. It takes an hour or two of remote, muddy roads to reach the bridge at Whitrigg, avoiding muck-spreading tractors racing down the lanes. It is a good place to stop and eat the rolls I fortunately bought earlier. I could have taken a shortcut, for the OS maps suggest a cross-channel route from Anthorn. But, like many old paths, it leads to a ford, still recorded on the map but no longer used, washed away. The contours of the channel now flow in a different harmony, the river whipping slowly as it seeks the sea, waiting one day to return to an earlier life, like an animated slow-moving dragon tail.

## THE COAST IS OUR COMPASS

Huge radio masts whistle in the wind as I ease around the coast on the only road possible. A bicycle would be nice, but walking allows me to absorb the rainbow beauty of the Solway Firth, lit by a rain-laden sky streaked with light, shadow and rainfall. The colours are vivid, the visibility crystal, in an air that is pure, unfiltered and fresh from the Irish Sea. I wander into the sleeping village of Bowness-on-Solway to find the B&B. The host invites me to the pub that evening to meet the locals, mostly retirees who have found a peaceful haven in this remote seaside village. They are interested in my long journey and share the simple bar snacks the landlord has prepared in the kitchen. I hear stories of the haaf fishermen, mastering tides and sea to catch salmon and sea trout in a tradition that dates to the Vikings and will shortly disappear.

The B&B is a treat, but options are limited. The accommodation is oriented towards Hadrian's Wall walkers, for this is where its western edge terminates in a mosaic-tiled hut on the shoreline. I am the first King Charles III England Coast Path walker to be hosted and sign the visitor's book to make my mark, although many others would have passed this way. My host, Barry, is keen to hear about my experience of walking from Silloth. 'It could be ideal for cyclists, as the area has wonderful quiet lanes,' I explain. He ponders a cycle-hire business with this news, ever entrepreneurial and excited to promote the area.

This will be my last day in England. The plan is to simply march down the minor roads to Gretna via Carlisle city centre. But new routes have opened, and I can cross the River Eden on the A689 earlier than expected and drop down to the riverbanks to join the brand-new King Charles III England Coast Path paths (signposts still covered). On one of my few field crossings I am thrilled to shepherd a family of stoats. A mother and four, possibly five kits, dance underneath the long grass, popping their heads up like meerkats to check me out. I ease my pace to enjoy every second until they pass through a hedge and are gone.

The River Eden flows to the sea, sure and steadfast. The evidence of its power lies high on the banks. Broken trees and storm-swept vegetation dries in the sun, awaiting the next high tide or flood. I meet a dog walker and ask if there are any shops nearby. He suggests a recycling plant pop-up cafe near the aptly named cross-border lorry village of Cargo, easily reached by a shortcut path. I trespass on to the site, following the smell of bacon, and order a haggis bap from Morag, who runs 'The Butty Monster'. Her Borders banter lifts the heart of every customer, their weary faces light up as they wait for their food – a highlight of their day and mine, and a culinary first for me. I am approaching Scotland; the accents change, and the humour flows easily.

The path follows Rockcliffe Marsh at the edge of the River Esk. I can hear the M6 road and mainline rail traffic funnel across their bridgeheads. I cross the intercity line and then follow an endless road into Gretna. It is marked as a minor road on my map but is a busy shortcut highway for those in the know, an alternate non-motorway route to Scotland. I reach the border bridge at the River Sark exactly when a fellow adventurer stops on his gravel bike. He is on a long journey to the Highlands, his sleeping bag and a tent strapped to the fork legs and frame, a lightweight rig in the spirit of an ultralight backpacker. We take photographs of each other at the 'Scotland welcomes you' sign. He has a long journey ahead, but mine has ended, other than a short stroll to the station.

I dream of walking to Ayr as the train rocks me to sleep, for Scotland is inviting me to explore. I wake a few hours later into the rush-hour madness of Euston and hustle through the London Tube to my connecting station. I'm in crowd shock, unable to comprehend what everyone is doing, outraged at their urgency. I can barely keep pace as the departing platform is announced – commuters sprint to their favourite carriage seats in a mass carnage of chaotic, competitive walking, as if they harbour a secret frustration to escape the city for the countryside.

# 15
# BERWICK-UPON-TWEED TO HORDEN
## A wind that carries the memory of coal

*'If you are lonely when you're alone, you're in bad company.'*
Jean-Paul Sartre

**Distance walked: 1,750 miles**

A female Harris's hawk has spooked the pigeons at King's Cross Station, staring down from the upper concourse, comfortable on her handler Matt's forearm. He is happy to talk to a group of waiting travellers, in awe of the raptor's aura:

'What's her name?' I ask.

'This is Aria; she's nine,' explains Matt as he adjusts her tether.

'I can't see a single pigeon; she is an effective deterrent,' one traveller replies.

'She's a bit lazy today, overweight. I weigh her each morning and keep her close to her optimal weight of 1,100 grams. Any heavier and she won't fly; any lighter, she'll be hungry and will hunt. I have eight of them, all trained for this work,' he beams with pride.

It is an impressive sight. I could watch the hawk's dagger gaze all day as she scans the huge expanse of the vaulted space adjacent to the train platforms, freaking out London's local bird – the ubiquitous mongrel pigeon. My departing train to Edinburgh is called, and I make my way to the platform. The tourists are back in numbers, ticking off the top 10 things to do in the UK. I suspect only a few have considered walking even a part of the coastline but may do so after seeing the glory of this East Coast LNER service. My destination, Berwick-upon-Tweed, is three hours and 37 minutes away, and I arrive on time. The carriages arc towards the gorgeous Royal Border Bridge across the River Tweed, their steel wheels squeaking a delightful welcome to this stunning seaside town.

It is three miles from the station to the Scottish border and almost five, returning around the headlands, to the hostel. I meet Stuart on the path, for this is his regular walk. Three times a week, he makes sandwiches and a flask of tea and catches the bus from St Abbs. He doesn't need to pay at his age, and the 40- to 50-mile walking week keeps him in good shape. He is completely transfixed by the beauty of the coastline.

'Every time is different: the weather, the sea state, the animals, birds and flowers. I love it. You should walk north to Edinburgh,' he suggests. 'The coast path links to the John Muir Way, and you can carry on to Fife if you fancy.'

'Sounds great, but I'm walking the English coast and will turn around at the border and walk south. The new King Charles III England Coast Path is now fully open to Bridlington.'

Stuart knows every gate, every step, every shortcut. I can identify with the joy of repeatedly walking the same path – a new experience each day, yet a constant route. You add your footsteps to its history and enrich your sense of place. I'd love to walk with him to learn all the details he can see, but I turn around at the Scottish swing gate and read the sign back to England. It says, 'English Border – Cuddy Trail', yet this is also the Forth to Farne Way, the King Charles III England Coast Path and the Berwickshire Coastal Path. I prefer the local name, as cuddy is a Scottish word for a donkey, or maybe it is an eider duck, or even an affectionate nickname for St Cuthbert (who I will encounter later). In Scotland, any word that sounds about right is acceptable if said convincingly – the tone conveys meaning as much as the word. Stuart would know the answer, but he is already along the way north.

Now I walk alone. The coastal seascape is enthralling, and I am delighted by the perspective of the east coast. Is it the light or the sea state as I head south, or maybe the different expectations of the terrain that lies ahead? Am I going downhill? Whatever it may be, there is something special about the orientation, as if you are looking out at time past, where the wind goes, and not the future, where the wind originates. In that moment of thought, I notice that the word *wind* has two related meanings: the movement of air and the verb to traverse a curving path. The intonation is different, but the motions are similar. In both cases, the topography governs direction – mountains, trees, hills and coastline. The air is being pulled towards lower pressure; the walker is moving towards rest. Each of us flowing and dancing with the passage of time.

The hostel in Berwick is huge, a former granary. It is modern, comfortable and buzzing with cyclists, walkers and adventurers. I am reading the YHA brochure and reflect on their strapline: 'Because where you go changes who you become.' A long-distance walker must have written that, as walking has undoubtedly changed me. My curiosity leads to adventures, where I learn something new, which makes me more curious. It is a virtuous addictive loop. As you explore new environments, meet new people, and explore new cultures, these journeys embody what it means to be alive. You are active, not passive, embracing change. It is the ideal human condition – living, not just existing. You must engage with your surroundings through sight, hearing, smell, touch and taste. You must engage with the people you meet, to avoid the atrophy of the mind and the body – you must walk just to stand still.

I idle across the old Berwick Bridge on to the Lowry Trail, which will steer me towards Spittal in the early morning light, introducing me to the works of L. S. Lowry, who painted several scenes around the River Tweed. His match-stick characters capture the everyday scene and are a little happier than his paintings of the poverty and gloom of industrial cities. Children play on the beach in these vacation paintings (depicted on information boards), and ships and sailboats drift into the bay you see before you. He left his black and grey crayons at home, for these colours are bright and breezy. The paintings cheer me up as the urban streets unfold to cliffside grass paths and open sands. The tide is rising, but I have enough time to sneak in a path to the sluice bridge beyond Cheswick Sands, waving to the LNER trains as they pass. Only yesterday, I would have stared back from the carriage window – contemplating my future self, striding along, heading south.

I arrive at the road causeway to Lindisfarne, but the tide is rising fast. I could make it across but would get trapped for several hours, waiting for it to ebb as darkness fell. You cannot camp on the island, so I'll save this delight for another day. A new King Charles III England Coast Path section circuits the island and is reached by following a pilgrim's path – a line of poles in the sands, not the road. My walk around England will come to an end in a few weeks, and I start to dream of a pilgrimage from Holy Island to Cape Wrath, taking St Cuthbert's Way into Scotland on a 500-mile journey, or even taking the Berwickshire Coastal Path, John Muir Way, Fife Coastal Path and the John o 'Groats Trail. My curiosity is storing up possibilities and options. I think more about the meaning of the word pilgrimage, a more spiritual journey that focuses less on where I walk, but why I walk.

I think about the meaning of the word pilgrimage, a spiritual journey that focuses less on where I walk, and more on why I walk. It is a pity, for I later explore Ross Back Sands and discover what must be one of the finest coastal beaches in the UK. Seals, terns and plovers breed on these shores and must be protected during sensitive periods. Other signs warn of the wildfowl shooting seasons in October. Once again, the juxtaposition between death and beauty is perplexing – the wildlife refuge and wildfowling marsh are side by side, not that the birds would know the difference. I later read that you can bid at auction for the 'fantastic' opportunity to blast teal or wigeon from the sky with a shotgun. A long weekend break for £3,500, requiring permits from Natural England. I am sure there is an explanation for this, and I will learn about the interplay between conservation and sport later when I reach the southern boundary of Yorkshire.

A tractor is ploughing up the footpath, disturbing the hares which scatter at speed in all directions, occasionally stopping to scan for threats with their huge sound-cone ears. Now flooded by the tide, the salt marsh fills with swans, gulls and wildfowl. The samphire and eelgrass is flushed again as the tide creeps into the creeks, disconnecting the community of Lindisfarne from the mainland for a few peaceful hours. Edwin Lutyens' remodelled Arts and Crafts castle stands sentinel, a prime position on the Northumberland coastline. But it is not as prominent as Bamburgh Castle, which commands all it surveys – a statement of northern power and one of the finest coastal scenes in England. It is built on the Great Whin Sill, a ridge of dolerite that arcs around the national park, underpinning many strategic defensive boundaries, notably Hadrian's Wall and other fortifications on the north-east coastline.

## THE COAST IS OUR COMPASS

Sleepy lanes bring me to Waren Mill campsite, which is perfect for an early start. I pitch and rest. As twilight falls, the sky fills with the skeins of geese heading north to roost. The chill air descends, and I wrap up in my sleeping bag and drop off to sleep, to be rudely awoken by a vicious fight erupting near the burn. I can only assume it to be a fox, badger, otter or combination thereof, but I am too tired and scared to investigate. I wake and depart early enough to see the wildfowl in Budle Bay and the returning chevrons of geese heading for the fields to feed. I curse my lack of binoculars, for little egret, shelduck, redshank, greenshank, plovers, merganser (or goosander), and many others are feeding at low tide. I could sit here for hours with a telescope, but I am eager to catch the early morning light that wakes the powerful mass of Bamburgh Castle each morning. It commands the landscape in a manner unmatched in England – a sight that belongs to Tolkien's imagined Middle-Earth world. No wonder it is often seen on film and television as a backdrop for an epic battle or fantasy kingdom. It is a view loved by all, one that brings together the beauty of the coastline with statement architecture – both powerful narratives in our lives.

I favour firm beach sands to the soft coastal dunes and make good progress into Seahouses to gather lunch before continuing to Beadnell Bay. I pace the miles, seeking the harder sands and walking inland when burn outflows are too deep to ford. Storm Agnes passed in the night, leaving clear skies and a gentle breeze until another front arrives to empty more rain on the approach to Dunstanburgh Castle. The empty paths were busy an hour ago, and now the streets of Craster are deserted too. Walkers hide now in their cars, inns or cafes for lunch. I shiver on a bench and eat the contents of my food bag, eager to get going and raise my core temperature by burning this new energy. I should have stopped at the welcoming golf club, inviting tired walkers for tea. There is a friendly vibe along the fairways, and the signs are considerate and helpful, unlike many notices in the south of England that tell you what you cannot do, not what you can do.

An unusual ridge curves and then descends into the village of Alnmouth, perhaps a continuation of Bamburgh's geology. It is a pretty seaside port – a romantic and beautiful view from the LNER rail service window as if someone had commissioned an artist to craft it for that purpose. The streets hold clues to its past, for it was once an important port for grain shipment from the fields of Northumberland. Even though it now relies on tourism, I search in vain for an open cafe while I wait for the late-afternoon 418 bus to the Alnwick YHA hostel. After a short journey, I dry off gear and clothing by draping it across the bunkbeds, for I have exclusive use of the dorm – a pleasant surprise for the time of year. I cook a meal in the communal kitchen that would shock any chef, but at least it is nutritious, calorific and hot. I return to Alnmouth in the morning, sitting next to a fellow passenger who must have cleared the shelves at Greggs. He demolishes three bacon butties and six sausage rolls, flushing them down with three large tins of high-energy drink. I count the calories as he screws up the empty paper bags and crushes the cans. His breakfast would keep me going for a week. I find a few foraged plums in the trees, which will supplement the porridge I had for breakfast, enough to keep me going to Amble.

The overcast sky has tempered the early morning sun, which tries to break through. Its intense light cuts a precise white two-dimensional circular hole in the cloud. It is an illusion of a portal to another universe. As I walk on to the hard sand, this vapour filter evaporates and a warmer colour spectrum shimmers across a sheen of water on a low-tide beach, mirroring the clouds. It is difficult to perceive perspective as I only have a horizon line as a mirror's edge reference. The bloom of the white clouds looks no less complex as a reflection; the billowing forms repeated at any scale. This empty, water-washed canvas clears my mind as I drift along its lonely shores to Amble, inducing a dream-like state. I awake when I realise I must double back to Warkworth. The North Pier lighthouse drew me towards the town, but I cannot cross the harbour channel.

The extra two miles would have been unnecessary if I had checked the map, but it is a price I enjoy paying. Reaching the outskirts, I cross the ancient bridge into the medieval village with its prominent castle, nestled in a defensive embrace by the River Coquet. Its ruined towers stare down an estuary full of migrating birds, cleaning their salty feathers in the freshwater weir. I am elated to come across a sculpture trail into Amble. The first installation, *Sea Pies and a Dokie's Egg,* is a calendrical poem housed in an auk egg-shaped shelter (a sea pie is an oystercatcher, and a dokie egg is an auk's conical egg that rolls in a circle to stop it falling from the cliff). September's curlews and October's lapwings are evident – you see what you read in the text on the benches, divided into the months of the season.

Further on, *Tern Wings* is an enormous stainless-steel open wing of the roseate tern that tempts you to fly as you stand beneath the four-metre-high reflective structure. Finally, the *Flock Sphere* is a globe of gulls. It begs you to clamber inside and immerse yourself in circling steel birds. These uplifting works are a part of the *Amble Bord Waalk* (or Bird Walk if ye divvent knaa hoo te' taak proppa), and they are a welcome sight as I walk to the quayside. Quite a few people have suggested I stay at the hostel, a unique building crafted by a passionate entrepreneur with care and artistic flair, but it is midday, and I must reach Newbiggin. My love of the place is sealed when the 'Geordie Banger' sausage roll pop-up hits the mark with a perfect spiced meat pastry. My bus friend would love the Greggs upgrade, as do the starlings who eat the crumbs from my hand as I smile at the lighthouse opposite that led me astray earlier.

Energised, my poles go into Nordic marching mode, sprinting along the vast expanse of Druridge Bay – the alternate left-pole, right-foot, right-pole, left-foot metronome slowing only as the sand softens. This must be a contender for the longest continuous beach walk in England, at an estimated eight to nine miles when the tide is out. I begin my final approach, banking around the biomass power station and dodging golf ball fairways to St Bartholomew's Church, whose graveyard is sliding into the sea. Ahead lies a view of the industrial north-eastern shores I will navigate in the coming days. I ponder this change as I nurse a fish supper in a takeaway with one free table for a tired walker. The pub and my accommodation have a quiz night that evening, and I would join had I not fallen asleep. The 1970s 'name-that-tune' round frustrates my dreams as I hear the quizmaster announce each track. I cannot name a song or artist, even though I recognise all the tunes from my teenage years.

My old boots are at the end of their life, and blisters are developing; their tired soles and cracked uppers no longer grip the rock or remain waterproof. I expected mud, but the paths are dry and the sand is hard on the beaches. Now, I suffer the roads and pavement around the industrial parks and trading estates of Blyth. Promises of battery and undersea cable factories are written on the construction site security fence posters.

Other developments look idle with expired EU funding. This former coal and shipbuilding port marks the southern boundary of a coastline that has taken me by surprise since Berwick. Its coal, grain, quarry, military, religious, shipbuilding and fishing heritage is framed by a stunning coastline that easily matches the south-west coast of England as it returns to its latent natural glory.

I cross the county border after Seaton Sluice, a coal port and a glass bottle empire in the 18th century – a superb beach if you like to collect sea glass. For the next four days, I will walk through an industrial heartland synonymous with the Industrial Revolution and the British Empire, the communities now finding solutions to the decline of coal and shipbuilding, which once fed the energy and sea transportation markets. The seaside resort of Whitley Bay, with its Spanish City, can't compete with Blackpool, yet it has a promenade, beach, and the charm of human scale. A rusting steel door secures the clubhouse of the Panama Swimming Club, established in 1930, some 90 years before wild swimming became so popular. It is a gentle introduction to Tynemouth and North Shields and the entrance to the River Tyne, protected by the pincher claws of the North and South Piers. The heritage density increases as the city of Newcastle is felt. The urban landscape replaces the remote coastline, but it is just as interesting to read its depth.

I aim for the ferry to South Shields, crossing to walk out again to the shoreline where I meet the weeble-wobble (if you can remember the famous toys of the 1970s) women on Littlehaven Beach. Their human forms invite me into a conversation, drawing me to social interaction and slowing my pace. I try to walk away, but they whisper to me and I walk back to study them, each unique, each with a story to tell and an invitation to know of my life's journey. The shape, structure and situation play with my behaviour in a disconcerting way. It is an excellent installation called *Conversation Piece* by a Spanish artist, Juan Muñoz. There is another artwork as I reach the polished, clean sands on Sandhaven Beach: blocks of stone that mirror the golden colour of the sand – warming you, inviting you to sit and rest.

I can see Souter lighthouse in the distance, and I wonder if there is enough light in the day to reach Sunderland. I haven't booked anywhere to stay, so I walk to Lizard Point, which the lighthouse defends, and take the bus towards Roker Park. This is the former home of Sunderland FC and the church for a legion of fanatical supporters for 100 years, before it was replaced by the nearby Stadium of Light. I get off at Seaburn, having hastily booked a B&B while travelling. I am lucky that a busy Italian restaurant has a last-minute cancellation. The food is superb, reasonably priced, and demands a large glass of red wine to complement the garlic and olive oil aroma. I can barely walk back to my B&B as my muscles have seized solid, and my feet hurt after a day of pounding promenades for 28 miles. Blisters need sorting tonight and may develop in a few days. I forget that prevention is better than a cure. This walker's self-harm is a curse that I have yet to overcome, and I know the consequences of not taking care of my feet. I know what to do but often can't be bothered.

Luckily, my daughter lives in Darlington, and it is the weekend so she has invited me to stay the following night. I can recover and try to replace my worn, heavy boots with trail shoes. As I board the bus to return to yesterday's end point, the driver recognises a fellow long-distance walker who, unknown to me, has a passion for coastlines. We chat as he heads north, and then he pulls into an empty bus stop on the pretence that he is ahead of schedule for he wants to know more.

'Whoa, you are walking the coastline of England,' he says. 'I'd love to do that when I retire. Where did you start? What's your favourite bit? How many days? How many miles a day? Where do you stay? Who do you meet?' The questions fire in rapid succession, but our conversation is interrupted by an annoyed passenger.

'What have we stopped for? I need to get to work.'

'He's ahead of schedule,' I offer in his defence, but that is a lie, and she is right to be annoyed. The driver needs to turn left and ends the conversation, stating the direction I need to take.

'You get off here. The lighthouse is a hundred yards up the road. Have a great day,' he calls, as the pneumatic door closes.

I leave him a card that links to my blogs and social media, which I do not update while walking as I am often too tired to write a coherent sentence in the evenings, but it will answer many of his questions. The lighthouse is only a short distance away, bathed in the warm early morning light. There is no wind, the sea is flat and calm, and the sun hangs like an Anglepoise light on the table of the North Sea, illuminating the coastline, waking the inhabitants of Whitburn as its spring-mechanism relaxes. Bird observers are up early, counting the inbound migrating geese in the distant sea, concentrating hard and not wishing to be disturbed, clicking their counters with their right thumbs as the other hand adjusts focus on the scopes. The pink-footed geese have arrived. Their 'wink-wink' cry differs distinctly from a tribble gargling of a brent goose or farmyard honk of a greylag goose.

Sunderland, or seagull city as it is known, has protective piers, taking the sting out of the swell. The northern arm retains its lighthouse, but the southern one was relocated to Roker in 1983. I take the long route around the marina and head towards Wearmouth Bridge, past the university campus and accommodation blocks, whose rubbish bins are plagued with enormous rats brazenly carrying lumps of protein to their dens. The southern bank is home to the homeless and addicts, who sit spaced out and holding tins of strong cider – too far gone to ask a coherent question. It takes an hour to leave the city and docklands behind and a further hour to reach County Durham and Seaham.

This coastline bears witness to the colossal scale of the mining industry; its shores blackened with the waste poured over the nutrient-rich magnesian limestone cliffs. It was once home to a diverse ecology, and it is returning slowly, over decades, as the community 'turns the tide' and cleans the beaches. The shoreline is unrecognisable from the final violent scenes of *Get Carter*, filmed along the blackened beaches near Blackhall Colliery. Jack Carter, Michael Caine's 1971 gangland film character, met his gruesome end on the polluted shore – a depressing metaphor for the sordid horrors of gangland Britain in the 1960s.

I walk south through a dene (like a mini-Devonian combe) and gill (like an Isle of Wight chine), both awkward scars in the geology that test the patience of a walker conditioned now to a flat North Sea coastal journey. My heart is lifted by a puff of goldfinches in the gorse, maybe 20 of them. They settle but erupt again as 50, then 100 and maybe more. I have never seen such a colourful spectacle. Their gold, red, yellow and white flight sparkles like your first kaleidoscope experience. It is a wonderful sign of a recovering coastline, where nature will reclaim her home from industrial brutality and vandalism. Coal has released its anthropogenic poisons, leaving a profound environmental debt in this geological era. A sign says it all – 'A wind that carries the memory of coal.' The evidence of industry slowly fades, but the impact remains with us to this day.

The rain starts, and a decision to walk inland for the bus is rewarded. There is a train strike on the local line, but the bus gets me to Hartlepool station and connects with the cross-country service to Eaglescliffe, where my angel of a daughter leans across to open the door of her warm car. The wipers beat buckets to the kerb, as I twist into the seat.

'You look a bit soggy, Dad,' she says, consolingly. 'I've made your favourite for tea. Fancy a pint tonight?' she adds. 'They have a good porter on tap.'

We spend a restful weekend in Darlington, home of ORB, a sublime micropub, and Up & Running, a proper, fashion-free, runners' paradise, open on a Sunday. My brand of trail shoes, the ever-wonderful Brooks Cascadias, are on sale. The micropub has a range of foaming pints, poured with skill from beer engines for the chatty customers unpacking and processing their week. My daughter's company, companionship and cooking spoil me in a way no B&B, hostel or hotel could ever match. My weary frame is restored for the final leg to Bridlington, where I will shortly join the Cleveland Way National Trail.

# 16
# HORDEN TO BRIDLINGTON
## Are you sitting down?

*'The secret to living well and longer is eat half, walk double, laugh triple, and love without measure.'*
                                                                    Tibetan proverb

**Distance walked: 1,870 miles**

I return to Horden through the Stockton to Darlington railway cuttings that held the world's first passenger rail line almost 200 years earlier. My daughter has challenged me to take pictures of the everyday rather than picturesque seascapes and artworks. Show me the real world, she suggests. I am not anticipating a shortage of subjects as I reach the path and head towards Hartlepool. The beach with coal dust leaching into the sand, creating fractal deltas – too arty. A friendly racing pigeon, ringed and hungry – a bit lucky to see. Boarded-up abandoned housing in need of decoration – clichéd social commentary. Lastly, the inside an empty carriage of the 08:37 from Thornaby – perfect.

It is difficult to take a dull picture, as there is so much interest. The sun lights the land, directly and indirectly, reflected from the calm sea and through white clouds. Kestrels are hovering, gulls glide along the cliffs, and passerines dance between the thorns in the bushes. There are gun batteries, poetry plaques, lifeboat murals, stories of mining heritage, tales of shipwrecks and storms and a sculpture of *Andy Capp*, the much-loved northern strip cartoon character. There is a full day of local interest here, worthy of its own walking trail, to discover the 800 years of history since King John granted a charter to the citizens of *Herterpol*.

The racing pigeon, sporting a green leg ring, walks with me along the path, probably resting after a sea crossing, looking for something to eat and someone to welcome it home. Weirdly, it stops as I study the *Waves* sculpture at Seaton Carew, a stylistic turbine sweeping sea glass from the shore. Another metaphor of renewal, set against a backdrop of Teesside Wind Farm in the distance. The pigeon gets bored and flies away; I walk on through the marshlands of Seaton Snook to be confronted by a power station, oil refineries, chemical plants and the prospect of an endless road walk into Middlesbrough. There is a new aroma, unnatural, sweet and sickly – a blended Billingham perfume that is unpleasant to breathe.

The walk to the Transporter Bridge is long and tedious. It is closed for repairs and I must walk a further four miles to the city centre to a hostel I have booked, which I realise on arrival is temporary housing for asylum seekers. An anxious family and I are trying to work out how the lock code works. I solve the problem with a phone call to a side-hustle entrepreneur, who answers with another business name. He reprogrammes the lock without knowing of my desperate neighbours. We all walk into a communal room, where they embrace other family members and friends. My room is without TV, biscuits, kettle, soap or towels, but I sleep well enough. I can light my stove in the shower basin to make a brew and rehydrate a simple meal.

The streets of Middlesbrough are deserted at 6am as I walk to the south gate of the Transporter Bridge and turn right. The huge Meccano-like structure is framed through the brick wall of former saltworks, ironworks and pottery factories. The Riverside Stadium sleeps, awaiting 25,000 football fans for the 19:45 kick-off against Cardiff City. The Navigation Inn pub nearby (with its 'no away supporters' notices) takes delivery of beer barrels for later celebrations, each landing with a thud as they are dropped on to the straw bolster by the drayman. It marks the start of the Black Path, a black cinder rail-side walk to the eastern end of the Teesdale Way, signposted with steel boots hanging from the fingerposts. Unexpected and poignant artworks line the path, local paintings and poetry that evoke recent memory:

*Night shift.*
*It's late, back ache,*
*Long shift, low mist,*
*Bird calls, dawn falls,*
*Heavy tred, soon bed,*
*I walk the Black Path home.*

I climb to the works road to escape the wet nettle paths and get a better view of Teesport and the remnants of the Redcar Steel Works that dominated this landscape for over 170 years. The demolition teams write the final chapters as blast furnaces, casting houses, charge conveyors, chimneys and towers are felled into a tangled mess of concrete and rusting steel. Net-zero projects are emerging like a phoenix from Europe's largest brownfield site, sequestering a cluster of local industry carbon emissions deep in the North Sea – a world-first CCUS (Carbon Capture Usage and Storage) facility.

Shepherding deer along the path, I reach a road and a pop-up cafe, busy with van drivers and workers seeking breakfast. The chatty chefs are keen to know the story of someone without a vehicle and with a backpack, as they expertly scrape and turn bacon and eggs with a jointing knife, flipping the perfectly burnt rashers into triangular fadgies (another new word for bread bun).

'We don't get many walkers stopping here. Where are you off to?' asks the chef.

'I hope to make Saltburn and the Cleveland Way for lunchtime, then maybe another three weeks to get to Cromer in Norfolk to complete my walk around England.'

'I'll add an extra rasher, you'll need it. Here you go, sauces and sugar on the table.'

Egg yolk oozes on to my sleeves as I bite – I never learn – and sweet tea refreshes my palate, the double pack of sugar far cheaper than an energy bar. I reach Redcar Sands and the familiar language of a coastal promenade, with its holiday furniture, sculptures and fishing heritage. A museum houses the world's oldest lifeboat, the *Zetland,* which was built in 1802 and saved 500 lives over a 78-year period of service. Her white clinker hull rests indoors, while the *Nicola Jane* and *Lady Maude* Yorkshire cobles, almost identical in design, lie in their cradles, waiting to be launched to fish the local waters.

It is a long beach walk to Saltburn, weaving through the wet channels on the hard sands. Juvenile gannets feed voraciously offshore. Their black wings moult feather by feather each year until they reach their full, six-foot wingspan, black-tipped, Persil-white adulthood. They are certainly my favourite seabird. It is a feeding frenzy, the enthusiasm of youth ruthlessly emptying the sea of fish. They flap purposefully into the wind and then twist and fold into the surf, emerging a moment later, facing the wind again, to take off and circle back. Their height and angle of attack adjust to the task, measured to intercept their prey in shallow shoals. I count a few successful catches, the flick of a neck instantly swallowing a mackerel head-first.

The Seaview chippy, a favourite my daughter suggested, is closed, but the Cat Nab takeaway has a table and satiates a hungry and tired walker. I need the meal, for the path ahead ascends into the cliffs of the Cleveland Hills, the first real test for my calves since Minehead in Somerset. Like the South West Coast Path, I am now back on a co-aligned National Trail but walking in the opposite direction from my route in 2016. The views are familiar yet unfamiliar, but just as breathtaking as I ascend the first cliff.

This new elevation is interrupted by Skinningrove's sandy shores: its modern steel industry hidden inland, alongside the remnants of the ironworks and mining heritage. Moments earlier, I stopped to photograph the famous steel *Circle* charm bracelet conceived and designed by artist Richard Farrington over a few pints in the local pubs. He welded and wrought the forms at the nearby works, forging charm objects representing the intersection of nature and industry – the mineral and the molecular – connected in a ring, framing the coastline. It is a replacement for the vandalised original that lies somewhere in the sea below.

The next ascent brings me to the highest point on the east coast, near Boulby, sitting above the deepest mine in the UK. It excavates potash and polyhalites that haven't seen daylight for 260 million years. This valuable nutrient mineral can, at last, sunbathe on the fields again, giving life to the crops and, ultimately, to us. A 50th-anniversary bench has a map showing layers of mine tunnels extending four miles out to sea. The scale is beyond my comprehension as I survey the coastline near the 213-metre summit, trying to imagine what goes on almost a mile below my feet in a multi-floor tunnel network of 297 square miles, seven times deeper than my elevation to sea level and over twice the distance to the village of Staithes, two miles away.

Staithes is impossibly pretty. The red-roofed, white-walled cottages hug the cliffs, using any available plot, forming a disorderly Tetris geometry that evolved unplanned. The tourists are absent, and the narrow streets are quiet, giving me space to find the exit back to the path without stopping at the inviting Cod & Lobster pub. If cobles were moored in the bay, you would know their fish was fresh, but nowadays it will come from a wholesaler's warehouse in a refrigerated lorry. After a nine-hour day the campsite is only a few weary miles further. A camper's kitchen, spacious showers and a rest hut are all that I need – perfect for cooking my dinner, showering my muddy legs and writing my journal before wrapping myself in goose down to sleep out a windy night in a shaking tent.

It is funny how towns and villages are often placed at 10-mile intervals. I can make Whitby for lunch and Robin Hood's Bay for tea, so there is no need to carry food. I could walk further, but that would mean wild camping, for Scarborough is too far in a day. I try to wake late, but like a dog needing a walk, I am wagging my tail with happiness. The seascape beckons, and the adventure pulls me like the wind. This is day 100 of my journey from Cromer, a satisfying milestone suggesting 2,000 miles completed. The coast has been my compass for over three months, on and off. I can sense the journey ending and savour each day, knowing I have fewer days left in my life than I have lived, making each moment more precious.

Walking is easy and pleasant. The paths are empty until I see a group of seven walkers ahead. My puppy-like behaviour activates to chase them down, a prey to be caught. I celebrate my fitness. Poles power me up the inclines and balance rapid descents. My new shoes make a difference; they are lighter, nimble and secure. I feel more like an athlete than a rambler. My first walker is overtaken, and I offer the casual 'Mornin'' greeting, but receive a gruff Yorkshire response from someone just as competitive but who can't keep up. This repeats until I meet John, a Scotsman, who leads the way. I slow down, match his pace and fall into a conversation, the race won for now. His pet spaniel explores every bush, hedge, field and fence, but he walks briskly on, knowing the breed will check with his master every few minutes. After the usual introductory exchanges, John talks about his career as a professional footballer.

'I passed the Riverside Stadium in Middlesbrough. Do you know the score from Saturday?' I ask.

'I think they beat Cardiff 2–0. I used to play for them,' replies John.

'Who, Middlesbrough?'

'Aye, in the 90s, scoring the last goal at Ayresome Park before they relocated to Riverside.'

'That's an impressive claim to fame.'

We chat for ages, exchanging life stories. He is fascinated by my walk, and I am fascinated by his story as a young lad coming to England at 16 and making his way through the leagues. He is an attacking player who would have made many a fan's Saturday dream come true. By this time, we have walked ahead of the group, so I continue into Whitby via the low-tide beach from Sandsend, eager to find a decent fish supper before the one-o'clock crowds fill the restaurants. The Magpie Cafe waiter looks at me, sucking through his teeth as if a table is a ridiculous ask, but he finds me a cosy seat on the top floor.

The fish pie is extraordinary, and I scrape every hint of burnt cheese sauce from the bowl. As I emerge on to the streets, the queues are building, for this is a popular restaurant. Crossing the bridge, I note the tide times that have been scratched on the blackboard a thousand times but are irrelevant now for the high-level walk to Robin Hood's Bay. I walk off the pie, climbing the 199 steps to the abbey. I count each of them, placing my foot on the final step as my inner counter clicks to 200. A whistle from the Whitby steam train is the starting gun that reignites my competitive pace – doubly so as I see the group again, who have taken a shorter lunch. It is one of those days when energy levels are high, and I intend to celebrate a century of days on the coastal paths.

The group merges with another, the path busy now with Cleveland Way and Coast to Coast walkers who have crossed the Pennines from St Bees Head. They have only a few miles to the finish at the bottom of the hill in the village. They are exhausted, having walked through Storm Agnes, the first named storm of the season.

'The route will be a National Trail in 2026. What was it like?' I ask a tired-looking gentleman.

'Tough going, buddy. The storm hit as we reached the moors. Up to our ears in the mud,' he replies with a distinct Australian twang. 'We're a group from New South Wales, with some Americans, too. We weren't expecting this. It has been a tough 17 days.'

'Well, at least the wind was behind you,' I offer in consolation. 'I think it's taken me 12 days to travel from St Bees around the coast of England – a sort of coast to coast, by walking around the coast.' It is then I realise I will walk from those start to end points twice on this journey.

The group leader gives me the details, telling me that it was one of the toughest conditions he had experienced. The wind, hail and rain were challenging, but the group held up, and he used all the contingency plans. That must have been a real test, and I admire his leadership skills in keeping a group together safely. It must have been a good mix of Type 1 and Type 2 fun, judging by their smiles.

The hotel arrives too early in a village famed for smuggling contraband, an illicit port for illicit goods from Europe for the north-east of England – tea, rum and tobacco would evade the customs men, who would meet silence from a community supplementing their meagre fishing incomes. My room is cosy, a good excuse for an early nap and time to check my gear. The shoes are working well, but my food reserves are depleted. However, that is no worry as Scarborough and Filey lie ahead, nicely spaced. The weather will turn, so I repack my waterproofs to the top of my rucksack and use rubbish bag liners at the bottom of my pack to double seal my gear.

Starting my descent to the Bay Hotel, the end (or start) of Wainwright's Coast to Coast walk, I read a memorial to the bravery of coxswain Henry Freeman, whose dogged determination saved the crew of the *Visiter* brig on 18th January 1881 by leading a team of horse and men to haul the Whitby lifeboat through a seven-foot snowdrift to launch at Robin Hood's Bay. Freeman almost lost his own life 20 years earlier as the sole survivor of a fateful rescue. He had been the only one wearing the new cork life jacket. No doubt, the earlier experience shaped his character. I cannot imagine the fortitude needed to venture into the sea in those conditions, as they frighten me when I stand on the shore on a calm day.

The path is muddy, more so when hedges and trees shade the path. My walking poles arrest slips as I engage four-wheel drive. Stepping into the puddles is safer than tiptoeing around the edges but it soaks my feet. I don't care – they will dry out soon enough on the promenades. After a while, I play with their depth like a toddler in wellies – reconnecting to the joy of splash and muck that thrilled me in earlier life. I can manage about an inch of depth until the water flows easily into the ventilated uppers. It flows easily out again, as liquid and vapour, unlike with the more expensive Gore-Tex versions I have tried, which the sales staff fail to remind you are waterproof in both directions.

Flagstones have been used in places, and landslides eat away at the cliff line, destroying compacted paths and forcing me into the fields. Setting off early, I am unlikely to meet walkers going in my direction and only one couple meet me in the other, stopping for a quick chat. The National Trust is opening its centre at Ravenscar, which tells the story of the alum works and the role of urea in creating aluminium sulphate – a mordant to fix colour when dyeing cloth. Huge volumes of human urine were collected in cities and shipped in barrels to the works, founded when a naturalist noticed the similarities in flora to that near a factory in Italy, betraying the underlying soil minerals. I can't imagine the smell. It seems the north-east of England was chosen for many industries emitting toxic or noxious by-products, so the wind could disperse the gases in the direction of Norway.

I touched the bench that inspired my journey around the North Sea by bicycle in 2017, and recall wearing out a full set of brake blocks descending along the cinder rail line into Whitby on a wet day. That was an epic journey, but it triggers another memory – the loss of my younger brother to cancer that same year. I am now seven years older, and that age gap chills me. As I continue to process that loss, I am unaware that there will be happier news in an hour.

I stop before turning the headland at a cafe run by the owner of the Magpie Cafe in Whitby. These small cluster businesses are a good sign, and the sister Wavemark Cafe is excellent, too – a perfect burger and chips. As I wait, I check my phone and see a message to call Emma, who contacted me a few weeks ago about an unknown first cousin DNA match on *ancestry.com*. We conclude that either my father was not my father or my first cousin's mother was my half-sister. 'Can she get a DNA test?' I suggested at the time. I ring her back as the results must have come through.

'Are you sitting down?' she asks. 'The match is 30%, about 1,995 centimorgans; that means Jenny is your half-sister; the TIMBER algorithm is 100% certain.'

'Wow,' I say. 'So it's true. I have an older sister. I'll ring her straight away. How does she feel about it? She now knows her father and has gained a brother; I have a sister. I am delighted.' A few moments later, I get her number by text. My burger can get cold. 'Hi, this is Martyn, I'm your younger brother,' I say. The words sound strange.

'Hello,' she answers in a soft Liverpudlian accent. 'I'm Jenny, your big sister.' Those words feel stranger.

'Just to say, I am so thrilled to know you. When can we meet? I could come up in a few weeks. I'm in Scarborough now, walking around England.'

'You are what?' she screams.

'We have a lot of catching up to do,' we say in unison.

'Yes, quite a bit. Emma told me a bit more about your family. It will take some time to explain things. To work out what we can and what happened decades ago,' she replies. I can hear her wipe the tears from her eyes.

A few weeks later, we meet in the Lake District. Our parents' stories align, and the parallels are spooky as I find more in common with her husband, Geoff. We were both born in the same hospital and went to the same school in Singapore in the late 1960s. He adores early Triumph Bonneville motorcycles, as I do, having ridden them in the White Helmet display team.

She married the likeness of a father she never knew. We each have families that need to get to know each other: new uncles, cousins, nieces and nephews (later we uncover even more parallels). This is bigger than I thought.

I finish the burger and coffee, and the waitress cleans the table.

'How was the meal?' she asks.

'Lovely, lovely, but sorry to burden you. I must tell someone. I have just learned I have an older sister after six decades.' Tears form. She tears up, too. I control my initial emotions to explain what happened, using a napkin to wipe my eyes. My father was in the right place and at the right time. Did my father know? Did my mother know? There are many unanswered questions without the possibility of ever knowing, as they are no longer alive.

'The swinging 50s and 60s, eh!' she giggles.

I walk out of the cafe on to the long promenade around Castle Cliff. Storyboards tell Scarborough's history, but I don't have the mind space to read them – I must process what has just happened and what better way to do that than to walk? A mile passes until my emotions are interrupted by a mechanical fortune teller speaking from a booth outside the Coney Island Amusement Arcade, probably triggered by a motion detector.

'You will have unexpected news today,' 'he' booms in a deep, creepy voice. I stop, having possibly misheard. 'Zoltar has more to say to you if you have a small gift for me.' I dare not feed a £1 coin into the machine, fearing what 'he' might say, but I make a mental note to buy a lottery ticket for the first time, believing luck comes in waves (it doesn't). I settle back into the walk and pay more attention to the path and landscape, thinking of the campsite ahead and the deteriorating weather.

The seascape looks like a rain-soaked watercolour painting – grey, washed out, with unnameable coloured tints a memory from an earlier sunny day. The sea has bolder tones: the offshore wind streaks converge to the distant horizon, playing with the surface waves, a mix of the deepest blue troughs to the spray-white crests. It is calm enough in the lee of the cliffs to see minke whale fins that I have been told are near, but I only glimpse a fulmar arcing through the undulating sea, hiding behind the waves and then twisting over the peaks within inches of its wingtips. I walk on to the astonishing sedimentary cliff patterns of Filey Brigg, a view I didn't see when walking north. Shades of gold, black and grey layer the horizontal, connected to the landmass with the green wind-blown grass at a lazy 45 degrees. It is a beautiful scene to end my walk, an evening light that clouds and rain will soon extinguish as the sun finalises the day and hides below the horizon.

Turning right after the rescue rocket pole and Cleveland/Yorkshire Wolds National Trail start/end stone marker, the heavens open. I aim directly for the reception building of the nearby campsite. After a *Catch-22* discussion to get my key return deposit in the morning, I walk on the damp grass to a sheltered pitch, picking up clods of fresh cuttings that will later decorate the shower cubicle. In a more comfortable tent, my neighbour sizzles sausage, bacon and eggs on his stove, casting an intoxicating aroma downwind as I pitch my ultralight one-man wonder. I peer out, nibbling an energy bar, and boil enough water for a mug of rooibos tea. My food bag is empty, and my stomach is empty, too. I should have popped into town for a meal, but tiredness and the day's emotions have overtaken me.

I wrap the returnable key fob and a note in a zip bag, not expecting to see my £10 deposit returned, and head for the centre of Filey for food. It is an early start, so I can catch a train from Bridlington in time for a proper home-cooked meal, which my taste buds crave. It is dark, and the rain is still washing the streets and windows. The neon chill of the supermarket aisles is uncomfortable: an unnatural spectrum of light and freezing air. I can't wait to return to the outdoors with warmer rain and light.

Walking out of town, I make the rookie mistake of religiously following the fingerposts, which navigate me in circles up steps and around parks. If I had looked up, I would have seen the flat sands of the beach and a low tide. A local assures me I can exit near Hunmanby, so I drop down to the sands and march on. As I climb the cliffs my shoes clog in mud, their block-pattern soles rendered useless by the chalk soils. I weave around the back fence of a compound of static caravans to reach the trig pillar at Speeton Cliffs, and easier paths.

Binoculars would be useful now. The seabirds are rafting at sea or soaring from their cliffside homes. The gannets hold court, but numbers are lower than I recall. There are more birds if you turn your view inland, rare migrating birds, warblers, larks and finches. If it were May, the skies and seas would be alive with breeding gannets, kittiwakes, puffins and guillemots. The birdwatchers are happy on a rainy day, some carrying enormous camera lenses wrapped in camouflage cloth. They are joined by a gaggle of fluorescent-vested schoolchildren on a field trip from RSPB Bempton Cliffs – little ducklings waddling along the mud paths to an observation deck. Their teachers and guardians do their best to highlight the flora and birdlife on a dreary day as the children scribble notes on clipboards, their pencils useless on papers dissolving in the rain.

The vertical cliffs diminish in height as I enter the chalkland peninsula of Flamborough. The waves carve the reefs and caves, and the competing currents bring nutrients to feed a diverse ecology. I am guided by the lighthouse I saw from the Filey campsite, its four-flash, fifteen-second interval light now resting until the evening. It has stood here since 1806, but it is modern compared to the stunning original white chalk tower lighthouse inland, completed in 1674 – one of the oldest in England. I rest in the lee of a wall and consume every crumb in my food bag, knowing I have a strong headwind into Bridlington. After climbing over Danes Dyke, a defensive boundary that once protected an ancient self-sustaining community of this peninsula, I ease my way into the delights of another eastern seaside town. A faux-tractor promenade train motors by, its carriages empty on a blustery day. I walk behind it to shelter from the wind and explore the seafront.

In among the cafes, chippies, amusement arcades and funfairs, my attention is drawn to a plaque. Who would have thought two Hawaiian princes would have introduced surfing to England in 1890? HRH Prince David Kawananakoa and HRH Prince Jonah Kuhio Kalanianaole missed their home breaks in the Pacific Ocean, so they commissioned a local builder to cut surfboards to their specifications while they studied in York. That must have been a sight in the Victorian era. Bronzed princes riding the breaks to the shore on timber planks.

I am too early for my train and wait in a cafe serving tiffin and tea – a reward for walking 245 miles from Berwick in 10 days. Cromer seems a step away now, but even though there will be no hills, the King Charles III England Coast Path has yet to open for much of the remaining route. The sections to Hull will be a challenge, as will the Lincolnshire coastline, but a path will make itself known, and I will find a way. I have a few days to research in the comfort of my home, study OS maps and talk to friends who have walked around the area. For now, I drift off to sleep with the train's rocking motion, until I change at Hull for the faster 'Land of Green Ginger' service to London.

# 17
# BRIDLINGTON TO BOSTON
## A Dead Bod and Oss Wash

*'To be everywhere is to be nowhere.'*
                                            Seneca

### Distance walked: 1,980 miles

I have butterflies again, and I cannot explain my pre-travel nerves. I know they will pass as I take my first steps, but I have yet to understand why I get them. It takes inward courage to set out on your own, to dare to live. Maybe it is a fear of the sacrifices made for the freedom of a long walk: fewer comforts, solitude, and leaving home and family. Whatever it may be, it works away in my unconscious mind, and I must find an answer.

It usually makes sense to book a return spilt ticket for only a little more than a single. With a little skill and a friendly chat at a ticket counter, it's surprising how cheaply you can reach a walking destination if you are flexible on travel dates and times. A collection of paper tickets facilitates my return to Bridlington and possible routes home from Boston.

I am greeted by a rainbow as I retrace my steps to the harbour and head south. My nerves fade as I walk the shallow grass cliffs and drop to the low-tide shoreline. With luck I can reach Hornsea without taking a messy and unmarked inland route by walking on the hard sands. Such conditions favour me one day but will defeat me the next and need careful research before the day begins. On this section I must also keep an eye open for jettisoned World War II ordnance from stricken bombers approaching the emergency airfield at RAF Carnaby.

To my right, the cliffs have the consistency of soggy digestive biscuits dunked in a tepid North Sea tea. Like the southern Isle of Wight, the rate of erosion is frightening. The cliffs are not as high, but high and slippery enough to thwart and escape if trapped by the tide. Maps are out of date, and the mean high water is at odds with my precise GPS smartphone. Holiday villages are being consumed, just like the medieval villages once were. The Domesday Book lists 30 or so, now lost to the sea. Wilsthorpe, Auburn, Hartburn and Hyde are now absorbed by nature; their foundations of sand and mud have found a new aquatic home. Two millennia ago, the Roman shoreline was as much as three miles away to the east. The soft clay left behind by the Ice Age dissolves easily, leaving only pebbles, sand and conglomerate stone.

The east coast is highly vulnerable to sea-level rise, where storm surges flow easily from the shallow coastal shelf. The North Sea was a landmass during the Ice Age. Dogger Bank is only 15 metres deep in places yet lies 60 miles offshore, ideal subterranean foundations for out-of-sight wind turbine arrays. Fortunately, I have the right tides and join oystercatchers, plovers, sanderlings and turnstones at the water's edge. My feet seek harder sand, while the birds' bills, all of differing lengths, probe the softer edges of the shoreline to find molluscs, worms, crabs, shrimps, larvae, cockles, ragworms and shellfish. The waves lap gently on the shore, and the wind is light in the lee of the cliffs, protecting me from occasional rain and hail. It is perfect relaxed feeding for them, and perfect walking conditions for me. We are both enjoying the day as we hear the sea whisper her secrets, blown gently by the balletic winds. Poems of the deep released at last to those who dare to listen.

Natural England will find it a challenge to establish an enduring path here, even though it has a right to rebuild routes inland as the coast erodes. For now, the route choice is dictated by tide and weather, and my judgement of the conditions. Caravan and static-home parks hold jealously on to their territory. I sense a bandit backcountry spirit, fighting a boundary dispute with nature with only one outcome. Like in Norfolk, the utility pipes and cables hang like wet-coloured spaghetti pasta from the cliffs, draping over the undermined tarmac and angular concrete foundations into the sea. It will be a familiar sight in the coming days as I navigate along the impermanent coast, mindful of my safety and the escape routes.

I'd thought a campsite might be reachable at Atwick, but I cannot climb the cliff. I pray I can exit at Hornsea, assuming beachgoers have some access. Fortunately a set of steps places me in a car park, where I can sit for a moment to search online for accommodation. I find the perfect B&B, and within two minutes of paying, I knock at the door. The owner answers, reading my confirmation email on his smartphone. 'Gosh, you're quick,' he says. This new means of securing accommodation is a wonder compared to the use of lists and telephones as recently as 10 years ago.

It is a fine breakfast the following morning, eaten early alongside contractors who have parked their vans on the street. I am going to need it, for the weather is foul. It is a strong north-easterly, pushing waves up the groynes. I pass the twin-sister start/end Trans Pennine Cycle Route sculpture, identical to the one on the east coast in Southport. It rotates with quantum-entangled harmony to welcome adventurers to the east coast. I study the tide times and consider it safe to reach Mappleton, but even though it is a good four hours before high tide, I only just make it past the crumbling cliffs. The digestive-coloured biscuits have been replaced with soggy Oreos: black and flecked with white-sugar-cream stones, consumed by the insatiable appetite of a foaming tea-brown milky sea. I am lucky to have an exit up a concrete ramp, marked by the warning sign leaving me in no doubt of the dangers of walking this shoreline. Now, I have no option but to find an inland route to Withernsea.

Looking at my OS map on a smartphone, zooming between the 1:50,000 and 1:25,000 scales, I try to discern paths to follow in the pouring rain. A road brings me to Aldbrough where I can turn towards the cliffs again. The views north are frightening as the hungry gale smashes endless surf into the cliffs for food. No one is about, except for a farm worker who stops in his tractor to confirm a muddy path towards a church tower in the distance, a brief respite from the B road. Old signs still point to destinations where the roads no longer go. Lanes lead to the sea but terminate at solid concrete blocks, to stop anyone driving over a 20-metre cliff face. I trespass where I dare, back to the truncated roads and more navigational church towers, before a long arduous road walk to Withernsea. The town's destiny seems sealed, and that fate somehow infects the inhabitants. It will join a list of many other forgotten communities. Owthorne, Waxholme, Newsham and Old Withernsea lie offshore in their graves.

I find a cafe which is about to close, and attempt to dry out on a concave polypropylene chair which puddles the day's rain and soaks my underclothes with cool water. The waitress looks at me as if I have lost my mind, for who would walk in this weather? She is right, for the next section to Easington is miserable. I begin to wave at the cars that slow to pass me, sometimes with an admonishing toot. The saving grace is lighter traffic at this hour, for I would fear the rush hour to the gas terminal facility. I have learned from my motorcycle training to navigate the curves and present maximum visibility, at times walking in the middle of the road. A flag would help, but I gave the one I borrowed from Fleetwood to Gretna back to its owner, Henry. Instead, I spread my fluorescent microfibre towel around my backpack. The rain eases, but my feet have taken a bashing and blisters are hiding in blood-soaked socks. I am fortunate to find a good campsite. The landlady asks for a car registration, and I tell her where I have walked from. 'You're mad,' she says.

I rest a day. My new sister Jenny lives nearby and has heard of my plight and offered to pick me up in Hull after a short bus ride to the city centre. It is a godsend, as she is an ex-army nurse and knows a thing or two about blisters. 'You're mad!' she says as if I need a reminder. She tapes up my wounds and I catch the bus back to Easington, taking a day's rest to natter and recuperate. At least the sun is shining as I walk to the tip of Spurn Head. The tide is rising but should not flood the spit path on my return, so I relax and pace my walk past the concrete fortifications that litter the beach. A Yorkshire Wildlife Trust warden greets me.

'Please keep to the shoreline, little terns and plovers are back, nesting,' he says. 'You'll be fine on Spurn Head – keep an eye out for short-eared owls.'

These dedicated volunteers put their hearts into protecting these vulnerable species. I am happy to comply, but others, with leadless dogs free to roam, cause untold damage in minutes. I plug away with poles in softer sand near the lapping waves, singing songs to the selkies (seals) who swim alongside. They are curious creatures, and it is easy to see why they captivate us. They are our sea-born spirits, reflections of our souls, a manifestation of opposites living in a secret world. Beach fishermen confirm the tides as I walk beneath their transparent mono-filament lines, waiting to haul in a flattie. Oystercatchers, dunlins and sanderlings sing their songs, as do the herring-ball shimmer puffs of the goldfinches inland. This is a rich paradise for a birder and joyful company for a lone walker.

## BRIDLINGTON TO BOSTON

Spurn Head is, by any standard, a stunning land spit, penetrating the mouth of the Humber Estuary. It was home to a lifeboat station and lighthouses, clinging to the shifting sand and shingle. It is a special place where people live, attending to the safety and navigational needs of Grimsby, Hull and Immingham. Buried villages lie within its embrace. Ravenser Odd, a recipient of King Edward I's royal charter in 1299, was more important than the ports of Grimsby and Kingston upon Hull until the sea consumed its sandbank foundations. At its southern tip my GPS suggests I am floating in the sea, for this is a dynamic landscape. The white sands are pristine, a place to sit and watch shipping enter the estuary under the careful eye of the pilot station radar. Harbour porpoises tease with their shallow breach breaths in the waves. A distance post announces that Sydney is 10,474 miles away, and New York is 3,437 miles in the opposite direction. I might as well be a similar distance from anywhere, as this is a lonely, peaceful and precious spot where time and distance are only human concepts.

I turn north into chilling later afternoon wind, following the orphaned railway and road paths that cling to the banks, turning to deeper 4x4 tracks where the sea occasionally breaches the shingle. Birds are nesting, and the Spurn Bird Observatory keeps watch as I head along the seawall path, unsigned, to Kilnsea. I had planned to wild camp in a few miles, but a small campsite appears. I ask the owner if I can stay. He switches off his lawnmower and finds me a simple pitch. He has moved here for the birds and spent years working hard to retire early to follow his passion. It is a blessing to have a shower and water to drink before the long, lonely walk along the northern banks of the River Humber to the city.

I wake early and depart along easy paths but then find the route a challenge at Sunk Island, its flank protected by impassible channels and fenced sluice gates. I explore options and bravely shimmy across a steel pipe to avoid a long walk. Dave, a local dog walker, tells me I must walk to Patrington, but I ignore his advice and almost fall into the ditch. On the opposite bank, a monument pays tribute to Stanley Duncan. He founded WAGBI (Wildfowlers' Association of Great Britain and Ireland) in 1908. It is now known as BASC (British Association for Shooting and Conservation), which on first read is an oxymoron, though it claims to promote a sustainable solution to the sport. Thinking this through helps me understand what I saw at Lindisfarne: we have the power to protect and destroy, and must take a balanced long-term view to protect nature's interest.

Yet these habitats are under an indirect, more concerning threat, for sea-level rise will impact this estuary. Major coastal defence works are evident. Diggers and bulldozers line the fields, waiting to rearrange the seawalls and landscape. I have no option but to follow the diversions in place, but they are signposted, with fully compliant health and safety notices. New sluice gates and pumps will be installed, and buffer zones will be established that permit controlled flooding of the marshlands. Over £150 million will be spent to protect homes and infrastructure, but it is not enough. It will never be enough. Commercial interests take priority in the less-populated areas, and these civil works will thwart my progress into Lincolnshire.

The sea will ultimately succeed, for it has eternity on its side, and future generations will not walk these paths. They will look back, as I do, on the fate of the estuary ports and communities. Nature is heartless and uncompromising, responding in her own way to climate change and the plunder of natural resources – mother Earth, or *Gaia*, as James Lovelock named her, will have the final word. Cod and herring were once abundant, supporting huge industries until their numbers plummeted. Our release of greenhouse gases into the atmosphere will raise sea levels, ultimately overwhelming our efforts to protect the land. Nature is acting over much longer timescales and will prevail as society makes short-term political decisions over the future of our planet – kicking a can down the road until that road ends.

Eventually, the seawall path resumes along gabion cages full of rocks, which are tricky to walk along. The hawthorn blossom is an intense brilliant white, and wildflowers are at their peak. Roe deer are everywhere, in pairs, hopping effortlessly over fences and hiding in the fields and sea marsh. Daytime barn owls glide along the ditches, harriers hunt, and shelduck swim in circles, upending into the shallow creeks to feed. Curlews call out as they fly, a sad call, a lament on the state of the world. Slowly, an overpowering smell reveals an enormous whale carcass, one of two I will see today and the first on my journey. The view to the south bank provides a clue to the flotsam that lives beside them. Cathode ray televisions, disposed of in favour of the latest QLED screens, are common. Then, the endless detritus of the fishing industry:

fish boxes, nets, lubricant bottles, oil containers, floats, rings, hooks, rope – all tangled into plastic Gordian Knot wreckage that grips the shoreline, strangling it in a deathly embrace.

I haven't met a soul since the morning; it is an utterly deserted, isolated and lonely stretch of path. I reach the public houses of Paull, after a nine-hour, 27-mile day. I walk towards the petrochemical plant and catch the X75 EastRider service to the city centre. Sitting on the top deck, I enjoy a panoramic view of Hull's traffic carnage. An anonymous cheap hotel is convenient, next to a Tesco Extra, whose aisles add a couple of thousand steps to my walking day and take ages to navigate to find a simple ready meal.

The same service returns me to Salt End, along a dual carriageway that will be the start of my walk. It is disheartening but surprising how quickly I return to the docks and turn to the quayside. I can barely comprehend the scale of the wind turbine blades at the Siemens Gamesa factory. Three 79.8 metre blades will extract seven megawatts from the air, each turbine enough to power 5,000 homes when the winds blow at an optimal speed. Each structure is taller than the Humber Bridge, thousands of them will be installed in the North Sea farms, named with a logical efficiency: Hornsea 1, Hornsea 2, Dogger Bank A, Dogger Bank B. A poet has taken a moment to reflect as I turn away from the blades:

*Keeping watch from the edge of our shore,*
*The tide is as constant as change.*
*The warp and weft, the ebb and flow.*
*Another rush recedes then is gone.*
*The moon pulls the season onward.*
*Time echoes in time with time.*

I think about the tides. Tides that caress time, a diurnal breathing, older than our consciousness – time echoes in time with time. I love this stuff, and it persists in my thoughts as I walk, calling me to seek and digest its meaning.

The quayside records the changes to the city, which has seen its fair share of industry, war and trade. There is sculpture, art and history at every turn. Of all the people I meet on my walks, the people of Hull stand out as the most friendly and welcoming. It is unsurprising to learn that Hull became the UK City of Culture in 2017, beating Dundee, Leicester and Swansea. I read about 'Dead Bod', and 'Oss Wash'. I am meeting my sister in an hour or so to walk across the bridge, and she will put me up for a few days at her home in North Lincolnshire, where I know our conversations will provide a deeper insight.

Until then, I have an elevated view from the Albert Dock walkways, which take the Trans Pennine Trail through the city to St Andrews Quay. Along the seawall, a sequence of stainless-steel origami triangles appear to fly as the light reflects on their frame-by-frame forms. It takes some research to read about *Migrating Zoetrope*, a public artwork by Adrian Riley and Annabel McCourt. It is a beautiful, moving installation that depicts either the migration of pink-footed geese or the sails of Humber sloops – showing us that we are both subjects in nature and are governed by its rules. Nearby, a more poignant installation tells of a campaign at the peak of the fishing industry – *The Winter of Discontent*. 'Big Lil', or Lillian Bilocca, and her head-scarfed ladies fought for safer working conditions for their menfolk aboard the trawlers. Their determination and demands for a charter resulted in changes to Maritime Law that has saved many lives. It is a tribute to the city's spirit, which I am sure remains, even though the industry has diminished.

I walk under the enormous Humber Bridge, the longest suspension bridge in the world that you can cross on foot. Its aircraft-wing form seems fragile but carries the A15 traffic between South Yorkshire and north Lincolnshire. I am walking briefly on the Yorkshire Wolds Way, another overlap with the King Charles III England Coast Path, before reaching the car park to meet my sister, Jenny.

'Ready for a walk?' she asks, as her husband, Geoff, takes the car to the opposite shore to meet us.

'Why not. It'll be a pleasure,' I smile. We embrace again as brother and sister. 'What's Dead Bod?' I ask.

She tells me the story as we walk on the western path between the towers, looking at artworks created by local children. It is a good mile between the pillars, so we have time. 'It's a bird, well, it was a bird,' she says. 'A seagull landed on a boat with a broken wing, and the captain took care of it for three weeks, nursing it back to health. When he released it, it flew briefly before a startled crewmate kicked it with a scream of "what's that!" "It's a Dead Bod now," came the reply from the captain.' A local artist then painted a depiction of the incident on the corrugated walls at the quayside, and it became a navigational mark. This response would follow whenever a vessel was asked how far along the Humber it had reached.

'I just passed Dead Bod,' was an answer that located a position precisely. It became a saying and a symbol of the city.

I am getting used to Jenny's scouse accent mashed with the local vocabulary. 'Oss Wash' is a horse wash at the docks. 'Breadcake' is yet another word for my white roll collection, and 'Yerolidze' means going on holiday. Jenny is a scream, and the conversation flows easily until we descend to the cafe at the Waters' Edge Country Park. I swap her to walk with Geoff and their dog, Darcy, who bounces up and down with excitement for the first mile to New Holland until his legs start complaining. Walking and talking is a great thing to do. We lose ourselves in conversation that evening, discussing our lives, passions and dreams. We have a lot of catching up to do after 60 years.

Early next morning, Jenny's Ukrainian-grandmother-accented sat nav gets me back to the shoreline for a long walk to Cleethorpes, constantly admonishing her for any wrong turns. I walk through the dockyard where they unload timber from *Lady Amalia*, just in from Scandinavia. The origins of each bundle load is stencilled on the end grain.

Soon, I lose myself in thought along the seawall. The path is peaceful. Sedge, reed and Cetti's warblers chatter in the hedgerow, and a distant cuckoo calls. This tranquillity does not last, replaced by the emerging hum from the Port of Immingham. Huge car transporter ships disgorge rivers of new Mercedes and Peugeots into the car parks. Suzuki and Volvos add to the vast arrays of cars awaiting transportation to dealers – all the same, and yet subtly customised for their new owners. The scale of production is immense; the material and energy costs are unfathomable. It is a sight not seen by the public, whose perception of the motor vehicle is formed by compelling brochures and adverts, promoting status-object desires and wants that are way beyond need.

I must turn inland near the former lighthouses, decaying with a noble patina. Their duties fulfilled, they sit in retirement, observing the overwhelming commerce of the new port. Oil refineries dominate the skyline, and the air hums with industry, chemical processes, trade and materials movement. The only option is to walk along a dual carriageway where the A160 terminates, for the King Charles III England Coast Path has yet to be determined on this stretch. A lone man, a lorry spotter, stands at the roundabout with a camera. He is waiting to photograph a heavy load that will depart soon. I am in luck, as roadworks batch the traffic flow. I can walk quickly into the traffic-free moments and then hide in the verges when I see the next queue released. On another day, this would be a very unwelcome few miles, but I reach the shore eventually and relax for a moment, believing I have an easy walk to Grimsby.

The Environment Agency has started huge coastal defence works at Stallingborough, and my path is blocked. No amount of discussion with the safety officer wearing a fluorescent jacket will get me through. I must walk inland, but fortunately a new cycle path has been built to take me to the fishing port. It is not shown on the map, but this new Immingham to Grimsby Cycle Superhighway guides me to the back streets, and along a rail line and a bridge to the promenade. Blundell Park football ground nestles in the middle of the back-to-back streets, with alternating one-way roads, the homes for the thousands of fishermen and port workers now employed in food industry logistics that remain to this day (Grimsby still processes fish, but it is landed elsewhere). The huge temperature-controlled warehouses dominate, yet I can only find one wet fish shop to meet local needs. The culture of earlier years must have been fascinating; even today, football is central to community cohesion. The pride of the fishing industry lives on, though the vessels no longer pack the harbour.

After a restful night at Jenny's home, I return to Cleethorpes station. I've been spoilt with an enormous curry, which wipes away any calorie deficit I have had since Bridlington. I'll need it as I walk into the remote and wild marshlands with only a seawall to guide me. The route is not clear on the map, but it is obvious on the ground – the freshly cut grass is easy to walk on, and the faint impression of earlier footsteps gives me confidence to proceed. My map misdirects me to Somercotes Haven, where a bridge has been removed. I backtrack through heavy nettles and curse the bloody-minded masochistic stupidity of walking in shorts through the poisoned overgrowth. I put on my waterproof trousers for protection, but the damage is done; the welts bubble on my legs, and I know I will sleep restlessly tonight. I'll never learn.

At Donna Nook the map suggests severe difficulty finding a path, but I need not worry. I will be fine if I keep the range warning signs to the east and follow the informal tide line desire paths. Thousands of seals will give birth to over 2,000 pups along these military shores between October and December. It is one of the largest seal colonies in England. The bombing range ironically gives them an undisturbed shoreline where people cannot tread. Unexploded ordnance litters the ranges, and the Lincolnshire Wildlife Trust manages this harmonious relationship. Redshank feed in the salt marsh, and partridge, skylark, dunnock, whitethroat, linnet and yellowhammer nest in the scrub. Little terns will breed too, beyond the severe notices that warn of death to humans. Not that a fisherman seems to care as he walks nonchalantly to the shoreline with his bait pump.

I am grateful for an easy path through samphire beds between the marsh and the scrub. I climb into Saltfleet and find a fish and chips takeaway embedded in a caravan park. It serves a simple but excellent fish supper, lifting my spirits. I relax a little along easier paths that connect shoreline car parks together. The rain eases as I venture on to the low-tide sands to Mablethorpe, where I am delighted to find a *Time and Tide Bell* in the sands. This is one of the most evocative public art installations on the coast, created by the sculptor and musician Marcus Vergette. The harmonic structure of the bell plays a beautiful tone – a message concerning sea levels. It is like a church bell calling, a warning, an artwork that connects to emotions, triggering, it is hoped, a call to action.

A group of walkers arrive, unsure of the object they see, their dog barking at its alien form. I ring the bell as the tide is out. To everyone's amazement, they pay attention and the chatter stops. The dog is silenced, not defensive or aggressive, as if it, too, understands what the bell is trying to say. Usually, the bell rings its harmonics as it is triggered by the ebb and flow of the tide. A conversation starts about its meaning; it is working as intended – stimulating thought and discussion of our future.

Religiously, I touch the fingerpost I'll return to in the morning before walking inland to a campsite. The host gives up looking for the category of 'senior backpacker' and lets me stay for free. His wife normally takes the bookings but the computer is a mystery to him, although he looks like he could rebuild his lawnmower in an afternoon and service his own car. He warns of the coastal defence work ahead.

'They're rearranging the sands over the next week or so,' he tells me. 'You'll see dredgers offshore, sucking up sand and blowing it on to the beach. The path should be ok, I hope.'

Sure enough, fluorescent-gowned grown men are playing with their enormous toys, digging, piping and combing sand along the beach. A small fleet of dredgers lies offshore, gurgling away. The Environment Agency has set up information boards about more lost villages and floods. Extracts from an 1863 poem recall the search for survivors, another bell ringing loudly from Enderby church, now lost to the sea, mimicking the earlier artwork:

*Then some look'd uppe into the sky,*
*And all along where Lindis flows*
*To where the goodly vessels lie,*
*And where the lordly steeple shows.*
*They sayde, 'And why should this thing be?*
*What dangers lowers by land or sea?*
*They ring the tune of Enderby!*

*'For evil news from Mablethorpe,*
*Of pyrate galleys warping down;*
*For shippes ashore beyond the scorpe,*
*They have not spar'd to wake the towne:*
*But while the west bin red to see,*
*And storms be none, and pyrates flee,*
*Why ring 'The Brides of Enderby'?'*

*'The olde seawall,' one cried, 'is downe,*
*The rising tide comes on apace,*
*And boats adrift in yonder towne,*
*Go sailing uppe the market-place.'*
*He shook as one that looks on death:*
*'God save you, mother!' straight he saith–*
*'Where is my wife, Elizabeth?'*

Jean Inglelow, extract from *The High Tide on the Coast of Lincolnshire* (1571)

## BRIDLINGTON TO BOSTON

Pictures of the 1953 flood give evidence of the destructive nature of this capricious sea. The combination of spring high tide, a low-pressure storm surge and northerly gales forced water into a North Sea geological funnel drained only by the English Channel. The effect was devastating, killing 2,500 people on its shores in the UK and in continental Europe.

The King Charles III England Coast Path is open from Mablethorpe to Skegness, so I feel more comfortable navigating to Chapel St Leonards and the North Sea Observatory. Unfortunately, the art space is closed at the UK's only purpose-built marine observatory. I continue along the promenade that separates acres of static caravans, almost a mile deep to the west. Their occupants explore the shops, pubs, amusement arcades and leisure parks. Butlin's is monumental, with the emphasis on those last two syllables. It is 11am, but it should be 11pm, for the party has started already. Ingoldmells's Rock City is bright, brash and in your face – strangely beautiful and compelling, channelling Las Vegas hedonism. The huge tents of Butlin's dominate, as do the Fantasy Island rollercoaster rides. I don't know if the security fences are to keep people in or out, for the site looks like an open prison. I look completely out of place as I walk past the diners, carvery, pubs, chippies, karaoke bars. The energy subsides briefly until I enter Skegness, where this unbridled fun returns.

I reach the car park near the lifeboat station and walk back into the salt marsh through a narrow gap. A switch flips, the sounds of party land have gone, and the light turns from daylight neon to a lower, natural colour temperature. I head for Gibraltar Point and unpuzzle a path to the visitor's centre, walking around deep water channels that have changed their course and dismantled the fence line. I can relax for a cuppa and light meal and contemplate my route to Boston across a remote and desolate marshland on a very long seawall.

I have arrived at the north-westerly edge of the Wash. This is England's sea lung, which breathes twice a day through its aquatic trachea, bronchi, bronchioles and alveoli – mimicking mudflat and marshland channels, creeks and streams. A timeless regular motion, the unstoppable rhythm of our planet, to which life has adapted. It is huge, and it takes a healthy walk of 100 miles to reach Hunstanton. But first, I must enter Wainfleet Sand by climbing a gate to cross a critical footbridge.

A barn owl watches me as I lever around its steel wire security fence protecting the gate; one slip and I'll be in a deep canal. I have fretted about this crossing for days, seeking advice, so it is a joy to escape along the seawall and turn inland to Wainfleet St Mary for a campsite. I hope the gate opens when the path is formally defined, as the inland routes are tortuous and unclear.

Trevor greets me at the campsite and refuses a fee to stay.

'You'll be fine now to Boston,' he says. 'I used to run the marathon from Skegness every year, but now that's stopped. Take the sea banks that have cut grass; it is hard going otherwise.'

It is a pleasant stay, and I fill up with enough water for the eight or nine hours to the Lincolnshire market town and inland port, for none will be found on the path. I sink a litre before I leave, knowing this will be a hot day. I march down to the seawall and head towards a bombing control tower, now obsolete since the range closed in 2010. Since World War I, fixed-wing and rotary aircraft have used this sand and salt marsh stretch to drop their munitions into the mud, attempting to hit ramshackle targets. Now, it runs quiet, and the risk of unexploded ordnance (UXO) will keep the people away, much to the delight of the wildlife.

You can now stay at the tower and sleep in an old Lynx helicopter or Jetstream aircraft, which have had their seats removed and replaced with bedding. The control tower has been converted to a living room, with views over the Wash – it is a quirky and unusual place. It would be perfect if you like military history and would appreciate some peace to reflect on its original purpose.

The seawall hugs the field boundaries. The ploughed fields vanish into the distance, the furrows convergent points moving as I walk. I can hear the flood tide move in from the sea, filling the salt marsh faster than I can walk. The birds flock inland before it engulfs them. This is a long and lonely section. There are no dog walkers or farmers for miles until I arrive at a road betrayed by a cloud of dust from a landowner's Toyota Land Cruiser. He is stopping with a farm manager to measure moisture in the crops. It looks as if they could spend the day doing this, for the size and number of fields are of an industrial scale. As I approach Boston, tractors pull picker frames over the fields, and cabbages and other vegetables or fruit are plucked and processed in a job yet to be mechanised.

The hours have ticked by easily as I reach the RSPB Freiston Shore lake. A little further on I am hoping to find cake and tea at the 'We'll Meet Again' World War II Homefront Museum. It is closed, so I walk on to meet a trail-angel couple digging out fence foundations at a cottage they are restoring.

'You look in need of a cuppa,' they suggest. 'How far have you walked?'

They know that my direction will mean I have had a long day and that no facilities exist along this long sea bank route.

'Fancy a biscuit?' the woman asks me, opening a large packet of shortbread. 'If you're off to Boston, you must visit the prison first. It's just down the road, and the path goes right through it.' I am not sure if she is joking or not.

As soon as I see the sentinel landmark that is St Botolph's Church (known locally as The Stump) I can gauge how far I have to walk, but its height deceives. Sure enough, I reach the prison, where a nurse emerges from a hut.

'Wait a moment,' she says. 'We'll ring a guard to walk you through.'

The guard, Neil, welcomes me, handcuffs and radio jangling from his belt, and walks me along the public footpath to the opposite outer boundary of the open prison. I am convinced this ensures I don't leave anything behind rather than protects me from the occupants.

'We don't see many walkers this far out,' Neil says. 'You are the first for a few days.'

I feel like an escapee as I clamber over the furrows in the field, baked hard by the sun. My route is blocked by the Haven, a deep channel that severs the salt marsh connecting Boston to the Wash. I walk with the incoming tide towards Boston Stump, knowing its form marks the end of my day. Along this waterway, in 1607, the Pilgrim Fathers would have sailed in the opposite direction to my walk, on a n ebb tide and in their first attempt to flee to Holland. They were betrayed by their captain and arrested. They would ultimately succeed in their quest to escape persecution, sailing across the Atlantic. In memory of that day, they would name Boston, New England, in the USA.

## THE COAST IS OUR COMPASS

I reach a cheap B&B, eat at the local pub, and contemplate the journey ahead. I decide to return in a few weeks as the spacing between accommodation options would work perfectly. It is a remote section ahead, and my wife has offered to bring the campervan to meet me in Norfolk, whose tree-lined shores I saw in the distance earlier.

# 18
# BOSTON TO CROMER
## Skinny rambling

*'As far as we can discern, the sole purpose of human existence is to kindle a light of meaning in the darkness of mere being.'*
Carl Jung

### Distance walked: 2,180 miles

My journey is coming to an end. 'The distance is nothing, only the first step is difficult' is an often-quoted maxim, but I am beginning to realise that it is the last step that will be the hardest. I will return to normality, I am getting older, and I might never walk this path again. Life is lived forward but remembered backwards and those memories become increasingly important, a reminder to treasure your remaining days that could end at any moment. These days near their goal, but I have some left to spend to complete my journey.

The accommodation options are limited until I reach King's Lynn, some 45 miles away. A wild camp is certain; therefore, I will walk until the evening light fades to sunset, or low energy suggests I stop. This is a remote path, and I should have no difficulties finding a wild camp spot. I walk out from Boston, its Eastern European markets and shops busy with customers. The market town is evolving, its roots and heritage in fishing and agriculture, whose fertile fields feed a nation still. A few remaining seafood and shellfish merchants sell directly to locals. Like the Grimsby wet market I passed a week ago, they depict a time past when the distance from net to table was minimal.

A sign marks the start of the 300-mile Macmillan Way, a route for sponsored walkers established by the cancer charity which follows the limestone belt across England, ending in Abbotsbury in Dorset. I use their waymarks to enter the square shape of the Wash basin, punctured by the Rivers Welland, Nene and Great Ouse. These manmade drainage channels define this landscape. Everywhere I look is at sea level, the difference between land and water being a sea bank, a sluice gate or an automated pump. Dutch engineers worked with wealthy landowners in the 18th century to tame an incredibly lush and abundant wilderness into profitable farmland. The Fen Tigers fought against this change and rising sea levels will one day reclaim it. Over 1,500 square miles of fenland are at risk, even with an audacious plan to seal the Wash with a tidal barrage.

Mother Nature has not been tamed yet, for the salt and marshland to Fosdyke Bridge harbour a proliferation of breeding birds. Avocets and Arctic terns pester me, protecting their nests. Inquisitive cows walk alongside, mixing their diet of grass with seaweed. They are unsure of this rare walker in their midst and want to introduce themselves, but I am nervous as I have nowhere to go if they decide to evict me. Sponsored cancer charity walkers will now head along the River Welland to Dorset, but I cross the bridge after collecting water at the marina.

The clouds are heavy, the south-westerly pushing their cargo of rain towards me. I head back on to the endless seawalls into serene emptiness, with no evidence of people or buildings. I pitch just as the rain starts, taking a snooze to a pitter-patter tune on my flysheet. The sun briefly appears before resting for the night, enough time to prepare a freeze-dried meal to satisfy my hunger. I peer out of the flysheet at the hunting barn owls patrolling the fields for their evening meal. The wind dies and silence descends, enveloping a lone walker into a deep dream world as the stars emerge in the night sky, so clear that I can count them just above the horizon. I awake later for a call of nature and exit the tent to stand unclothed to pee. The Milky Way shines above me, revealing colour in the constellations, galaxy and nebula. A shooting star underlines the awe I experience, for this theatre is a common church for all the inhabitants on our planet and one we should attend more often to be reminded of our scale in the universe.

On days like this you get up early, allowing nature's clock to ring the alarm. The quiet psithurism, a whispering of the reeds along the dykes, changes tone with the variations of the wind. The paths are ready to walk as the cut sea bank grass dries quickly. I pack the tent, and I lift the pack to my back. I tick off my last-minute checks: switching my phone to airplane mode, looking for buried tent pegs and clearing any litter before grabbing my trekking poles, left plugged into the soil the night before. Only human-shaped pressed grasses remain as evidence of an overnight stay and will soon recover to leave no trace of my passage.

At this hour, the paths are deserted – the sea bank is a dividing line, extending endlessly into drained fields and marshlands. Inland, I can see the regular matrix of drainage channels and ploughed fields to my right, and to my left, the Mandelbrot marsh fractal patterns of the estuarial channels. One landscape has been painted by man, the other by the tides. One reclaimed for agriculture, the other as nature intended. Marsh harriers hunt along the tree line, and grey herons glide down the channels, calling loudly as they lift into the air on massive wings. I don't think I have walked in such isolation before, but this tranquillity is shattered when a BAE Hawk T2 advanced jet trainer screams from the clouds on a high-angle strafing run to a target in the salt marsh. I have arrived at the RAF Holbeach Air Weapons Range and should have paid more attention to the signs and red flags. The jet rises and curves into the sky to loop around for a second run – their true menacing power revealed, unlike their PR-orchestrated acrobatic behaviour at an airshow.

The YouTuber Ted Coningsby, a passionate follower of military air movement, is filming. His teddy bear mascot dances across the screen before each clip, carrying an RAF flag. His VHF radio squawks unintelligible commentary between the aircraft and the control tower, his excitement palpable.

'They are not kinetic today, only practice runs for new pilots,' Ted tells me. 'But you should have seen the F-15E Strike Eagles the other day dropping their Paveways. Here he comes again!' he screams, panning the camera in their direction. The T2 emerges from the cloud in silence, until its sound cone reaches you. I get drawn into Ted's excitement, for much of my youth was spent at RAF bases worldwide, and the display awakens those memories. The strong contrast to this morning's walk could not be more unsettling, but I am thrilled.

We chat for a while, and his passion and enthusiasm are undeniable. A few others are recording footage, aeroplane spotters highly addicted to the awesome power of modern aeronautical engineering and weaponry. The birds benefit too; the weapons are not armed and so cause little damage, but their presence is very effective at keeping people away. The brent geese will nibble their *zostera marina* weed in winter – the seawrack or eelgrass that thrives in the mudflats alongside unexploded ordnance. These contrasting worlds coexist, each benefiting the other in unusual, unexpected ways.

I meet the first dog walker since Boston, his pair of spaniels unusually obedient, betraying their gun dog training. After explaining my walk, he urges me to keep an eye out for the lighthouses ahead, which mark the entrance to the River Nene.

'Peter Scott lived there in the 1930s, collecting wildfowl birds, writing and painting,' the dog walker tells me.

'I thought his home was in Slimbridge, Gloucester?'

'Yes, later, after the war.'

'I've been there. Didn't he have something to do with saving a Hawaiian bird?'

'Yes, the nēnē, a goose, he collected and bred them before extinction; there were only 30 pairs left, now there are 3,000 after he sent pairs back to the Big Island in Hawaii.'

'What a coincidence, that's the name of this river, the River Nene; surely those names are not connected? I must find out.'

It is a happy coincidence, as a quick Google that evening confirms no apparent connection. I also learn more about Scott's origins as a wildfowler and how he became the world's pre-eminent conservationist, once more illustrating the important connection between sport and conservation. The lighthouses are beautiful, gatekeepers to the fens and now private homes. The one on the western side is empty; Scott's former residence is opposite on the eastern bank.

Crossing the swing bridge, built in 1897, I follow a road until I pass his lighthouse and enter the familiar remote sea bank landscape again. A sign warns of no facilities for 10 miles. I had a good night's rest at the B&B, demolished a full English and ate too many chips with my battered fish, so I'll be fine until King's Lynn. I walk deeper into a remote and featureless landscape, the only foreign form the weird Outer Trial Bank island, a prototype landmass experiment for a freshwater lake. I cannot see a building, tractor or any evidence of walkers, farmers, birdwatchers or anyone else. In that moment of isolation, I have a compelling urge to walk naked. Why not? I skinny dip; why not skinny ramble? It is warm, the winds are slight, a little more suncream in the right place and I'll be fine.

Removing all clothing except my hat and shoes, I haul my pack to my shoulders and walk on with poles in each hand. The experience is immediately delicious, thrilling and liberating, just like a naked swim in the sea. It connects you to your environment; you are vulnerable, exposed, and free. I vow to keep going like this but scan the horizon for any voyeur and rehearse the hasty sequence of putting my shorts back on. At first, the fear of discovery is naughty, magical, rebellious, subversive, but it becomes natural to walk naked after an hour. The fear of discovery is replaced by a fear of forgetfulness and images of me standing before a stranger talking about the weather, not realising I am in the buff. My experience is Schrödinger's cat experiment – I walk in a landscape box where I am neither naked nor clothed until observed. This makes me feel less guilty, and that guilt subsides further as I feel the utter joy and liberation it brings.

In proper attire, I arrive at the West Lynn Ferry, having crossed into Norfolk naked. Now, I walk the streets of King's Lynn, a fenland port and market town not unlike Boston in Lincolnshire, both anchoring the Wash to the landmass. It is an opportunity to stock up before an equally remote walk north. My wife has driven up in the campervan and will solve the accommodation problem for a few nights. I plan to meet her at Shepherd's Point, a good walk towards Hunstanton. The King Charles III England Coast Path is fully open for the remainder of the Wash shoreline, and then the Norfolk Coast Path National Trail will take me to my destination, now open along the full county border. After walking around the docks and attendant industrial parks, I return to a seawall that offers views of salt marshes before it dumps me below to the path between the wall and the drainage ditch. The local KLWNWA (King's Lynn and West Norfolk Wildfowlers Association) club seem reluctant to give up their sea view, and their old signs still warn of trespass and the need to carry a membership card. Cattle roam freely, with their water butts located on the path. Unnecessary gates and fences would trap you if they were taking a drink, as there would be no option but to walk through them at close quarters or return to King's Lynn. Other signs make me feel unwelcome; it is not until I reach RSPB Snettisham that I feel comfortable. It is a pity, as nearby you can see one of the most spectacular wildlife displays in the British Isles. During spring high tides, knot and oystercatchers are forced inland in huge numbers and have nowhere to go other than the gravel shores of the inland lakes. What you may perceive as a grey beach is in fact, thousands of knot huddled together. The slightest disturbance and they lift into the sky in dense clouds. Today, they are out on the mudflats, and I can only see a few shelducks tending to their impossibly cute humbug-coloured chicks on the shoreline.

My wife is sipping a beer as I walk to meet her at the campsite. Showered and fed, I sleep deeply in the comfort of the van after another nine-hour day. I look at the map and realise I can reach Wells-next-the-Sea, some 30 miles away, tomorrow. The path will be flat and easy-going on a familiar route, part of the Peddars Way and North Norfolk Coast Path, the 19th National Trail I completed a few years ago. I know the paths well, and I can carry a day pack. Plenty of refreshments are on the route, so I can lighten my pack further. A coastal bus can take care of any contingency.

I leave early, which is a top tip if you plan a long day. The high tide is hard against the shoreline, quite different from yesterday afternoon's low-tide scene, where you would struggle to see the sea. A few hours ago, the featureless mudflats would have seemed benign, now, waves crash into the breakwaters. Where shingle beach remains, nesting spots are roped off to protect the plovers. Inland, the marshland is home to waders, wildfowl and the occasional raptor. Through Heacham, the holiday shacks are exposed to the elements, ramshackle and uninsurable temporary beach dwellings. I smile at an artist painting, the perfect bohemian resident connecting with the beauty of the seascape and seemingly unconcerned with the material comforts of a modern home. Unorganised paint tubes, pots and brushes spill out of the doorway. Her mind is focused on the moment of creativity as she interprets the colour in the morning sky.

Hunstanton, pronounced 'huns-stun', is nearby. I marvel at the lazy Norfolk accent that seeks to reduce any complex noun to two syllables. The town is waking slowly, a pocket-sized resort that could never compete with Skegness on the opposite shore. To my surprise, I see fulmars glide by and then find myself climbing above the unusual iron-pigment-stained red chalk cliffs where they nest. My calf muscles haven't seen such elevation for weeks. I walk to the lighthouse, long since decommissioned, and take a moment to reflect on my walk from Gibraltar Point. If someone were to ask me which part of the coast was my favourite, I might answer the Wash. It has been a unique experience to walk around – manmade geography with a latent natural energy. You can sense the fecundity beneath the soil, waiting to be free again – the largest expanse of littoral landscape on my walk. If the Fen Tigers had their way, the ghosts of eels, birds, fish and other sea creatures would return to replace the incredibly productive industrial agriculture – Mother Nature temporarily captured to feed us.

The coastline turns to sand, endless beach penetrated by shifting channels and impermanent dunes and a dangerous landscape to navigate. The huge expanse of Holme Dunes, Scolt Head and Holkham Beach forms an uninhabited world where birds, seals and wildflowers thrive. The path weaves around the creeks, and occasionally I am forced deep inland away from the coastline. A volunteer ranger is speaking to as many dog walkers as possible, encouraging owners to keep pets on leads, for the terns and plovers are breeding in the dunes. Beach areas are roped off to protect the oystercatchers sitting on their nests. The shoreline is overlaid with thousands upon thousands of razor-clam shells, which crunch beneath my feet. The skyline is open, and the sea breeze fills my lungs with the North Sea air.

The Crab Hut at Brancaster Staithe is busy with appreciative customers ordering crayfish or crab specials, and tea in a proper mug that you recycle at the return window. The holidaymakers and tourists are out in force, arriving by the coach load for boat trips, bird sanctuary excursions, woodland and beach walks – clutching ice creams or paper coffee mugs from other vendors. With their remaining hands, they tap away at smartphone screens, rendering them unable to swing their arms as they walk. I am in a similar dream state but plugged into the surrounding landscape, head high, mind open. I arrive at Wells and walk past another Zoltar, who offers no free advice on my penultimate day. My wife waits at the campsite, beer in one hand and a book in the other.

'Walked far, dear?' I giggle at her gentle sarcasm. 'There is a beer in the fridge. Have a shower, and I'll start the meal.' This is an unexpected luxury for a lone walker who normally struggles to resist a need to lie down and fall asleep after a 30-mile day.

## THE COAST IS OUR COMPASS

My wife will meet her good friend after I leave early for Cromer on my final day. I am full of energy and march at a pace that celebrates the general fitness that has developed. I pass other walkers, teasing an occasional competitive streak in them to keep pace with me. I am light and move fast on easy paths. My progress is not just a function of fitness but of developing proprioception (the body's awareness in space), foot placement and rhythm that has developed over thousands of miles. More than that, I am in some sort of hurry to finish, but don't know why. It is not a race. Walking is not a sport, but my psyche urges me to complete this epic journey around the coast of England.

This is day 116, or a total of 110 days of walking if I count the half-days travelling to the path. I have recorded 2,300 miles and 830 active hours in my diary, but it is not necessarily accurate, as I do not use a fitness tracker. I have missed an island or two and crossed estuaries by public ferry services. That explains the shortfall, and I'll walk those estuaries and islands later. I am not pedantic, and anyone circumnavigating the coast of Britain will understand how conditions impact distance. After many years of walking long distances, I start to measure progress in hours rather than miles, and even that consideration becomes irrelevant as I harmonise with the natural rhythms of nature.

What does matter to me is the joyful experience of walking alone along a diverse coastline – seeing, listening to, smelling, touching and feeling nature and the outdoors in various weather conditions. This experience is enriched by all the people I meet along the way, their humour, their insights and wisdom. I have listened and learned a great deal about art, nature, science, industry, environmental impact and social issues, and the interplay between those realms. I hope I have developed a balanced understanding of our future challenges – a story that can be told, not to those who already accept the scientific evidence and impact, but to those who choose not to accept, or have yet to understand the consequences of inaction. Art in all its forms has the power to change the world, and for me, walking is an artistic expression that connects people with place.

A movie of the entire walk plays in my head, the life of my journey sensing the end. I celebrate the emotions that surface as my mind circumnavigates from the rump of Norfolk, around the eastern and southern coastlines to Cornwall, where I turned right to follow the western shores to Gretna. Tears are building as the scenes play from Berwick, recalling the north-eastern beauty to the Wash, and those final miles I took just a week ago. I stop and breathe deeply, an intermission to catch those feelings until the path pulls me forward. My life is in natural motion again; walking to stand still – a simple act of placing one foot in front of the other.

The swallows are looping turns in the creeks. The marsh harriers are patrolling and pouncing on their prey. Black-headed gulls and terns search for food. Warblers whistle, bearded tits ping, robins sing, and goldfinches fill the air with colour. They have become friends, and I will miss them – earlier than expected, for they hide in the rain as the sun is extinguished by a weather front. The early morning warmth has gone, and the paths turn to wet shingle along a misty beach occupied only by hardy fishermen who have retired to their triangular poly-shell tents. As if by magic, the sun returns at very moment my shoes touch firmer grass paths. The brief annoyance of damp pebble-skating is replaced by easier strides up the hill to the Sheringham lookout station above the golf course.

As I enter West Runton, I descend to the beach for a final mile, passing one more number 103 beach hut for my photographic collage. I can now see Cromer Pier. As I get closer, my wife and her friend appear, waving at me. Before I know it, we are embracing, but our elations are overtaken by the town's festivities, for a 1960s-style carnival is in full swing. Quite literally, as Lindy Hop dancers twirl on the boardwalks of the pier and jazz bands play. Mods on scooters mingle with their former Rocker enemies on classic motorcycles, sharing their passions and polishing regimes.

I am swept up in the celebrations, displacing my own thoughts and emotions, which will take months to process. Writing this book is a start, a cathartic experience, forcing me to understand and process the memories that have been gently laid with such care by the act of walking. Those memories are secure for now and will entertain me as they re-emerge in the coming years, making connections with the future, activating my curiosity, leading me to further adventure and learning.

I am reminded of the words of Gwyn Thomas – 'But the beauty is in the walking, we are betrayed by destinations.' I will reflect on how my journey has shaped me, changed me, and taught me what it means to be alive. Arriving back at the beginning of my journey connects me to a younger self. I hope I am wiser, more tolerant and happier. I feel a deep and satisfying serenity, earned through the achievement. It is a feeling I want to experience again as another journey takes shape in my mind; another coastal journey guided by my inner compass.

## Distance walked: 2,290 miles.

# FURTHER READING

It is easy to Google, use social media or an AI chatbot to find information about the coast paths and the people that use, manage and protect the coastal margin, wildlife and landscape. I curate pages on my website that try to keep step with their activities over time, with useful links to further information. If you want to know more, along with an approach to planning, safety, navigation, accommodation and the gear I use, then visit this website: *trailplanner.co.uk*.

Via this site you can find a series of digital maps that show most of the locations mentioned in my writing, plus path news, stoical quotations and information on public art, nature organisations, nuclear sites, ferries, geology and nature zones. It's updated regularly, with more information about other coastal journeys in Scotland, Wales and beyond. You can subscribe to this WordPress site to keep in touch.

I want to highlight the work of a new charity, National Trails UK, who have in scope the national designated long-distance routes with a mission to bring together many organisations to conserve, promote and make accessible these iconic trails for all. Many of their aims align with my goals for this book, not least to inspire others to experience the coastline. One of their initiatives will explore the opportunity to leverage the newly designated coastal margin, a landscape established when the King Charles III England Coast Path was opened and roughly defined as the land between the path and low tide. This important biodiverse habitat for wildlife and nature (some 950 square miles) is a landscape threatened by coastal erosion and rising sea levels. Together with the National Trails (almost 6,000 miles), Parks and Nature Reserves, this forms ecological corridors and areas that, if properly managed, can contribute significantly to the protection of our precious ecosystems, loved by so many who inhabit these islands. Over the coming years, a new initiative – the Coastal Wildbelt – will build a movement to unify, celebrate and develop the ambitions of many individuals and organisations that share a passion for this littoral space. In doing so, nature will connect, people will connect, and we will all thrive to protect and understand this precious world. What could be more important for our own wellbeing and survival? More information about this work can be found at *nationaltrails.uk*.

# ACKNOWLEDGEMENTS

After publishing *Tales from the Big Trails* in 2021, I have learned a great deal about the publishing industry and have met so many people who share my passion for walking in nature. Doors have opened, new avenues of curiosity have been revealed, and my appreciation of nature and community has grown. Together with the countless interactions on the coast path, I have had time, while walking, to reflect and process a myriad of conversations into the words you will find in this book. I must thank everyone in this community. Many of you may recognise your contributions, although not necessarily in the location we met.

A few close friends need a special mention: Jackie, Fiona, Betsy (and her wonderful book club), Stuart and Tony. They have contributed, challenged and inspired me in ways they cannot imagine, often triggering new ideas and concepts that have found their way into the chapters. The same can be said of the numerous artists I have spoken to, whose names are mentioned elsewhere in this book. Their work is a catalyst that unlocks what I see and what I feel as I walk – changing my beliefs and values, challenging me to go further and examine the world we live in, and the threats to our environment.

The greatest contribution, and acknowledgement, must be to my family. Foremost, my wife, Alison, who has helped me process the fundamental importance of a meaningful connection with nature, community and family. It helps that she is a professional therapist, and if her peers recognise her input into this work, played back through the artistic practice of walking, then we will be thrilled. She has endured long conversations, patiently listened, and allowed me to spend so much time outdoors. I revisit special locations with her, ones that only a walker discovers, so she can experience the beauty of the coastline. Both of my daughters have reviewed the chapters and helped me polish the sharp edges. I am immensely proud of them, for they are now giving back wisdom, maturity and emotional intellect that makes me gasp at times. They too, appear in *The Coast is Our Compass*, more than they know.

Lastly, special thanks go to the team at Bradt Guides, who helped me bring this work to publication. We all seem to share a passion for curiosity, learning and adventure.

# LIST OF ARTISTS

The public art installations on the coast of England had a big influence on my journey, stimulating thoughts and emotions that I processed as I walked. Art is often ambiguous, so my interpretation of the work will not necessarily resonate with others; they played to my state of mind at the time they were encountered and are personal. I want to thank all the artists mentioned in the book and list them, and others I learned of later, below. They can also be found on the digital map mentioned in the introduction, with links to their individual websites. I'm adding more artists to this map as I continue to explore the coastline of England, Scotland and Wales – coastal public art is powerful and necessary.

**Adam Bridgland** *adambridgland.co.uk* – YOU ARE THE DAWN AFTER MY DARK. This work remains with me still, years after I encountered it on the beach. It is an optimistic post-pandemic statement.

**Maggi Hambling** *maggihambling.com* – SCALLOP. A symbol of pilgrimage and of the sea, and a shelter, which is how I used it. The echoes of the sea reflected in its feminine form, a symbol of fertility and for me, the evolution of our life from the sea.

**J. A. Baker** – THE PEREGRINE. A work that at first I found fascinating and then started to question. Did he really experience those events, or did he imagine them? I learned that the longer you spend in nature, the more you see. So perhaps it was I who was blind.

**Ali Pretty** *beachofdreams.org* – BEACH OF DREAMS. A public community art project that started in 2021 with a walk from Lowestoft to Tilbury, a 500-mile journey with 500 silk flags. The project still grows, with events beyond the timeframe of this book.

**Cornelia Parker** – FOLKESTONE MERMAID. The symbolism of the mermaid, in the context of climate change. It reminded me of *Jibaro*, an episode of Love, Death + Robots on Netflix, which I took to be a metaphor for the destruction of nature, defended by a siren.

**Derek Jarman** – PROSPECT COTTAGE. This was a delight to find on the shingle expanse of Dungeness. The garden blends into the landscape and occasionally the wonderful interiors are open to the public.

**Luke Jerram** *lukejerram.com* – MUSEUM OF THE MOON. One of many spheres installed in a variety of locations as part of a touring exhibition. I have yet to see GAIA or MARS, but the placement of these artworks in a cathedral setting is very powerful.

**Thrussels** *thrussels.com* – ROOK WITH A BOOK. Completed in 2018, named Isla. A giant rook holding a book celebrating the famous writer Daphne Du Maurier, who lived in Fowey. The book is titled *The Birds* – one of her short stories. It looks quite sinister.

**Carole Vincent and Anthony Fanshawe** – THE BUDE LIGHT 2000. A millennium needle of rock, with internal LED lighting to celebrate the invention of the Bude Light in 1830 by Sir Goldsworthy Gurney. I haven't seen it by night, but it was my touchstone between my walks on the South West Coast Path.

**Damien Hirst** – VERITY. I am someone who does not like this public artwork, so take a trip to Ilfracombe and see for yourself which side of the fence you sit. It'll be moved soon.

**Louise Butcher** – a double mastectomy marathon runner. An inspiration to do your thing. I saw Louise running near her hometown of Braunton. Running as artistic expression.

**Svetlana Kondakova Muir** *svetlanakondakova.com* – BURNHAM-ON-SEA LIFE (MUDFLAT). There are many mosaics along the coastline, but this work is one of the finest I have seen. I depicts the ecology of the landscape you see in front of you, revealing hidden secrets.

**Graffiti Artists** – M4 UNDERPASS. Celebrating Chepstow, constantly changing. Many underpasses are heavily graffitied, but these works are examples of beautiful street art. See also *lucanart.com*.

## LIST OF ARTISTS

**Peter Blake** – DAZZLE FERRY. *Snowdrop*, a ferry with a stunning colour scheme and a wonderful pop-art public artwork that transports passengers every day between Birkenhead and Liverpool.

**Antony Gormley** *antonygormley.com* – ANOTHER PLACE. Another representation of his bodily form, like the Angel of the North and many other works. The local council fought hard to get this installation, which has now found a home at Crosby. It is very moving, and worth exploring at different times of year, in different light and weather conditions.

**Morecambe Bay Partnership** *morecambebay.org.uk*. A charity dedicated to connecting people with nature, culture and heritage. Their *waysaroundthebay.org.uk* website gives information about the bay for anyone who would like to explore this area.

**Stephen Broadbent** *broadbent.studio/the-mythic-coast* – MYTHIC COAST – SEA SWALLOW. A collection of works at Cleveleys, commissioned by Wyre Council to illustrate the coastal defence works. Worth a day just to explore them all and to reflect on the power of the sea.

**Chris Drury** *chrisdrury.co.uk* – HORIZON LINE CHAMBER. One of only two camera obscura art installations I have come across. The other was a temporary installation in North Berwick in 2024, during the Fringe by the Sea Festival – *fringebythesea.com/the-forecast*. *The Forecast: Imminent, Rising, Becoming Severe*, by Karen Lamond and Philip Pinsky. Meeting them helped me reinterpret Chris's work.

**Anthony Padgett** – THE PRAYING SHELL. Gifted by the sculptor, a work to commemorate the loss of migrant cockleshell pickers. It opens its heart to a larger power – the tide as it comes into the bay.

**Henry Fletcher** *henryjf.xyz*. Henry's personal flag from the collection by the *Beach of Dreams* project, which I carried after the Morecambe Bay Project walk. It features a cairn he built at Thorpeness – the Coralline Cairn.

**Bridget Riley** – an artist who captures waves, rhythms and shimmers in nature in stunning abstract paintings, many influenced by her time spent in Cornwall. I seek out her work at galleries, where I am transported back to my journeys around the coastline.

**Christine Boyce** –STAINED GLASS/NORMAN NICHOLSON. A stained-glass artist who has interpreted the works of Norman Nicholson – *normannicholson.org*.

**Fire Pit Design** – ALAUNA AURA. A sculpture on South Quay, Maryport.

**Various artists** – AMBLE BORD WAALK. A trail of public sculpture in the seaside port of Amble. Spend a pleasant afternoon finding all 16. There is an app to download, which tells you about each installation and artist. Just search for Amble Bord Waalk in your app store.

**Juan Muñoz** – CONVERSATION PIECE. A captivating work that demands you stop and hold a conversation with the sculpted forms, each different, each with character. A Spanish artist who died in 2001. His work remains, known locally as the Weebles.

**Reg Smythe** – ANDY CAPP – *fabulousnorth.com/andy-capp-statue*. The start of a pleasant day walking around Hartlepool.

**Richard Farrington** *sculptors.org.uk/artists/richard-farrington* – CIRCLE. A quite wonderful charm bracelet. Second edition, after the first was vandalised and thrown down the cliff. See also, *northeaststatues.com/2022/02/07/circle/*.

**ZOLTAR** *zoltar.org*. A fortune-telling robot, often seen at seaside amusement parks. One day I will feed it with a £1 coin, but I am too afraid of what it might say. Made famous by the film *Big*, starring Tom Hanks.

**Annabel McCourt and Adrian Riley** *annabelmccourt.com* and *electricangel.co.uk* – MIGRATING ZOETROPE. A collaboration for a public artwork near St Andrews Quay, Kingston upon Hull. In the right light, and if you walk/run fast enough, the stainless-steel forms move, representing geese in flight. I turned around and did it twice.

**Marcus Vergette** *timeandtidebell.org* – TIME AND TIDE BELLS. One of my favourite coastal artworks which embodied my walk in many ways, connecting the land and the sea, communities and the environment, around the UK coastline. I almost want to reconstruct a walk or cycle which visits them all in a single journey. If you are alone next to a bell that starts to ring as the tide rises, it is an emotional moment.

**Debbie Lyddon** *debbielyddon.co.uk*. A remarkable artist combining walking and coastal art, based in Wells-next-the-Sea. I came across her work after the walk, and it resonated with my experience of the east coast of England. One image, *Day Moon*, from the Fragments series, is the cover for this book. To quote Debbie:

> *This work is about experiencing place, about the consequent memories of that place, of recollection and of imaginative re-creation. It is about how memory underpins the imagination and how new work is developed by the reshaping of what has been remembered. I have called the body of work Fragments, and it is a response to diverse recollections of my experience of walking the coast, both during the day and at night. I have created word-sketches, drawings, and 2-D and 3-D textile works that explore evidence of natural phenomena and the continuous, and often infinitesimal, processes of change that transform the landscape and the objects in it. The landscape has spoken – I have listened, remembered and responded.*

# ABOUT THE AUTHOR

After 40 years as a multinational technology executive, Martyn Howe rediscovered his passion for the outdoors, walking all of Britain's National Trails and writing about that 3,000-mile journey in his first book *Tales from the Big Trails*. On reaching Cromer, he realised he could not stop and set off to walk the new King Charles III England Coast Path National Trail, a further 2,700-mile journey around the coast of England.

In 2019, he walked the Wales Coast Path, and recently, he completed a walk along the east coast of Scotland, from Berwick-upon-Tweed to John o' Groats, a journey of a similar length to the South West Coast Path. In between these expeditions, he cycled 4,000 miles around the North Sea Cycle Route and completed two journeys from Land's End to John o' Groats, one via Ireland's Wild Atlantic Way and the other taking in the four cardinal points of Britain – another 2,000 miles.

This wanderlust of over 13,000 miles has left an indelible imprint on his psyche. He writes about how he has change in *The Coast is Our Compass*, hoping that others will be inspired to experience the power of nature's blue spaces and coastal margins. His ongoing adventures can be found at *trailplanner.co.uk*, which includes new digital maps that show the interplay between art, culture, geology and society along the routes he has taken.